The Country of Memory

ASIA: LOCAL STUDIES/GLOBAL THEMES

Jeffrey N. Wasserstrom, Kären Wigen, and Hue-Tam Ho Tai, Editors

The Country of Memory

*Remaking the Past
in Late Socialist Vietnam*

EDITED BY
Hue-Tam Ho Tai

Foreword by John Bodnar

UNIVERSITY OF CALIFORNIA PRESS
Berkeley • Los Angeles • London

University of California Press
Berkeley and Los Angeles, California

University of California Press, Ltd.
London, England

© 2001 by the Regents of the
University of California

Library of Congress
Cataloging-in-Publication Data

The country of memory : remaking the past in
late socialist Vietnam / edited by Hue-Tam Ho
Tai.
        p.   cm.—(Asia—local studies/global
themes)
    Includes bibliographical references and index.
    ISBN 0-520-22266-0 (cloth : alk. paper).—
ISBN 0-520-22267-9 (pbk. : alk. paper)
        1. Vietnam—Politics and government—1975–
        2. Vietnamese Conflict, 1961–1975.   3. Vietnam—
Intellectual life.   I. Tai, Hue-Tam Ho, 1948–   II.
Series.

DS559.912.C69 2001
959.704'4—dc21   00–046705

Contents

Illustrations

Foreword

The world we live in is encased in memory projects, undertakings designed to reconstruct versions of the past suitable for a myriad of purposes in the present. The cohesive narratives and glorious monuments that punctuated the culture and politics of nation-states now appear as mere options on a lengthy menu of books, films, sites, and images of times gone by. Scholars have not been reluctant to advance explanations for this cultural discord. Many have argued that the rise of memory, with its links to individual and group subjectivity and its disdain for the domination of officials, has exploded in the aftermath of the decline of the nation-state. In the most powerful nations in the world, traditional accounts of the relationship between the past, present, and future have withered. In the United States this has given rise to voices that contest interpretations of change over time that have venerated the nation as a source of material prosperity or democratic rights for all. In many nations, images of heroic men who defeated a country's enemies now must fight for cultural space against stories and symbols that expose the evil ways of a nation's leaders themselves. Thus, today in France, Germany, and Japan, significant political debates occur over the degree to which these nations were responsible for violence directed not only toward outsiders but also toward their own citizens.

Hue-Tam Ho Tai's masterful collection of essays that explore how the past is being remade in contemporary Vietnam constitutes a welcome addition to study of the larger problem of engineering memory, especially in political cultures where the identity of the nation-state is in a considerable state of flux. This collection tells us that the struggle over the past is no less difficult in smaller nations. In some ways, these essays remind one of issues faced elsewhere, such as the tension between familial and state cultures and the increasing importance of formulating a past suitable for tourist consumption. And the dramatic shift in official priorities, from an economy of socialism to one that is market driven, offers much insight into the relationship between state power and public forms of remembering. But no one who reads these essays can escape the fundamental connection the book makes between the tortured history of Vietnam and the modern clashes over what most needs to be recalled. Professor Tai makes it clear that the twisted course of events in this century in Vietnam, from battle against the French, to the War of National Salvation Against the Americans, to the decision to pursue market reforms has left the Vietnamese with an assortment of issues regarding their past. It is for this reason that she is more than justified in arguing that public memory in Vietnam today is characterized "as much by confusion as by profusion."

This book also suggests that the "commemorative fever" that is sweeping Vietnam is about more than Vietnam's history. It also has a great deal to do with the problems premodern cultures presented to those who promoted the creation of contemporary states. In this regard both Vietnam and this book offer all scholars of nationalism and remembering in the West a fascinating perspective on their own nations. Traditions of public debate over commemoration or monuments did not exist in totalitarian regimes; the cultural distance between peasant societies and modern states was immense not only because totalitarian governments could not promise a democratic future but also because they were so far removed from people steeped in premodern traditions. Thus, we can see in this volume that the incredible force of cultural domination in peasant societies produced a countermovement to hold on to memory in unique and compelling ways. When the Vietnamese government attempted to honor the dead who had fought the Americans, they cast their commemorations in predictable tropes of patriotism and heroism. Such images, however, held only a limited value for families deeply attached to rituals that signified that the dead would be reborn in an "otherworld" where they would join a community of ancestors. Thus, in a local community in northern Vietnam studied in this collection, families found official ceremonies for the war dead did not satisfy their needs, and they mounted their own efforts to commemorate the dead and reintegrate them into their own ancestral beliefs. State-sponsored ways of knowing the past were simply insufficient to meet the imperatives of local cultures. Similar tensions between secular and religious cultures are noted in this book in attempts to commemorate a communist revolutionary. It is evident from the larger study of nationalism and memory that tensions between local and collective cultures were abundant, but this collection reminds us that true comparisons of these questions across boundaries of time and space have yet to take place. Thus, this study of one "country of memory" admonishes us to reflect upon how much our experiences are similar to tensions found in Vietnam and how much they differ.

John Bodnar

Acknowledgments

The present volume grew out of a double panel at the 1996 annual meeting of the Association for Asian Studies. It could not have been put together without the assistance and inspiration of numerous individuals and institutions across several continents. In addition to the acknowledgments included in individual chapters, the authors wish to express their thanks to the two panel discussants, Marilyn Young and Rubie S. Watson, for their insightful comments on the papers. We record as well our appreciation for the very lively interventions by members of the audience. The incisive critiques of Michael Robinson and another reader for the University of California Press greatly improved the original manuscript. Duong Ngoc Dung compiled the glossary. Natalia Puchalt supplied many of the beautifully evocative photographs in the book. Sheila Levine, Juliane Brand, and Rose Anne White of the University of California Press patiently shepherded the manuscript through the many stages of the publishing process.

While we gratefully acknowledge our numerous debts, we also take full responsibility for errors of fact or interpretation. Above all, we hope that our collective effort will inspire others to delve more deeply into issues of history and memory in Vietnam. The present volume should thus be seen as a beginning, not an end.

Hue-Tam Ho Tai

Situating Memory

Hue-Tam Ho Tai

Commemorative fever is threatening to blanket the Vietnamese land-scape with monuments to the worship of the past. Every year, it seems, another museum opens, a new memorial is dedicated. Temples are re-furbished, and rural roads bristle with signs pointing to historical sites. Volumes of memoirs are constantly being churned out, cemeteries to the revolutionary dead dot the country from north to south. If it were not for the equally ubiquitous symbols of the global economy, such as Coca Cola bottles, karaoke bars, golf courses, and computers, Vietnam would appear to be living in the past.

This upsurge of commemoration is a paradoxical by-product of the program of economic reforms known as *Doi Moi* (lit., "changing for the new"), which was launched in the late 1980s. Coming barely fifteen years after the country was unified under communist rule, these reforms were designed to transform its economy from a socialist, centrally planned economy to one driven by the market. Yet the commemora-tive fever is not just a salvage operation designed to preserve traces of a fast-vanishing past before they are obliterated by the forces of relentless capitalist-style modernization. As the chapters in this volume suggest, the stakes involved in public memory are far more complex. What is being remembered? Who does the remembering? How is it done, and why? What is the context in which memory work is being carried out? These are some of the questions raised in the present volume. Its goal is to present analyses of how Vietnamese pasts have been constructed by different actors over nearly four decades, with particular emphasis on the postwar period. I propose, in this introduction, to provide a glimpse into the historical and cultural contexts that are shaping memory and the study of memory in Vietnam.

READING THE FUTURE INTO THE PAST

Public memory in present-day Vietnam is characterized as much by confusion as by profusion. A key to understanding this situation lies in the difficulty of assigning historical meaning to the upheavals that form the raw materials of modern Vietnamese history. The divisions they have engendered suggest the need to follow in the footsteps of Maurice Halbwachs and study the social context in which Vietnamese public memory is constructed.[1] There is, however, another dimension of memory that needs to be attended to as much as the social one: it is the historical context in which remembering takes place.

The Greek playwright Agathon is reported by Aristotle to have declared: "Even God cannot alter the past." Samuel Butler answered back across two millennia: "It has been said that though God cannot alter the past, historians can."[2] Others, besides historians, can and do alter it as well. "It's a poor sort of memory that works only backwards," remarks Lewis Carroll's Queen in *Through the Looking Glass*.[3] Indeed, memory works forward as well as backward; the past is shaped by the future as much as the future is shaped by the past. Memory creates meaning for particular events or experiences by inscribing them in a larger framing narrative, be it personal or collective. Whether implicitly or explicitly, in this larger narrative is embedded a sense of progression and vision of the future for which the past acts as prologue. In *Penser la révolution française,* François Furet pointed out how the political sympathies of different actors, including historians, led them to conceptualize the French Revolution either as the end point of the narrative of the French nation or as the beginning of the Republican narrative.[4] In Vietnam, deciding how to remember a century's worth of historical change is a matter of grave difficulty for a society filled with uncertainty about its future and only just beginning to rethink its past.

The larger narrative capable of giving meaning to otherwise random experiences has changed abruptly over the course of the twentieth century. Vietnamese have experienced imperial and colonial rule and have gone through a prolonged struggle for independence, a Communist-led revolution, and several wars. They are currently living through a slow and fitful transition from a centrally planned economy to a market-driven one. At the turn of the century, Vietnamese reformers thought they had found in social Darwinism the key to understanding their country's fall to colonial conquest. Three decades later, their spiritual heirs discovered in Marxism-Leninism a way out of the dismal national future that social Darwinism seemed to predict. And yet, only fifteen years after the country was unified under communist rule, the revolutionary leadership committed itself to implementing a market economy governed by the ethos of social Darwinian competition.[5] Each struggle to create a new future through revolution, war, and counterrevolution has been accompanied by attempts to redefine historical meaning and, in the process, to remake the past. The past, like the future, is an eternally unfinished project, constantly under construction and constantly being revised.

The political liberalization that is a by-product of economic reforms is widely credited with opening a space for revisiting the past. Yet it is not only the loosening of state control over cultural life that has allowed discrepant interpretations of the past to come to the fore; new historical conditions are forcing them into the open. In opting for Doi Moi, Vietnamese leaders were implicitly setting aside a socialist vision of the future that had sustained them through decades of struggle; nonetheless, they did not abandon their claim to historically based legitimacy, continued monopoly on power, or formal commitment to Marxism-Leninism. Even now that the need to mobilize for war is gone, the leadership retains a stake in promoting a version of the past that inscribes it as the legitimate inheritor of the Vietnamese patriotic tradition and the dominant force in the recent history of the country. Such a version of the past tends to empty the historical stage of alternative scenarios and actors. Yet the decline of High Socialist orthodoxy, relative prosperity, and prolonged peace have encouraged other actors besides the state to try to occupy the space of memory. The new visions of the past must take their place alongside old ones that continue to give solace not only to the state but also to important segments of Vietnamese society. The deconstruction of the official past is thus an untidy, sometimes surreptitious, seldom openly confrontational by-product of economic reconstruction.

UTOPIA AND ITS AFTERMATH

To understand how the past is being reimagined, it is important to know how it was constructed to begin with, for the socialist telos of the old historical narrative has never been repudiated, and new visions of the future—and thus, discrepant versions of the past—must be told around it rather than in open challenge to it.

In the midst of the War of National Salvation Against the Americans (Chien Tranh Chong My Cuu Nuoc), as the Vietnam War was known in North Vietnam (and now in the whole country), the scholar-activist Pham Huy Thong gave an interview in which he declared: "History is a source of comfort to us."[6] Previously an aide to Ho Chi Minh and later director of the Institute of Archaeology, Pham Huy Thong was a key actor in the efforts of the North Vietnamese state to use history as an instrument for mobilizing popular support during wartime. By the time the interview took place in January 1973, on the eve of the signing of the Paris Peace Accords, decades of living through war and revolution had turned these experiences into seemingly normal states rather than extraordinary events. Making history serve wartime purposes was achieved by writing the past (history in the lower case) as a narrative of heroic and ultimately triumphant struggle against foreign domination and inscribing the future as a vision of communist utopia achieved through the inexorable workings of History with a capital *H*, Marxist-style.[7] Both time past and time future, so it seemed, was on the North Vietnamese side and firmly under control.

When peace finally came, socialism was on the wane worldwide. Even in Vietnam, where the revolutionary generation remained in power, the future had to be rethought. The Doi Moi reforms saved the Vietnamese communist leadership from historical irrelevance when other socialist regimes throughout Europe were being toppled. But with Doi Moi, History lost its capital *H*. If revolutions aim to transform the future, and in so doing rewrite the past, so do counterrevolutions. The end of utopia has taken away the telos that had made possible a particular writing of Vietnamese history. One Vietnamese historian told me: "Now we are at peace, we need a new theme around which to organize our historical narrative." Unlike history, memory is not weighted by the need to unify the past, and its production is proceeding at a faster pace than the re-writing of history. Yet memory does not exist without reference to history. The unmooring of the historical past from its predicted end has undone the carefully erected structures of memory.

GEOGRAPHIES OF MEMORY

Nearly a century after the end of the American Civil War, William Faulkner wrote: "The past is never dead, it's not even past."[8] In Vietnam as in the American South, the past remains a live presence, impossible to ignore, difficult to assimilate. With its share of winners and losers in what, increasingly, is recognized to have been a civil conflict as much as a war against foreign intervention, postwar Vietnam, at first glance, offers striking parallels with postbellum America; yet the issues involved in grappling with the past are quite different in the two countries.

Some Vietnamese families begin their collective narratives of living with and through conflict in the nineteenth century, when the French conquered Vietnam. For many, that narrative did not end until 1990, when Vietnamese forces finally pulled out of Cambodia. While some rejoice in their improved situations, others mourn accumulated losses. Answers to queries about a person's current circumstances are often prefaced with "After 1975" or "Before Doi Moi." Temporal references such as these function not merely as markers of time gone by but also as indices of economic and political gains and losses and of personal experiences of war and revolution. Gains and losses, triumph and tragedy, however, do not align neatly and predictably on either side of the national divide that was the seventeenth parallel. The postwar era has also become the postrevolutionary era, in which it is unclear who won and who lost, as it was in the American Civil War. This complicated geography of triumph and setbacks has a profound impact on how the past is reimagined.

The complex intertwining of geography and time in Vietnamese memory is illustrated in one of the earliest novels of the Doi Moi period, Duong Thu Huong's *Paradise of the Blind*. This book was published in 1988, when the Doi Moi reforms were just being launched, and is widely seen as a revisionist account of over forty years of Communist rule in North Vietnam by a veteran of the War Against the Americans.[9] At the end of the novel, the heroine decides not to accept the house bequeathed to her by her aunt because she is unwilling to take on the burden of bitter memories that goes with it. The house in question had been confiscated during the Land Reform campaign of the 1950s, and the once prosperous lineage to whom it had belonged had been destroyed. Later, thanks to the Doi Moi reforms and her own unceasing efforts, the aunt was able to rebuild the family fortune and recover the house. It is thus full of ghosts and painful memories, a reminder of the toll of revolution on a single lineage as well as the eventual triumph of a lone individual. It is also concrete testimony to that individual's insistence on passing on her memories of bitter loss and vengeful triumph to the new generation. The narrator thus speaks for many when she decides to refuse "to stay here beneath the roof of the ancestors," as enjoined by her aunt: "I can't squander my life tending these faded flowers, these shadows, the legacy of past crimes."[10] The rejected house functions as an ambiguous symbol of the past. For the heroine, it contains the bitter ghosts of the revolution, but for her aunt who had schemed for decades to recover it, it had represented as well the glory days of her family before Land Reform.[11]

While it is conceivable that alternative interpretations of the past would not have surfaced into public life had it not been for the reforms, it would be misleading to infer that the "orthodox" narratives all belong to the pre–Doi Moi period. As some of the chapters in this volume suggest, the perpetuation of the state narrative—though sometimes modified—is made possible by enduring collective and personal concerns that have not been rendered moot by reforms even as other actors with different interests have come forth with their own re-visions of the past. Everywhere, the prerevolutionary tradition is being revived (and, in many cases, invented wholesale), but its function is highly ambiguous. It is revived by some as an alternative to the cultural legacy of the communist era, and by others as a means of entrenching that legacy even more firmly in the national consciousness. As the heroine of *Paradise of the Blind* realizes, the struggle over the past is an aspect of the struggle to control the future.

A complicating factor is the emergence of an art market and the growth of the tourist industry. These are allowing international actors as well as domestic ones to play a role in this work of re-vision. The battle sites visited by French tourists are not the same as those that bring back American veterans, to cite two groups of foreign visitors with their own time-specific memories of "Vietnam," while others without personal ties to the country are drawn to the "timeless" beauty of its landscape and recreational facilities. More important, there is a definite tension between the uses of the past as a legitimating device and as a means of constructing community and its repackaging as a marketable commodity.

OWNING AND DISOWNING THE PAST

"Who owns the past?" Scholarly attempts to address this question began with a critical look at the politics of historiography and have since moved on to the study of the politics of memory. Efforts to rescue the past from the clutches of the state or of national elites have led some scholars to discern a tension between history and memory. The latter is considered more authentic and more democratic because it is more dispersed and, supposedly, less likely to be controlled from above. This, however, is to ignore the interest of the state in shaping not only written history but popular memory as well. In socialist systems, public activities are ordinarily conducted with close reference to official cultural policies. But a state-imposed narrative that was totally at odds with preexisting beliefs and practices would have a short shelf life. Moreover, the strict dichotomy between official history and personal memory overlooks the ways in which particular social contexts and historical conjunctures help shape memory and how often it aligns itself with the national narrative.[12] Official history and public memory thus are as likely to coexist in symbiotic fashion as to be in tension with each other.

Much has been written about public memory and commemoration in various geographic and temporal settings. By "public," I refer to ritual performances, speech acts, visual media, and other cultural activities that are articulated and made available or accessible to others rather than kept secret. These representations may be the works of single individuals or the products of collective efforts. I am thus not referring to clandestine counterhegemonic communities of memory on which Milan Kundera or James C. Scott focus,[13] but to individuals and groups who openly try to claim a piece of the past. It would be tempting to study the relationship between history and memory in Vietnam in terms of hegemony and counterhegemony pitting the state against individuals, losers against winners, North versus South. But, although it is certainly possible to study memory and countermemory through these analytic lenses, Vietnamese attempts to come to grips with the legacy of a century's worth of war and revolution raise issues that are far more complex than a simple story of tension and opposition might suggest.

Since Ernest Renan, scholarly attention has been paid to the "collective amnesia" that makes possible national memory.[14] Milan Kundera considers memory a powerful weapon against the totalitarian conspiracy of silence: "The struggle of man against power is the struggle of memory against forgetting."[15] This struggle can be waged by constructing a counternarrative out of the suppressions and silences in official history. This counternarrative would have to be lodged in the realm of private memory or to circulate among small, clandestine, counterhegemonic communities in order to endure. In Kundera's novella "Lost

Letters," the hero began by openly taking notes at meetings and keeping a diary; in other words, he tried to construct his own counterhistory. But soon "he decided he'd better put the incriminating papers in a safe place."[16] While these secreted papers may allow future generations of historians to reconstruct a past that is more in line with the hero's own interpretation, in the present they cannot become the stuff of public memory. Yet, resistance to an oppressive and ubiquitous master narrative may manifest itself differently: not by fighting one's way out of the enveloping shroud of official history into the refuge of private memory but through willed amnesia. While Kundera's hero is concerned with filling the silences of official history, it is as well to remember the coercive intensity of totalitarian commemoration. It is this very intensity that provokes its opposite, the wish to escape into oblivion. This may explain why public memory in Vietnam combines two distinct and opposite phenomena: hyper-mnemosis and willed amnesia. By hyper-mnemosis, I allude not just to the inability or refusal to let go of the past but also to the intense, even obsessive, effort to keep it at the forefront of consciousness, to shape it and to exploit it for a variety of purposes. Forgetting may be the only escape from the tyranny of enforced memory, a refusal to internalize the script that is being pressed by a totalitarian state or overbearing individuals. Easier said than done. As the heroine of *Paradise of the Blind* laments, "Memory refuses to die."[17]

Depending on their age, sex, regional origins, political sympathies, and experiences, different Vietnamese have different versions of what happened over the last century and different ways of dealing with its legacy of memories. The aging southern revolutionaries in Christoph Giebel's chapter, who fought to extend the revolution southward, are now engaged in the struggle to have their contribution to local history remembered by a grateful nation and incorporated in its larger narrative. The desire to make local, and even personal, history align with the national script may explain the production of southern revolutionary memoirs well after 1975, in which the tropes that are used are remarkably similar to those discussed by Peter Zinoman in his analysis of northern revolutionary prison memoirs from the 1960s. *Paradise of the Blind,* however, features a heroine who embodies a totally different attitude toward this revolutionary past. She belongs to a younger generation of North Vietnamese who do not strive to preserve the revolutionary legacy or to rebuild a prerevolutionary culture they have never experienced. Whereas for her aunt, undoing the revolution had meant restoring the family's fortune, for her it means vowing to "sell the house and leave all this behind."[18] She seeks closure to her family's encounter with revolution and even tries to take herself outside the national geography of memory by forging for herself a global identity: "I sat down, cupping my chin in my hand and dreamed of different worlds, of the cool shade of a university auditorium, of a distant port where a plane could land and take off . . ."[19] Revising the past is thus a matter not only of disagreement over what is supposed to have happened but also the expression of yearnings for different futures, however inchoate.

STYLISTICS OF COMMEMORATION

Studying memory in Vietnam presents its own set of challenges. Vietnam today is characterized by neither full-blown totalitarianism nor total democracy. In democratic societies, it is possible to explore the commemorative project from the initial proposal through the process of negotiation among various groups of actors to the end result: a new public holiday, a monument, or the naming of an already existing structure. This can be achieved by following records of public debates over budget, design, siting, timing, and wording, reports of protests as well as rituals of celebration. In the United States, monuments such as the Vietnam War Memorial ("The Wall"), special displays such as the Enola Gay exhibit, commemorative occasions such as the Christopher Columbus quintecentennial, the decision to honor Martin Luther King Jr. through a public holiday, and attempts to create theme parks out of hallowed sites such as Gettysburg have all been the focus of intense scrutiny, negotiation, and contestation. Debates over each of these projects reveal profound and lasting disagreements over the meaning of important historical moments, however far removed in time. The Vietnamese, however, do not have a similar tradition of public participation in decisions over official commemoration. Lacking a sanctioned outlet for debating political and cultural differences, Vietnamese public discourse often has an oblique quality; it is full of hidden meanings and allusions. Since substance so often must be presented in oblique fashion, the stylistics of commemoration are an important marker of meaning. Obliqueness depends on deep cultural familiarity.

Through their checkered history, the Vietnamese have acquired a wide array of cultural resources with which to construct discrepant representations of the past, each fraught with multiple interpretive possibilities. The experiences of over a century and a half of exposure to imperial rule, colonial conquest, war, revolution, communism, and capitalism have made of Vietnam a true contact zone. Its culture has been shaped by influences from China (both classical and revolutionary), France, the Soviet Union, and the United States as much as by internal sources. The complexity of these experiences and encounters ensures an abundance of commemorative resources. The chapters in this volume draw on a wide range of evidence: memoirs, fiction, poems, public pronouncements, paintings, tourist brochures, films, architectural structures and public sculptures, funerary rites, and other commemorative occasions. The decline of socialist realism, with its promotion of linear narrative and surface unity, has made recourse to different types of resources acceptable: among those discussed here are Vietnamese folk art, Sino-Vietnamese elite classical culture, French romanticism, and the global popular culture that has spread since the launching of reforms.

THE ESSAYS

This book is divided into three parts. The first three essays focus on what might be termed an orthodox construction of the past. They are followed by two analyses of the effect of the emerging art market and tourism on representations of the past. The last two essays focus on the use of gendered images to discuss both remembering and forgetting.

In the first chapter, Peter Zinoman takes a new look at a peculiar literary-historical subgenre called the revolutionary prison memoirs and shows that, despite their first-person presentation, they are far from unmediated. Instead, they seek to advance a political agenda; they are structured along a specific model and draw on a variety of literary sources for inspiration. As Zinoman points out, production of these memoirs began in 1960, just as the population of North Vietnam was fully mobilized in preparation for the War Against the Americans. The memoirs were thus an important tool in generating support for the government and Communist Party. Since they were intended to shine the spotlight on the heroic sacrifices of their leaders during the War Against the French, they created a certain vision of the prison population as a microcosm of the larger revolutionary community, which excluded not only common criminals but also anti-Communist or merely non-Communist political inmates. Similarly, the everyday texture of prison life was largely absent from narratives of prison-as-school designed to bolster the leadership credentials of their authors. To construct these variations on a single master narrative, Zinoman suggests, the Vietnamese Communists drew on a wide variety of literary inspiration, including socialist realism, but also Sino-Vietnamese classical culture and French romantic literature. To the extent that they succeeded, therefore, the memoirs did so because they drew on familiar plotlines and images.

This narrative of revolutionary heroism constructed through the memoirs continues in the commemoration of Ton Duc Thang, the southern revolutionary who succeeded Ho Chi Minh as president of the Democratic Republic of Vietnam and became the first president of a unified Socialist Republic of Vietnam. In his chapter, Christoph Giebel shows that the museum-shrine that has been erected in Ton Duc Thang's native village in the far south harks back not only to communist practices and symbols but also to a far older commemorative language. And while the memoirs analyzed by Zinoman were produced by members of the Communist Party with a view to securing its monopoly on power during wartime, Giebel suggests that an important aspect of the Ton Duc Thang shrine, constructed just as the Renovation policy was being launched, is to preserve the revolutionary legacy in times that have become decidedly unrevolutionary. One may ask who is the intended audience for the message embedded in the cult of Ton Duc Thang. Unlike the memoirs, which can be considered as emanating from the center of power, the museum-shrine represents an appeal by individuals who have been doubly marginalized—by their southern origins and the turn toward a market economy—to keep alive the revolutionary flame. Their message is not necessarily addressed to the southern population, but to those in power in faraway Hanoi, reminding them of the contributions of southern guerrillas. The shrine thus stands not as a counternarrative but as a corrective to the Hanoi-centered interpretation of war and revolution.

A similar urge to complement rather than contest can be discerned in the dual sets of commemorative rituals designed to honor the war dead in northern Vietnam. While Shaun Malarney details the elaborate measures the North Vietnamese state took to honor the war dead and succor their survivors, he also shows why these measures did not address some fundamental concerns of the latter and describes the steps they took to remedy the situation. In particular, while the state ensconced fallen soldiers in a national pantheon of heroes, their relatives were often more interested in ensuring their safe passage into the otherworld through the proper performance of funerary rites. Yet, as Malarney explains, these rites, which were appropriate for times of peace, were inadequate when it came to the violent deaths far away from home of young men whose remains were not always available for burial or were not intact. There was another area in which the state's concerns did not neatly dovetail with those of the families of the dead soldiers. In a nutshell, this was the definition of community that was constructed through the two sets of rituals. From the perspective of the state, those who died fighting the French and the Americans belonged to a national pantheon of heroes. This pantheon united the recent dead and the heroes of bygone eras in a community of unrelated strangers; but, while proud of the honor bestowed on their own dead, the survivors also sought to incorporate them in a different community, made up of kin, both heroic and unheroic: the blood that had flowed in their veins being more important than the blood they had shed. In both cases, the dead and the living were united in a great chain of being, but the continuity they represented was different: one was national, the other patrilineal and local. This difference replicated earlier tensions between state and society, tensions that certainly antedated the advent of communism but were played out in North Vietnam during the 1950s in particular, when the state tried to substitute class for kinship as a basis for social organization. Heroism replaced class in this new attempt to transcend the bonds of kinship and locality through patriotism rather than ideology.

Although the remaining chapters in this collection address a wide variety of issues, they share one theme. In one way or another, different pasts are offered as alternatives to the narrative of heroic sacrifices in the noble cause of war and revolution explored by Zinoman, Malarney, and Giebel. In Nora Taylor's study of the art scene since World War II, one can see clearly the continued politicization of aesthetics, even or especially when a particular painting seems to lack overt political content. As she explains, when the dominant style was socialist realism and the task of the artist was to support the war effort, portraits of gaunt artists or paintings of empty city streets were considered unacceptably decadent. But now the zeitgeist has changed, and what was once deemed lacking in "national essence" is currently praised as more true, more authentic, than the heroic and cheerful paintings of now discredited masters. There is no better illustration of the idea that while the past may live in the present, it is the present that constructs the past and is constructed in the past. The empty streets in Bui Xuan Phai's paintings are reminders of the dire poverty of wartime Hanoi, and their bare electric poles subtly mock Lenin's description of communism as "Soviet power plus electrification of the whole country." But this recasting of wartime as a period of unheroic privations would not have been possible had the people of northern Vietnam not jettisoned the revolutionary ethos of self-sacrifice in favor of the ethos of acquisitive capitalism.

While the emergence of an art market replacing the previous system of semiofficially sponsored art may have something to do with the decline of socialist realism, it does not quite explain the embrace of folk art. Nora Taylor sees a likely reason for this phenomenon in the desire of artists to strike out into new artistic directions while still working within the context of "national essence." One can also detect in this rediscovery of folk art an attempt to leapfrog the recent revolutionary past in favor of a more ancient and idealized one, emptied of both ideology and conflict.

The same impulse may also underlie the colonial nostalgia documented by Laurel Kennedy and Mary Rose Williams. But it is not just a means of erasing war and revolution from memory, of turning Vietnam into "a country, not a war" in the fond slogan of the tourism industry. Tourism is the chief means by which the country is going to extricate itself from the poverty that Bui Xuan Phai captured in his paintings. Yet this strategy of modernization depends on the nostalgic exploitation of French colonial architecture. This strategy contains several implications: it projects an image of calm luxury, it helps to gloss over the last half century of warfare, and it replaces peasant guerrillas with sophisticated urbanites as the dominant image of the country. Longings for the trappings of modernity are expressed in a picture of urbanism of the past, while all around the future is being built. What better illustration of the cosmopolitan aspirations of postwar middle-class Vietnamese than the twin attempts to preserve the architectural relics of French imperialism and to erect high-rise towers in the new idiom of architectural internationalism? To be sure, the landscape is also an important lure, but it is a landscape emptied of menace. Where once Vietnamese peasants were mobilized to repulse foreigners, now they are expected to welcome them. Visual reminders are in fact everywhere, but the pain has largely been anaesthetized. In the Cu Chi tunnels, tourists—including returning American veterans of the Vietnam War—are greeted by young men and women clad in the drab guise of Communist guerrillas who point out the spots where American B-52s rained bombs on the site and the underground chambers where the Tet Offensive, with its memorable attack on the American embassy, was plotted. In the compound's kitchen, visitors are invited to taste samples of the grim diet of taro roots and salt that guerrillas ate every day; in the souvenir shops, they are invited to purchase silver opium pipes or wooden Disney figures. Shell casings are made into souvenirs tanks, empty soft drink cans turned into miniature helicopters. Commemorative sites such as these play a double function: as building blocks in the state's narrative of glorious war and triumphant revolution, and as fodder for entertainment. In an uneasy combination of the epic and the ironic, they are expected to sustain memory and generate money all at once.

Tensions between images of Vietnam as either an urbanizing, modernizing country or a fundamentally peasant one are sometimes couched in gender imagery, as Mark Bradley and I suggest. In the last two decades, Drew Faust, Catherine Clinton, Claudia Koonz, Nina Silber, and others have tried to reinsert women's voices into overwhelmingly masculinist visions of war both as experience and as memory;[20] Maurice Agulhon has analyzed how the figure of Marianne has been utilized in French public discourse to galvanize the public behind efforts to save the embattled Republic.[21] Unlike in the West, however, Vietnamese images of war are not so overwhelmingly masculine, and women have long been symbols of heroism in the face of foreign conquest even as they also represent peace and stability. Both Bradley and I point out some ways in which female images can be deployed to symbolize remembering as well as forgetting, peasant Vietnam as well as the new consumerist cosmopolitanism. Issues of morality are also often presented in gendered terms, as Bradley's chapter demonstrates. This deployment of female imagery stands in contrast to the relative insignificance of women in commemorative rituals, alluded to in Malarney's chapter. It is to the parents of the dead soldier, not his wife, that the task of ensuring his safe passage to the world of the dead and the annual ritual of remembrance is entrusted by the community. His widow plays a secondary role in this commemorative exercise. In my chapter, I try to suggest why, when that is so, it is the mothers of dead soldiers who have been honored by the state, and who have become the keepers of memory. But, given traditional Vietnamese gender ideology and attitudes toward trade, I also suggest why young women can also represent contemporary amnesia. The acquisitive urge may be seen as a reaction against the poverty-stricken past, an antidote to the pain of memory. In families with divided loyalties and divergent pasts, poring over new purchases is a far safer strategy for retaining some semblance of unity than contemplating old wounds. Indeed, in order for family communities to include all their members, the dead and the living, it is necessary to forget, or at least to seem to forget, past divisions and rancor.

In the final chapter of the collection, Mark Bradley takes up a number of representational issues touched on in previous chapters. Here the representational language is that of film. Given that medium, it is not surprising that the idiom of gender would be deployed conspicuously to make points about both past and present. The films analyzed by Bradley use different generations of women to represent memory (the mother in *Brothers and Relations*), forgetting (the sister in the same film), heroic self-sacrifice (the peasant woman stricken by leprosy in *How to Behave,* the prostitute in *Girl on the River*), and capitalist greed (the middle-class woman in *How to Behave,* the sister of the dead man in *Brothers and Relations*). In *Brothers and Relations,* Bradley suggests, the keeper of memory is a relative by marriage rather than a blood kin of the dead man; his wish to recover the bones of his brother-in-law stems from his own war service. Through him, the military is presented as the bastion of revolutionary morality in a world where the amorality of the market (represented by his briefcase-toting wife) is on the rise. The climactic scene takes place in Noi Bai airport outside Hanoi. Since air travel from North to South was impossible during the War Against the Americans, airports are symbols of national unification and peace. They are also openings to foreign influences and thus represent a turning away from the national narrative of resistance against foreign conquest. In his discussion of another film, *When the Tenth Month Comes,* Bradley complicates the commemorative dichotomy set up by Malarney. To whom does the memory of fallen soldiers belong? In the film, the local party representative, the parents of the dead man, his grieving widow, his kin and neighbors, all are seen to have a claim. Whereas widows play a relatively minor role in the funerary practices of the patrilineal family and the nationalizing policies of the state, the bonds of conjugal love, the film director suggests, give them a starring role in the commemorative project. In another film, *Girl on the River,* gender gives a new twist to the regional perspective that Christoph Giebel discusses with respect to the commemoration of Ton Duc Thang. The film director Dang Nhat Minh (who also directed *When the Tenth Month Comes*) makes use of a stock figure in Chinese and Vietnamese classical culture, the patriotic prostitute, to critique postwar amnesia. The twist is that, though she is from the South, in her destitution she does not embody the supposedly southern ethos of corruption that has been widely blamed for the loss of morality among formerly upright cadres. Instead, it is the prosperous and powerful cadre who represents the careless forgetting by former revolutionaries of the services that ordinary Vietnamese once rendered them. The film's effectiveness rests partly on its upending of some stereotypes about region and about gender, which I discuss in my chapter.

No single collection of essays could possibly do justice to so contested a set of experiences as those of twentieth-century Vietnam or to the vast complexity of memory. This volume is thus offered as a small contribution to the ongoing Vietnamese search for usable pasts.

NOTES

I gratefully acknowledge helpful comments by Jeffrey Wasserstrom and Rubie S. Watson on an earlier version of this introduction.

1. Maurice Halbwachs, *Les Cadres sociaux de la mémoire* (Paris: Mouton, 1976).

2. Samuel Butler, *Erewhon Revisited* (New York: Modern Library, 1955), 468.

3. Lewis Carroll, *Through the Looking Glass and What Alice Found There* (New York: Morrow, 1993), 95. " 'That's the effect of living backwards,' the Queen said kindly: 'it always makes one a little giddy at first . . . but there's one great advantage in it, that one's memory works both ways.' "

4. François Furet, *Penser la révolution française* (Paris: Gallimard, 1978).

5. See Hue-Tam Ho Tai, *Radicalism and the Origins of the Vietnamese Revolution* (Cambridge, Mass.: Harvard University Press, 1992), 4–5, 20–22.

6. Quoted in John K. Whitmore, "Communism and History in Vietnam," in *Vietnamese Communism in Comparative Perspective,* ed. Wm. S. Turley (Boulder, Colo.: Westview Press, 1980), 11.

7. I am borrowing the elegant title of Nancy K. Florida, *Writing the Past, Inscribing the Future: History as Prophecy in Colonial Java* (Durham, N.C.: Duke University Press, 1995).

8. William Faulkner, *Requiem for a Nun* (New York: Random House, 1968), 92.

9. Duong Thu Huong, *Paradise of the Blind [Nhung Thien Duong Mu]* (Hanoi: NXB Phu Nu, 1988), trans. Phan Huy Duong and Nina McPherson (New York: Morrow, 1991).

10. Ibid., 258.

11. Ibid.

12. William C. Spengemann and L. R. Lundquist, "Autobiography and the American Myth," *American Quarterly* 17 (fall 1965): 501–2. The authors explore the parallels to be found in individual autobiographies and what Benedict Anderson calls "national biographies." See Benedict Anderson, *Imagined Communities* (London: Verso, 1991), 204. I am grateful to Benjamin Wilkinson for bringing this article to my attention.

13. James C. Scott, *Domination and the Arts of Resistance: Hidden Transcripts* (New Haven, Conn.: Yale University Press, 1990).

14. Ernest Renan, "What Is a Nation?" (lecture given at the College de France, 1882), translated by Martin Thom in *Nation and Narration,* ed. Homi Bhabha (London: Routledge, 1990), 19; Anderson, *Imagined Communities,* chap. 11; Mona Ouzouf, "Le Panthéon: l'Ecole Normale des morts," in *Lieux de mémoire,* vol. 1, ed. Pierre Nora (Paris: Gallimard, 1984), 157; John Gillis,

ed., "Introduction," in *Commemorations: The Politics of National Identity* (Princeton, N.J.: Princeton University Press, 1994).

15. Milan Kundera, *The Book of Laughter and Forgetting* (New York: Knopf, 1981), 3.

16. Ibid., 4.

17. Duong Thu Huong, *Paradise of the Blind,* 258.

18. Ibid.

19. Ibid.

20. Drew Faust, *Mothers of Invention: Women of the Slaveholding South in the American Civil War* (Chapel Hill: University of North Carolina Press, 1996); Catherine Clinton, *The Other Civil War: American Women in the Nineteenth Century* (New York: Hill and Wang, 1984); Catherine Clinton, *Tara Revisited: Women, War and the Plantation Legend* (New York: Abbeville Press, 1995); Catherine Clinton and Nina Silber, eds., *Divided Houses: Gender and the Civil War* (New York: Oxford University Press, 1992); Nina Silber, *The Romance of Reunion: Northerners and the South, 1865–1900* (Chapel Hill: University of North Carolina Press, 1993); Claudia Koonz, *Mothers in the Fatherland: Women, the Family and Nazi Politics* (New York: St. Martin's Press, 1987).

21. Maurice Agulhon, *Marianne au combat: L'imagerie et la symbolique républicaines de 1789 à 1880* (Paris: Flammarion, 1979).

PART ONE

CONSTRUCTING MEMORY

ONE

Reading Revolutionary Prison Memoirs

Peter Zinoman

A remarkable feature of the personal memoirs (*hoi ky*) published in northern Vietnam following the establishment of the Communist state in 1954 is how little they have to do with personal memories. Like virtually all forms of writing about the past that were sanctioned by the cultural authorities of the Vietnamese Workers Party (VWP) during the 1950s through 1970s, autobiographical memoirs were fashioned to shape a collective public memory rather than to express an individual private one. As a result, Communist Vietnamese memoirs from the era tend to provide much greater insight into the thinking behind official state projects than the putatively timeless and subjective dimensions of human experience.

Prison memoirs (*hoi ky nha tu*) form an important subgenre of revolutionary memoirs (*hoi ky cach mang*), a new literary form pioneered and promoted by the VWP after it came to power. While they describe the party's leading role in colonial-era labor and peasant movements and during the heady days of the August Revolution in 1945, a striking number of revolutionary memoirs relate tales of political imprisonment and episodes of prison resistance. Indeed, the genealogy of the genre is often traced back to two classic first-person prison narratives from the late 1930s. According to one party literary critic, "Le Van Hien's *Kontum Prison* (1938) and Cuu Kim Son's *Prison Break* (1939) mark the beginning of the genre known today as the revolutionary memoir."[1] These works, along with a handful written during the anti-French resistance, anticipated the vast quantity of revolutionary prison memoirs produced after 1954.[2] With the publication and massive dissemination in 1960 of Ho Chi Minh's *Prison Diary*—a poetic rendering of the sub-genre—the prison memoir emerged as the primary autobiographical vehicle for the leaders of the Democratic Republic of Vietnam (DRV).

It is tempting to read Vietnamese revolutionary prison memoirs as part of a rich transcultural and transhistorical tradition of writing from confinement. Indeed, the themes that have dominated prison writing historically—prison as a refuge, prison as a catalyst for intense friendship, prison as a matrix of spiritual rebirth—may also be found in the Vietnamese texts.[3] More remarkable, however, is the absence within the subgenre of what W. B. Carnochan has called "the larger metaphorical pattern" of prison writing—the theme of artistic expression itself as liberation or freedom from constraints.[4] While this absence may be difficult to discern within any single text, a consideration of the subgenre as a whole brings it into sharp relief.

A survey of revolutionary prison memoirs reveals little variation in terms of form, content, or thematic orientation. Virtually all works within the subgenre highlight the political education and successful resistance efforts of jailed Communist activists. They employ structurally identical episodes to illustrate colonial cruelty and Communist heroism. In some cases, different memoirs even use the same stylized language: poor sanitary conditions in colonial prisons are part of a strategy to "murder inmates bit-by-bit" (*giet dan giet mon*); Communist prisoners, however, maintain an "indomitable spirit" (*tinh than bat khuat*) and struggle to "transform the imperialist prison into a revolutionary school" (*bien nha tu de quoc thanh truong cach mang*).

The proliferation of such narrative and linguistic repetitions implies that works within the subgenre should not be read—like the *Autobiography of Malcolm X* or even Gramsci's *Prison Notebooks*—as acts of individual resistance to the coercive power of a total institution. On the contrary, they suggest that revolutionary prison memoirs must be understood as versions of the "revolutionary master-scripts" that Christoph Giebel finds in the commemorative installations exhibited in the official museums built by the Communist state.[5] Like museum exhibits, they function to "trumpet the accomplishments of the Party, provide shining examples of anti-imperialist heroism, and teach the younger generation the lessons of past struggles."[6] This is not surprising, since they were commissioned, subsidized, and sometimes even transcribed or ghostwritten by state-controlled publishing houses and literary associations under the authority of the same Ministry of Culture that supervised museum construction (fig. 1.1).

Given the circumstances in which revolutionary prison memoirs were produced, an analysis of the subgenre yields insight into the efforts of the leaders of the new Communist state during the late 1950s and 1960s to construct and promote an official public history of their rise to power. As I will suggest, there are several reasons why prison narratives by Communist leaders played an important role in these efforts. First, images of confinement figure prominently in two literary traditions that were familiar to the reading public: the classical Vietnamese tradition and the French romantic tradition. Second, the notoriously brutal colonial prison system provided a particularly dramatic setting in which to stage heroic revolutionary performance. And third, an emphasis on prison experiences drew attention away from the upper-class backgrounds of Communist leaders during an era in which the party's proletarian and peasant origins were an important component of its public image. In addition, I will suggest how the subgenre systematically highlighted certain features of colonial-era juridical incarceration while simultaneously suppressing others to accomplish the goals it had been created to accomplish.

THE LITERATURE OF CONFINEMENT
IN THE CLASSICAL TRADITION

Before examining the way in which political considerations during the 1950s and 1960s shaped the conventions of Communist prison memoirs, it is useful to consider how older literary traditions may have influenced the genre. It is significant that many of the party leaders who determined the parameters of cultural production during the early years of the DRV came from literati families and therefore possessed some familiarity with a classical literary tradition in which images of exile and incarceration figured prominently. Such images anticipated some of the thematics of Communist prison narratives in their emphasis on displacement, isolation, and spiritual resistance. Hence, when the party began to promote the prison writing of its leadership in the mid-1950s, it benefited from the fact that the political classes, if not the reading public more generally, possessed a cultural familiarity with the basic conventions of the genre.

Images of confinement first appear in the classical tradition through poetic depictions of Buddhist monasticism. As with Communist prison

Figure 1.1. Hoa Lo Prison, known during the American War as the Hanoi Hilton, is now a museum. Photograph by Hue-Tam Ho Tai.

writing, early Sino-Vietnamese Buddhist poetry frequently portrayed scenes of enclosure and segregation. A good example is Le Thieu Dinh's fifteenth century quatrain, *The Cloister on Mount Le De*:

> Deep in the mountains runs a crystal brook.
> Above the ancient cloister drift white clouds.
> To visitors the monks won't say a word—
> wind's blown through pines and opened their closed gate.[7]

By emphasizing the remoteness ("deep in the mountains") of the "ancient cloister," the poem recalls important similarities between monastic and prison life. Further affinities can be found in the distinctly carceral image of the "closed gate" and in the sharp contrast drawn between insiders ("monks") and outsiders ("visitors"). This reading of the poem follows David Marr's provocative analysis of the connection between Buddhist monasteries and colonial prisons:

> Colonial jails in Indochina might be described as fulfilling a religious function. They forced a significant segment of the Vietnamese intelligentsia to withdraw from the world, endure privation, sort out their thoughts and attempt to master the self and external reality. In this sense, prisons were not unlike Zen monasteries except that the acolytes were not there by choice and those in charge were not seen as teachers but as the enemy.[8]

Images of confinement in Buddhist poetry extended beyond perceived similarities between jails and monasteries. Compassion for human suffering prompted poets working within the Buddhist tradition to focus on the plight of the poor and destitute. Three centuries before Le Thieu Dinh, the Venerable Huyen Quang, the third patriarch of the Truc Lam Buddhist sect, composed a poem about the emotional devastation suffered by the families of prisoners. Entitled *Pity for Prisoners,* it is among the oldest surviving Vietnamese poems about jail and prisoners.

> They write letters with their blood, to send news home.
> A lone wild goose flaps through the clouds.
> How many families are weeping under the same moon?
> The same thought wandering how far apart?[9]

While the thematics of early Buddhist poetry may recall features of twentieth-century prison writing, the Vietnamese Confucian literary tradition anticipated the modern genre more directly. This tradition included a subgenre of plaintive appeals by imprisoned scholars, a good illustration of which is Nguyen Trai's *A Cry of Innocence,* produced after the famous scholar was arrested for treason in 1430.

> Through ups and downs I've drifted fifty years.
> My love for my old mountain I've betrayed.
> False honors bring real sorrows—such a joke!
> Many traduce one loyal man—woe's me!
> When I can't dodge what comes, I know there's fate.
> If culture will survive, it's Heaven's wish.
> In jail, a shame to read the overleaf:
> how is my plea to cross the Golden Gate?[10]

The prison poetry composed by Cao Ba Quat in the mid–nineteenth century offers another example of writing from confinement within the Vietnamese Confucian tradition. An influential official during the 1850s,

Quat was imprisoned, tortured, and eventually executed for launching a popular insurrection against Emperor Tu Duc. Quat's depiction of his own personal state in jail contrasts sharply with the overwhelmingly defiant tone of Communist prison writing. In *Benighted*, for example, the prisoner's feelings of impotence and liminality are explored:

> Night falls, the flood spills over,
> Cold winds have driven Autumn hence.
> My eyes are weary with following the days
> Suspended between heaven and earth, a poet lies in jail
> Pillowing my head, I see my sword lying there inert.
> By the dim light of the lamp, I contemplate my ragged coat.
> Full of the ardent force of life
> I must remain walled in, voiceless and mute.[11]

Imprisoned Vietnamese poets sometimes reflected on their own confinement by conjuring up sympathetic images of caged animals. Around 1750, the scholar Nguyen Huu Cau led a failed revolt against the Trinh family in the North. Cau, who was arrested and eventually put to death, is credited with writing the poem *The Bird in a Cage* while in jail awaiting execution.[12]

> In all the world one cage holds this small self
> whose eyes once roamed the space of winds and clouds!
> But why, oh, why did I get snared and caught
> to brood, to moan, to mourn my gift of flight?
> I used to preen my feathers, flap my wings—
> and now I sing of freedom in a jail!
> Orioles dip and dart by the north hedge.
> Phoenixes chirp and coo on the south branch.
> Let carpers, east and west, all wag their tongues.
> At my first chance, from bondage I'll break loose.
> Straight-winged, I'll soar and race toward yonder blue.
> I'll smash my chains and visit the sun-crow.
> Upon this earth, who knows my heart?[13]

Echoes of Cau's imprisoned but undefeated bird can be found in The Lu's well-known poem *Memories of the Jungle,* in which a caged tiger is employed to symbolize the predicament of Vietnam under the French.[14] Another metaphorically pregnant caged tiger appears in *What's My Crime,* a revolutionary poem penned by Tran Huy Lieu in 1938.

> You've bolted me in prison—What's my crime?
> I love my country—do I break the law?

A furnace tempers iron into steel.
Fire tests true gold and leaves no room for doubt
A tiger waits his chance to flee the cage
The dragon bides his time to break the lock
Pull any dirty trick you may devise—
just try and shake my purpose, I dare you.[15]

For Communist literary critics, the insertion of prison writing by party members into an older, indigenous literary tradition brought Vietnamese Communism's nationalist character into sharp relief. For example, in 1960, Tran Huy Lieu likened the spirit of Ho Chi Minh's *Prison Diary* to the "strong and proud will" of Nguyen Huu Cau's imprisoned bird.[16] In 1966, the poet and critic Xuan Dieu drew similar comparisons between Ho's poetry and Nguyen Trai's *A Cry of Innocence*.[17] The most elaborate effort to place revolutionary prison poetry within an indigenous literary lineage was carried out by Dang Thai Mai,[18] who traced "a long and powerful tradition of prison poetry" from a handful of classical Chinese and Japanese prison poets (Lac Tan Vuong [Lo Xinwang], Ly Thai Bach [Li Po], and Van Thien Tuong [Wen Tienxiang]) to the nineteenth-century prison verse of Cao Ba Quat and his nephew Cao Ba Nha.[19]

Communist prison writing also drew on a more recent tradition of prison poetry produced by patriotic scholar-gentry who had been arrested and jailed for political subversion in the early decades of the twentieth century. Much of this work emerged after 1908, when French security forces cracked down on the Eastern Travel Movement (Phong Trao Dong Du), the Eastern Capital Free School (Dong Kinh Nghia Thuc), and an outbreak of antitax demonstrations in Annam. Several dozen scholars involved in these movements, including the influential anticolonialist Phan Chau Trinh, were deported to penitentiaries at Con Dao and Lao Bao and held for the following decade.[20] To pass time in prison, the scholars formed poetry-writing clubs, which they ironically referred to as *thi dan* after the literary associations for cultivated men that were popular during the imperial era.[21] Although many of the poems composed in the prison *thi dan* were lost (or never written down to begin with), some were preserved in memory, copied down, and published by prisoners after their release.

The most energetic anthologist of this early twentieth-century prison poetry was Huynh Thuc Khang.[22] In 1904, Khang turned his back on a superb educational career and promising prospects in the imperial bureaucracy to join forces with other Confucian literati devoted to modernizing Vietnamese society and expelling the French. After serving thirteen years on Con Dao for political activity between 1908 and 1921, Khang founded *Tieng Dan* (*People's Voice*), which became Indochina's longest-running Vietnamese-language newspaper. Between September 1937 and April 1938, *Tieng Dan* published a large body of poetry composed by scholars who had been imprisoned with Khang in Con Dao.[23] In 1939, he republished many of the poems in an anthology entitled *Thi Tu Tung Thoai* (*Prison Verse*). Khang provided both Chinese and Vietnamese versions of the poetry, annotated and explained numerous classical references in the verse, and supplemented the collection with a host of anecdotes about prison life.

While the poetry of imprisoned scholar-gentry tended to convey a more melancholy tone than the relentlessly upbeat writings produced by Communist prisoners in the 1930s, the traditions shared certain thematic preoccupations. For instance, the Communists' attempt to link incarceration and education originated with the writings of Huynh Thuc Khang's generation. On Con Dao in 1908, Phan Chau Trinh advised Khang to try to turn the prison into a "natural school" (*truong hoc thien nhien*), a comment that anticipated a common trope within Communist prison writing that linked incarceration and political education.[24] Moreover, the emphasis in Communist prison writing on spiritual resistance despite physical confinement mirrors a common theme in scholar-gentry prison verse. It can be seen, for example, in Phan Chau Trinh's *Dap Da Con Dao* (*Breaking Rocks on Con Dao*):

> A man stands tall upon Con Dao
> he makes a din that makes the mountain shake.
> Hammer to shatter heap on heap of rocks.
> Break stone by hand to hundreds of small chips.
> To granite turn your body day by day.
> Can sun or rainstorm daunt an iron heart?
> When they're laid low, those who will save the world
> endure and let no trifle bother them.[25]

Although the popularization of scholar-gentry prison poetry intensified with Huynh Thuc Khang's efforts in the late 1930s, political prisoners jailed earlier in the decade were not unaware of the older tradition. In a memoir of his incarceration for political activity published in 1935, future Communist Party member Ton Quang Phiet recalled speculating that imprisonment will make him as famous as Ngo Duc Ke and Le Huan, two prominent prison poets from the generation of patriotic scholar-gentry.[26] Likewise, in the prison memoir *Doi trong Nguc* (*Life in Prison*), the militant Nhuong Tong described how he quietly recited Phan Chau Trinh's *Breaking Rocks on Con Dao* as he was hauled off to jail in 1929.[27]

FRENCH ROMANTICISM
AND THE CULT OF INCARCERATION

Just as the early cultural czars of the DRV were exposed to images of confinement from an older Vietnamese literary tradition, they were also familiar with a wealth of prison narratives found in nineteenth-century French romantic literature.[28] During the early twentieth century, Vietnamese students studied Michelet's famed account of the storming of the Bastille and Pascal's depiction of spiritual redemption in a solitary cell.[29] In the 1920s, Ho Bieu Chanh became Indochina's first broadly popular prose novelist by rather shamelessly adapting plots from Alexandre Dumas and Victor Hugo.[30] His first blockbuster, *The Ship Master of Kim Quy Island* (*Chua Tau Kim Quy*), lifted completely the narrative structure of *The Count of Monte Cristo,* including a melodramatic version of the spiritual rebirth in confinement of the hero Nguyen Van Anh (Dantes in the Dumas novel).[31] Chanh's second commercial success, *Ngon Co Gio Dua* (*Blades of Grass in the Wind*), a Vietnamese reworking of *Les Misérables,* followed the tribulations of Le Van Do, a petty thief whose fortunes take a dramatic turn after he, like Jean Valjean, escapes from prison.[32] The aquatic prison escape in Nguyen Hong's classical colonial novel *Cua Bien* (*The Ocean's Mouth*) is also frequently compared to Jean Valjean's.[33]

Victor Hugo, whose "life-long obsession" with the death penalty and images of crime and punishment is well documented, was perhaps the most beloved writer in the colony.[34] First translated into Vietnamese in 1913, his novels were serialized repeatedly in newspapers and magazines, and his poetry became a staple of the elite Franco-Vietnamese educational curriculum.[35] By 1925, Hugo had developed such a reputation among the budding southern middle classes that the Saigonese bureaucratic functionaries who founded the syncretic Cao Dai religion in 1925 placed him alongside Jesus, Confucius, and Buddha as a patron saint of the faith.[36] His portrait still graces the entranceway of the Holy See in Tay Ninh.

In a revealing interview conducted in 1991, party General Secretary

Nguyen Van Linh forthrightly claimed that Victor Hugo was his favorite novelist and that "Hugo and *Les Misérables,* not Karl Marx and *Das Kapital,* pointed him toward communism."

> I started reading *Les Misérables* and the image of Jean Valjean was very striking to me—a poor man, so poor he had to beg for his daily bread. . . . It touched the strings of my heart directly—I was very moved. I decided, I could not be satisfied with a society where there is an enormous gap between the rich and the poor.[37]

Linh's affection for Hugo's tales of crime, punishment, and redemption may also be connected to the fact that he spent over ten years in colonial prison prior to 1945.

Evidence suggests that French romantic carceral images exerted a powerful influence over the well-educated Vietnamese youth who entered radical politics in the 1920s and 1930s.[38] Such influence is apparent in the widespread use of the Bastille as a potent symbol within left-wing anticolonial rhetoric. In 1925, the fiery radical journalist Nguyen An Ninh published a provocative account of the storming of the Bastille in his Saigon newspaper, *La Cloche Fêlée (The Cracked Bell)*, and questioned why Vietnamese history had never witnessed an equivalent event.[39] During the 1930s, revolutionaries intensified their employment of Bastille imagery in the legal oppositional press and in underground publications.[40] Consider the following Vietnamese-language leaflet seized by the Security Police (Sûreté) at a Bastille Day parade in Qui Nhon in 1931:

> Brothers and sisters. Each year in Indochina, as in France and her other colonies, the imperialists spend hundreds of thousands of piasters to commemorate the 14th of July. As spectators, our compatriots unconsciously assist in the celebrations. Here is the origin of this observance, which we mistakenly call French Tet. On July 14, 1789, the Republican Party revolted in Paris. An armed mob demolished the monarchy's great prison, the Bastille, released the political prisoners who demonstrated in the streets. The French decided to celebrate annually, July 14, in order to commemorate their great victory and the triumph of liberty over the absolutist regime. Brothers and sisters, in celebrating July 14, French imperialism extols its love of liberty but conceals its ferocious and barbarous sentiments evidenced here by the prisons of Hanoi, Saigon, Quang Ngai, and all the provinces and in which suffer a considerable number of our compatriots. Brothers and sisters, rise up. Unite with one heart and protest against these arrests and imprisonments, overthrow French Imperialism, and in the spirit of the Parisian revolutionaries on July 14, 1789, destroy the prisons of Hanoi, Saigon, and the provinces and deliver our brothers and sisters who are condemned there.[41]

Other evidence exists of the popularity of French romantic prison imagery among radical Vietnamese youth. In 1928, the Sûreté seized a Vietnamese-language copy of Silvio Pellico's *My Prisons* from an illegal publishing house in Saigon.[42] This account by the Milanese liberal who spent a decade in Metternich's political prison, the Speilberg, had enjoyed a stunning success in nineteenth-century France, where five separate translations had been completed following its publication in the 1830s.[43] Dang Thai Mai, the dean of party literary critics, claims to have read Pellico's memoir while a student in Hue in the late 1920s.[44]

Still, the sensational prison narratives of Dumas and Hugo, replete with dramatic escape attempts and feats of great personal courage, appear to have exerted the widest impact among Indochinese youth.[45] In his 1929 memoir *Sitting in the Big Jail,* Trotskyist Phan Van Hum compared his own predicament to that of the protagonist of Hugo's *The Last Days of a Condemned Man.*[46] Hugo and Dumas also figure in Pham Hung's 1960 prison memoir, *In the Death Cell.*[47]

> In the Central Prison there was a library for the French. I borrowed some books and after reading them, summarized the stories for the other prisoners. To their delight, we read *Les Misérables* by Hugo and *Les Trois Mousquetaires* by Dumas.[48]

REVOLUTIONARY SCHOOLS AND HEROIC PRISONERS

The central theme of revolutionary prison memoirs is the transformation of colonial jails into revolutionary schools. Education and imprisonment are prominently linked in titles such as Hoang Anh's *Nha Tu De Quoc Tro Thanh Truong Hoc cua Chien Si Cach Mang* (*Imperialist Prisons Become Schools for Revolutionary Fighters*), Tran Huy Lieu's *Tu Hoc trong Tu* (*Self-Study in Prison*), Nguyen Luu's *Nha Tu Son La, Truong Hoc Cach Mang* (*Son La Prison: A School for Revolutionaries*), Nguyen Thieu's *Truong Hoc trong Tu* (*Prison School*), Nguyen Duc Thuan's *Truong Hoc Xa Lim* (*Cell School*), and Nguyen Duy Trinh's *Lam Bao va Sang Tac Tieu Thuyet trong Nha Lao Vinh* (*Writing Newspapers and Novels in Vinh Prison*).[49] In the scholastic prisons of such accounts, revolutionaries spend their first months in confinement studying Marxism-Leninism and practical skills and then apply what they have learned to protest poor conditions, organize fellow inmates, and convert non-Communist offenders to the revolutionary cause.

Tran Huy Lieu's depiction of Communist prisoners in Con Dao penitentiary in the early 1930s is exemplary:

> Under French colonialism, owing to powerful conviction and innovative and skillful organization, communists turned prisons into schools for the study of literature and revolution. The imperialists tried to use prisons to kill revolutionaries, but we made prisons into a place to recruit and train cadres. After graduating from such schools, many cadres displayed not only a heightened skill and an indomitable spirit but an increased cultural level as well.[50]

Tran Huy Lieu's reference to the "powerful conviction" and "indomitable spirit" of imprisoned cadres points to another preoccupation in revolutionary prison memoirs. Successful resistance, in these accounts, is always a function of the superior will and psychological doggedness of Communist prisoners. Le Duan's recollections of his experience on Con Dao make the point:

> In prison, wherever we chanced to meet, we, brothers and comrades from the north, center and south, spent our time pondering, planning, discussing how to struggle to defeat the imperialists and colonialists. Right from the outset, we decided to turn the prison into a school. When still at large, we had joined the revolution out of love for our country and hatred for the imperialists. But in prison, thanks to our indomitable will, we were able to read, and study and consequently to understand Marxism-Leninism, and thus we became confident in the victory of the Vietnamese revolution.[51]

In addition to drawing attention to the importance of revolutionary training and political commitment, another concern of revolutionary prison memoirs is to portray Communist prisoners as dauntless and heroic figures. Many accounts contain clearly hyperbolic depictions of physical endurance and courage or episodes in which Communist prisoners masterfully, almost effortlessly, outwit their guards. Elaborate depictions of dramatic escape attempts, a ubiquitous feature of the genre, most clearly reflect this tendency.[52] For example, in *We Escape from Prison,* Nguyen Tao fills nearly three hundred pages with three separate accounts of Communist prison breaks, each more daring and odds-defying than the last.[53]

DISTORTIONS AND ELISIONS

Revolutionary prison memoirs function not only through the experiences they repeatedly convey but also by those they continually suppress.

For example, despite the fact that ordinary lawbreakers made up the overwhelming majority of the colonial penal population, revolutionary prison memoirs give the impression that most inmates were political offenders. Based on memoirs set in Con Dao Penitentiary immediately following the suppression of the Nghe Tinh Soviets in 1931, one would never guess that, even after the massive crackdown on suspected "subversives," political prisoners remained in the minority on the island. In 1932, roughly 75 percent of the penitentiary's population had been jailed for common-law offenses, most for crimes against property.[54] Naturally, in periods of relative political calm, the proportion of common-law to political prisoners was even greater.[55]

Compounding their neglect of common-law prisoners, revolutionary prison memoirs never mention that the punitive regime applied to ordinary lawbreakers was considerably more onerous and brutal than the one to which political prisoners were subjected. Transported to an inhospitable frontier region, fed an insufficient diet, and forced to perform dangerous corvée labor from which political prisoners were normally exempt, common-law inmates had few opportunities to embark on the ambitious program of self-improvement and personal cultivation compulsively described in revolutionary prison memoirs. For most uneducated and impoverished petty lawbreakers, it is likely that a stay in a colonial prison was less like a semester in school and more like a nightmarish term in a concentration camp.

Exemplary is the tragic experience of Con Dao prisoner Nguyen Van Vien, whose case was brought to the attention of a colonial inspector in 1932. Caught stealing a buffalo in 1898 at the age of twenty-three, Vien was exiled to Con Dao by an indigenous provincial tribunal. As a result of a series of bureaucratic mishaps, Vien remained confined on Con Dao for the same theft almost thirty-five years later. That Vien is rescued from historical oblivion by virtue of an apparently sympathetic passage culled from a French inspector's report and not from the voluminous writings of fellow political prisoners is symptomatic of the limited field of vision exhibited by revolutionary prison memoirs.[56]

While "revolutionary prison memoirs" typically ignore the existence of common-law prisoners, several are instructive in the open contempt they display toward criminals. Such an attitude is evident in one of the genre's progenitors, Huynh Thuc Khang's *Thi Tu Tung Thoai* [*Prison Verse*], first published in Hue in 1939:[57]

In prison there are gangs of scoundrels so violent-tempered that a dirty look or a small comment will provoke them to fight. For prisoners to be murdered in their sleep is unexceptional. During the initial months of our captivity with the common prisoners, we felt miserable. During the day we would rest and at night we'd discuss literature and talk politics—we didn't dare to interact with the common-law prisoners.[58]

To further explain the absence or denigration of nonpolitical prisoners in revolutionary prison memoirs, it is important to recognize how strictly the VWP's cultural authorities policed the content of published material in general and prison narratives in particular after coming to power in 1954.[59] A pertinent example is the party's heavy-handed response in 1955 to Phung Quan's loosely fictionalized adventure novel, *Vuot Con Dao* (*Escape from Con Dao*).[60] In a disapproving review article published in *Van Nghe* (*Literary Arts*), critic Vu Tu Nam chided Phung Quan for subordinating the heroism of imprisoned Communists to the courage and savvy of common-law prisoners:

> Phung Quan's book depicts party leaders on Con Dao as excessively simple-minded and naïve. In reality, the ward of solitary-confinement cells, where our best and brightest cadres were concentrated, was the nerve-center of the island. According to Phung Quan's description, inmates in this ward were demoralized and broken in spirit. Phung Quan deliberately glorifies common soldiers and ordinary prisoners while ignoring the mighty political strength of cadres and party members.[61]

Vu Tu Nam's critique was buttressed and elaborated in attacks launched by powerful cultural officials such as To Huu and Tran Do, who, unfortunately for Phung Quan, were also former political prisoners.[62] As Phung Quan was besieged by the ideological assaults and prison credentials of his critics, *Escape from Con Dao* fell into disrepute, and he was forced to undergo public self-criticism.[63] Apparently, Phung Quan's reprimand was not lost on future authors of fictional and putatively nonfictional prison narratives, virtually all of whom made sure to relegate common-law prisoners to the distant margins of their accounts.[64]

Like common-law offenders, non-Communist political prisoners are also underrepresented in the accounts of revolutionary prison memoirs. From the 1920s through the 1940s, the colonial state imprisoned anticolonialists of different political persuasions, including various kinds of anarchists, Stalinists, Trotskyists, nationalists, and radical Buddhists, as well as members of syncretic religious sects, secret societies, and underworld gangs. During the late 1930s, French-language newspapers in Sai-

gon aggressively covered the arrest and imprisonment of such unortho-
dox non-Stalinist radicals as Nguyen An Ninh, Phan Van Hum, Ho Huu
Tuong, and Ta Thu Thau.[65] However, other than the well-documented
armed conflicts between Communists and members of the rival Nationalist Party (Viet Nam Quoc Dan Dang) on Con Dao in 1934, non-
Communist political prisoners barely appear in revolutionary prison
memoirs.[66]

In the rare cases when non-Communist political prisoners are mentioned, it is only to compare their feebleness in captivity with the
strength of the Communists. Le Duan's recollections are typical in this
regard:

> Among the political prisoners, there were also non-communists, such as
> members of the Nationalist Party, adherents of the "national revolution"
> tendency such as Mr. Nguyen An Ninh, and Trotskyists such as Phan Van
> Hum and Ta Thu Thau. But none of them could equal the communists in
> endurance, dauntlessness and self-sacrifice. The more difficulties and hard-
> ships they met, the more the communists were steeled and tempered. They
> survived the most atrocious ordeals while others did not.[67]

An irony of Le Duan's comments is that Trotskyists Phan Van Hum and
Ta Thu Thau did in fact survive the "atrocious ordeal" of colonial imprisonment, but upon release in 1945 they were executed by Le Duan's
Viet Minh during sporadic roundups of prominent figures from rival
nationalist groups.[68]

The tendency of revolutionary prison memoirs to focus solely on
Communist prisoners further distorts the historical record by conflating
the eighty-year history of imprisonment in Indochina with developments
after 1930, the year the Communist Party was founded. While the highly
organized defiance of Communist inmates after 1930 represented a qual-
itative change in the nature of colonial prison resistance, it is important
to recognize that the colonial penal system had been generating significant levels of collective violence since its foundation in 1862. In fact, it
is arguable that the sporadic and largely uncoordinated resistance to the
penal system spearheaded by prisoners during World War I actually surpassed the level of violent opposition attained under Communist leadership in the 1930s. Moreover, enduring features of the colonial penal
system that promoted successful Communist activity in prison (i.e., architectural shortcomings, administrative instability, discontented
guards, confused and neglected systems of classification, inadequate
supervision for forced labor) were equally responsible for facilitating

collective resistance during earlier eras.[69] One effect of revolutionary prison memoirs, therefore, is to elide such continuities and to convey the questionable impression that the effectiveness of Communist prison agitation developed independently of the chronic dysfunctions that had long plagued the colonial prison system. In revolutionary prison memoirs, successful prison resistance does not grow out of the defects of the colonial penal system but derives solely from the uniquely prescient tactics and iron discipline of the Communist Party.

Also missing from revolutionary prison memoirs are vivid depictions of the texture of colonial prison life or evidence of the development of distinct subcultural formations behind bars. Descriptions of food, labor, discipline, hygiene, and the complex triangular relations obtaining between guards, prisoners, and French penal officials, for example, seem schematic and vague as compared with the meticulously detailed accounts of political education, self-improvement, and collective resistance. Moreover, revolutionary prison memoirs pay little or no attention to the prurient obsessions of French prison writing; there are few tales of betrayal, corruption, or rivalry among inmates and virtually none about suppressed desire, rape, or homosexuality.[70]

In 1991, following the first significant relaxation of state censorship in northern Vietnam since the mid-1950s, the Institute of History posthumously released a brief prison memoir by Tran Huy Lieu, an important revolutionary from the 1930s and the DRV's most prolific historian. Originally written in 1950 and entitled *Tinh trong Nguc Toi* (*Love in the Dark Prison*), the account detailed Lieu's own loneliness and unrequited longings while incarcerated on Con Dao during the early 1930s. In one unusually frank passage, Lieu admitted to a temporary fascination with "brother T," a fellow prisoner who had performed in drag in a play staged within the ward:

> After viewing the play performed during Tet in Bagne II, I sent a letter over ten pages long to brother T, who, on that day, had played the role of a female courtesan. As the prison regime suppressed family sentiments and petty bourgeois romantic sentiments, we were often forced to seek other outlets.[71]

The meaning of the passage is arguably ambiguous, but it is instructive that while many of Lieu's prison accounts were published during the 1960s, the memoir containing this passage was not released until after the Renovation (Doi Moi) policy of 1986. It is tempting to conclude that the decision to suppress its publication during the late 1950s and early 1960s was driven by a perception that the memoir alluded to the existence of homoerotic impulses among political prisoners, during a period in which the party was promoting a distinctly sexless image of the "new socialist man."

MORALE-BUILDING AND PROLETARIANIZATION

To further understand the most prominent elisions and distortions characteristic of revolutionary prison memoirs, it is useful to reconsider the genre's function within the political culture of the DRV. As has been suggested, one reason for the wide dissemination of the genre is that naked oppressiveness of the colonial prison system provided a dramatic setting for heroic performance. Revolutionary prison memoirs depict Communist militants fearlessly confronting the colonial state's most thoroughly repressive apparatus. They often juxtapose denunciations of sadistic guards, torture, and cramped quarters with celebrations of mass demonstrations, hunger strikes, and prison riots. "Prison writing," according to party critic Hoang Dung, "simultaneously denounces the cruel crimes of our enemies, describes our intense feelings for the landscape of our homeland, and relates the miseries endured by martyred comrades in prison."[72]

In the early 1970s, the Institute of Party History and the Youth Publishing House endeavored to gather and publish Communist prison verse from the colonial era. Anthologists solicited submissions through literary newspapers and, in some cases, visited ex-prisoners in their homes to record poems that had been committed to memory but never written down.[73] Prefacing their two-volume collection, *Tieng Hat trong Tu* (*Songs Sung in Prison*), the editors justified their efforts on didactic grounds: "The poetry of revolutionary fighters created in the prison of the French imperialists, from the foundation of our party to 1945, holds excellent educational value for the younger generations who grew up after the August Revolution."[74] At the time, the party's need to harness the "educational value" of prison poetry was based on anxiety about public morale raised by the American War. Thus, the compilation concluded by drawing links from colonial-era prisons to those of the American-backed South Vietnamese regime: "Over the past few years, similar verse has unceasingly echoed in prisons of the American puppets in the south."[75]

Representations of revolutionary heroism were thought to possess a unique capacity to motivate and inspire in wartime. During Vietnam's war with China in the late 1970s, the Culture and Information

Committee of Son La Province published an annotated collection entitled *Tho Ca Cach Mang Nha Tu Son La 1930–1945* (*Revolutionary
Poems and Songs from Son La Prison 1930–1945*).[76] In the introduction, editor Nguyen Anh Tuan linked the timing of the anthology's publication to the national mobilization effort then under way to resist "the
hegemonistic expansionism emanating from Beijing."[77] "Today, we re-
read prison stories from a period of 'blood and chains,'" Tuan wrote,
"and we find the precious souls of imprisoned communist fighters in the
pages. Each of us must use this opportunity to reexamine ourselves, to
cleanse and purify our souls in order to fortify our courage and expand
our love for the entire nation."[78]

Besides portraying the VWP's leading figures as heroic, courageous,
resourceful, and unswervingly dedicated to the revolutionary cause, revolutionary prison memoirs serve the party in another important way.
By depicting colonial penal institutions as schools, revolutionary prison
memoirs help conceal from their readership something particularly un-
settling for the party about the social composition of its founding members. One of the striking things about the VWP is the high percentage
of its early leaders who sprang from an elite background.[79] According
to Bernard Fall's comprehensive study of party leadership in the 1950s,
approximately 75 percent of high-level party cadres come from solidly
middle-class or upper-class families.[80] This is clearly reflected in the privileged educational backgrounds many of them possessed. For example,
Pham Van Dong and Truong Chinh received baccalaureate degrees from
the exclusive Lycée Albert Sarraut in Hanoi. Vo Nguyen Giap and Ho
Chi Minh, among others, attended the prestigious Franco-Vietnamese
Quoc Hoc high school in Hue. And numerous top-level cadres, including
Pham Hung, Le Duc Tho, and Le Duan, came from low-ranking mandarin families who ensured that their sons received significantly more
education than did most Vietnamese at the time.[81]

Not only are the exalted educational careers of Indochinese Communist Party (ICP) leaders passively ignored in revolutionary prison
memoirs; they are actively obscured by the obsessive comparisons offered between prisons and schools. In other words, a depiction of
colonial prisons as the "universities of the Vietnamese revolution" conveniently draws attention away from the fact that the leaders of this
explicitly proletarian and peasant revolution were products of the most
elite educational institutions the colonial state had to offer. In this sense,
revolutionary prison memoirs should be understood as serving a function similar to the party's well-documented proletarianization (*vo san*

hoa) movement of the late 1920s and early 1930s.[82] That is, it allowed party leaders to reconcile their inherited class background with their adopted ideological inclinations.[83] Significantly, though, whereas proletarianization involved, in some cases, a genuine attempt by self-consciously elite party members to effect a transformation of their own "class outlook," revolutionary prison memoirs were penned by party leaders not to change their own perceptions but to reshape the public's.

It is in a similar context that the publication and massive dissemination of Ho Chi Minh's *Nhat Ky trong Tu* (*Prison Diary*), also in 1960, might be understood.[84] During the 1920s and 1930s, when his future colleagues in the Politburo were earning revolutionary credentials in French jails, Ho was abroad carrying out Comintern directives. The fact that Ho did not possess the same colonial prison record as virtually all his colleagues was neatly effaced by the public appearance of the *Prison Diary*, which he supposedly wrote while incarcerated in 1942 by a warlord in southern China. Released almost twenty years after it was allegedly written and at the outset of a campaign to spread revolutionary prison memoirs of ICP leaders, the *Prison Diary*, which is easily northern Vietnam's most widely published and translated literary work as well as a core secondary-school text, suggests an explicit attempt to bring Ho's revolutionary credentials in line with those of his comrades.

CONCLUSION

Revolutionary prison memoirs reveal much about the forces shaping cultural production in the Democratic Republic of Vietnam. The party's need to reassert the legitimacy of its monopoly over political power required a popular literary form that cleaned up, embellished, and celebrated the history of its heroic struggles and sacrifices. The "prison-as-school" trope not only could play such a role but also proved useful in its capacity to obfuscate the exalted family and educational backgrounds of many party leaders. Moreover, revolutionary prison writing could draw on colonial and precolonial literary traditions that were both familiar to the reading public and genuinely popular among the Western-educated but nevertheless traditionally oriented leaders of the party. In short, while revolutionary prison memoirs may obscure more than they reveal about the history of imprisonment in French Indochina, they do reflect the political strategies, class anxieties, and distinctive sociocultural background of the first generation of the Communist Party leadership.

NOTES

1. Tran Huu Ta, "Doc Hoi Ky Cach Mang: Nghi ve Ve Dep cua Nguoi Chien Si Cong San Viet Nam" ["Reading Revolutionary Memoirs: Thoughts on the Beauty of Vietnamese Communist Warriors"], *Tap Chi Van Hoc [Journal of Literature]* 2, no. 164 (1997): 17–28.

2. See, for some examples, Nguyen Tao, *Trong Nguc Toi Hoa Lo [In the Dark Prison, Hoa Lo]* (Hanoi: NXB Van Hoc, 1959); Tran Dang Ninh, *Hai Lan Vuot Nguc [Two Prison Escapes]* (Hanoi: NXB Van Hoc, 1970); Tran Cung, "Tu Con Dao Tro Ve (Hoi Ky)" ["Return from Poulo Condore (Memoirs)"], *Nghien Cuu Lich Su [Journal of Historical Studies]* 134, no. 9 (1970): 18–26; Bui Cong Trung, "O Con Dao" ["In Con Dao"], in *Len Duong Thang Loi* [On the Road to Victory] (Hanoi: NXB Hanoi, 1985); Ha Phu Huong, "O Nha Tu Lao Bao" ["In Lao Bao Prison"], *Tap Chi Cua Viet*, no. 3 (1990). The following (some reprints) can be found in *Suoi Reo Nam Ay [The Bubbling Spring That Year]* (Hai Phong: NXB Thong Tin-Van Hoa, 1993): Dang Viet Chau, "Nguc Son La 1935–1936" ["Son La Prison 1935–1936"]; Van Tien Dung, "Niem Tin La Suc Manh" ["Belief Is Strength"]; Xuan Thuy, "Suoi Reo Nam Ay" ["The Bubbling Spring That Year"]; Nguyen van Tu, "Toi Lam Cau Doi Tet o Nha Tu Son La" ["I Make Rhyming Couplets on New Year Occasion in Son La Prison"]. The following can be found in *Tran Huy Lieu: Hoi Ky [Tran Huy Lieu: Memoirs]* (Hanoi: NXB Khoa Hoc Xa Hoi, 1991): "Tinh trong Nguc Toi" ["Love in the Dark Prison"], "Duoi Ham Son La" ["In the Son La Hole"] "Xuan No trong Tu" ["Spring Blooms in Prison"], "Tren Hon Cau" ["On Hon Cau"]; "Phan Dau De Tro Nen Mot Dang Vien Cong San" ["Striving to Become a Communist Party Member"].

3. Martha Grace Duncan, *Romantic Outlaws, Beloved Prisons: The Unconscious Meanings of Crime and Punishment* (New York: New York University Press, 1996).

4. W. B. Carnochan, "The Literature of Confinement," in *The Oxford History of the Prison: The Practice of Punishment in Western Society*, ed. Norval Morris and David Rothman, (New York: Oxford University Press, 1995), 427.

5. See the essay by Christoph Giebel in this volume.

6. Tran Huu Ta, "Doc Hoi Ky Cach Mang," 17.

7. Huynh Sanh Thong, ed. and trans., *The Heritage of Vietnamese Poetry* (New Haven, Conn.: Yale University Press, 1979), 22.

8. David Marr, *Vietnamese Tradition on Trial, 1925–1945* (Berkeley and Los Angeles: University of California Press, 1981), 308.

9. Nguyen Ngoc Bich, *A Thousand Years of Vietnamese Poetry* (New York: Knopf, 1975), 32.

10. Huynh Sanh Thong, *The Heritage of Vietnamese Poetry*, 41.

11. Nguyen Khac Vien and Huu Ngoc, ed. and trans., *Vietnamese Literature: Historical Background and Texts* (Hanoi: Red River, 1980), 383.

12. For a biographical sketch of Nguyen Huu Cau, see Tran van Giap et al., *Luoc Truyen Cac Tac Gia Viet Nam [Sketch of Vietnamese Authors]* (Hanoi: NXB Khoa Hoc Xa Hoi, 1971), 298.

13. Huynh Sanh Thong, *The Heritage of Vietnamese Poetry*, 57.

14. Nguyen Khac Vien and Huu Ngoc, *Vietnamese Literature: Historical Background and Texts,* 574.

15. Tran Huy Lieu, "What's My Crime?" trans. Huynh Sanh Thong, *Vietnam Forum,* no. 13 (1990): 140.

16. Tran Huy Lieu, "Doc Tap Tho Nhat Ky trong Tu cua Ho Chu Tich" ["Reading Chairman Ho's Prison Diary"], *Nghien Cuu Van Hoc [Journal of Literary Studies]* 6 (1960): 21.

17. Xuan Dieu, "Yeu Tho Bac" ["Loving Uncle's Poetry"], in *Tap Nghien Cuu Binh Luan Chon Loc ve Tho Van Ho Chu Tich [Selected Commentaries and Studies on Chairman Ho's Poetry]* (Hanoi: Giao Duc, 1978), 79–81.

18. Dang Thai Mai, *Van Tho Cach Mang Viet Nam Dau The Ky XX (1900–1925) [Vietnamese Revolutionary Prose and Poetry in the Early Twentieth Century]* (Hanoi: NXB Van Hoc, 1964), 158.

19. Ibid., 154.

20. David Marr, *Vietnamese Anticolonialism: 1885–1925* (Berkeley and Los Angeles: University of California Press, 1971), 241–44.

21. Huynh Thuc Khang, *Tu Truyen [Autobiography]* (Hue: Anh Minh, 1963), 66.

22. See ibid.

23. Nguyen The Anh, "A Case of Confucian Survival in Twentieth-Century Vietnam: Huynh Thuc Khang and His Newspaper *Tieng Dan,*" *Vietnam Forum,* no. 8 (1986): 182.

24. Huynh Thuc Khang, *Thi Tu Tung Thoai [Prison Verse]* (Hue: NXB Tieng Dan, 1939, 42.

25. Translation is from Huynh Sanh Thong, ed. and trans., *An Anthology of Vietnamese Poems: From the Eleventh through the Twentieth Centuries* (New Haven, Conn.: Yale University Press, 1996), 118.

26. Ton Quang Phiet, *Mot Ngay Ngan Thu [The Eternal Day]* (Hue: Phuc Long, 1935), 11.

27. Nhuong Tong, *Doi trong Nguc [Life in Prison]* (Hanoi: Van Hoa Moi, 1935), 12.

28. Literary scholars point out that prisons and imprisonment have figured prominently in the French literary tradition. Victor Brombert writes of an "explosion of prison literary images in nineteenth-century France." Victor Brombert, *The Romantic Prison: The French Tradition* (Princeton, N.J.: Princeton University Press, 1978). According to W. B. Carnochan, "From the Royal hostage Charles d'Orléans (1394–1465) to Genet . . . the prison has always been a more fertile source of poetry in France than in England and America." Carnochan, "The Literature of Confinement," 432.

29. "In the area of literature, what the youth of Vietnam had available to read in school and out of school were works of French Classicists and Romantics." Cong Huyen Ton Nu Nha Trang, "The Role of French Romanticism in the New Poetry Movement in Vietnam," in *Borrowings and Adaptations in Vietnamese Culture,* ed. Truong Buu Lam, Southeast Asia Paper No. 25 (Honolulu: Center for Asia and Pacific Studies), 52–62.

30. See John Schaffer and Cao Thi Nhu Quynh, "Ho Bieu Chanh and the

Early Development of the Vietnamese Novel," *Vietnam Forum,* no. 12 (1988): 100–10.

31. For a discussion of the novel and its debt to Dumas, see Alexander Woodside, *Community and Revolution in Vietnam* (Boston: Houghton Mifflin, 1976), 268.

32. See Tran Hinh, "Victo Huygo va cac Nha Van Viet Nam" ["Victor Hugo and Vietnamese Writers"], in *Hugo o Viet Nam [Hugo in Vietnam]*, ed. Luu Lien (Hanoi: NXB Vien Van Hoc, 1985), 418.

33. Ibid., 420–21.

34. On Hugo's preoccupation with crime and punishment, see Brombert, *The Romantic Prison,* 91–117.

35. Dang Anh Dao, "Victo Huygo va con Nguoi Viet Nam Hien Dai" ["Victor Hugo and Vietnamese Today"], in *Hugo o Viet Nam,* ed. Luu Lien, 367. In 1926, Pham Quynh introduced Hugo's work to the readers of the influential journal *Nam Phong.* Portions of *Les Misérables* were serialized in *Tieng Dan* in the early 1930s. In 1936, novelist Vu Trong Phung published a Vietnamese translation of *Lucrèce Borgia* entitled *Giet Me [Matricide].* According to Nguyen Dang Manh, Phung also translated (but never published) *Le Dernier jour d'un condamné.* See Nguyen Dang Manh and Tran Huu Ta, eds., *Tuyen Tap Vu Trong Phung [Collected Works of Vu Trong Phung],* vol. 1 (Hanoi: NXB Van Hoc, 1993), 12.

36. Victor Oliver, *Cao Dai Spiritism* (Leiden: E. J. Brill, 1976). For more on Cao Dai, see Jayne Werner, *Peasant Politics and Religious Sectarianism: Peasant and Priest in the Cao Dai in Vietnam* (New Haven, Conn.: Yale University Southeast Asia Studies, 1981).

37. In the same interview, Linh discussed his admiration for French romanticist Hector Malot. The interview appears in Neil Sheehan, *After the War Was Over* (New York: Vintage, 1993), 75.

38. Tran Hinh argues that Hugo influenced the poetry of To Huu, the ICP's most celebrated poet. He also notes that Ho Chi Minh often recalled reading *Les Misérables* while a student in Hue. Tran Hinh, "Victo Huygo va cac Nha Van Viet Nam," 412.

39. Tran Van Giau, "The First Propagandist for the Ideas of 1789 in Vietnam," *Vietnamese Studies,* no. 21 (1991): 12.

40. For an examination of Bastille imagery in political rhetoric during the 1930s, see Peter Zinoman, *The Colonial Bastille: A History of Imprisonment in Vietnam, 1862–1940* (Berkeley and Los Angeles: University of California Press, 2001), 256–57.

41. Dépôt d'Archives d'Outre-Mer (AOM) in Aix-en-Provence: Service de Liaison des Originaires des Territoires Français d'Outre-Mer (SLOTFOM), Series 3, Carton 49 Dossier: Les Associations Anti-Françaises et la Propagande Communiste en Indochine, July–August 1931.

42. Daniel Hémery, *Révolutionaires vietnamiens et pouvoir colonial en Indochine* (Paris: Maspéro, 1975), 155.

43. Silvio Pellico, *My Prisons* (London: Oxford University Press, 1963).

44. Dang Thai Mai, *Van Tho Cach Mang Viet Nam Dau The Ky XX,* 76.

45. Nguyen Van Vinh translated Dumas's *Les Trois mousquetaires* into *quoc*

ngu in 1921. His *La Dame aux camélias* strongly influenced early attempts at Vietnamese prose fiction. Maurice Durand and Nguyen Tran Huan, *An Introduction to Vietnamese Literature,* trans. D. M. Hawke (New York: Columbia University Press, 1985), 117.

46. Phan Van Hum, *Ngoi Tu Kham Lon* [*A Stay in the Central Prison*] (1929; reprint, Saigon: NXB Dan Toc, 1957), 129.

47. An early revolutionary and longtime Politburo member, Pham Hung eventually became head of the Central Committee Directorate for the South (COSVN).

48. Pham Hung, *In the Death Cell* (Hanoi: Foreign Languages Publishing House, 1960), 75.

49. Hoang Anh, "Nha Tu De Quoc Tro Thanh Truong Hoc cua Chien Si Cach Mang" ["Imperialist Prisons Become Schools for Revolutionary Fighters"], *Tap Chi Cong San* [*Communist Review*] 1, no. 40 (1990): 3–9; Nguyen Luu, "Nha Tu Son La, Truong Hoc Cach Mang" ["Son La Prison, School for Revolutionaries"], *Nghien Cuu Lich Su* [*Journal of Historical Studies*] 103 (1975): 57–71; Tran Huy Lieu, "Tu Hoc trong Tu" ["Self-Study in Prison"], Nguyen Thieu, "Truong Hoc trong Tu" ["Prison School"], Nguyen Duc Thuan, "Truong Hoc Xa Lim" ["Cell School"], Nguyen Duy Trinh, "Lam Bao va Sang Tac Tieu Thuyet trong Nha Lao Vinh" ["Writing Newspapers and Novels in Vinh Prison"], all in *Truong Hoc sau Song Sat* [*School behind the Iron Bars*] (Hanoi: NXB Thanh Nien, 1969).

50. Tran Huy Lieu, "Tu Hoc trong Tu," 142.

51. "Le Duan Recalls Days as Prisoner on Con Son," Foreign Broadcast Information Service–East Asia Service-76 (9/3/76, Hanoi Vietnamese News Agency in English, 1454 GMT).

52. Escape attempts figure in most "revolutionary prison memoirs," and a sizable number are concerned almost exclusively with the planning and execution of breakouts. For examples, see Nguyen Tao, *Vuot Nguc Dak Mil* [*Escape from Dak Mil*] (Hanoi: NXB Thanh Nien, 1976); Tran Dang Ninh, "Vuot Nguc Son La" ["Escape from Son La Prison"], in *Suoi Reo Nam Ay,* 176–208; Ngo Van Quynh, "Am Vang Cuoc Vuot Nguc" ["Echo of an Escape"], in *Suoi Reo Nam Ay,* 208–18; Vu Duy Nhai, "Nho Lai nhung Ngay Thoat Nguc Son La" ["Recalling the Days of Escape from Son La Prison"], in *Suoi Reo Nam Ay,* 264–83; Tran Huy Lieu, "Nghia Lo Khoi Nghia—Nghia Lo Vuot Nguc" ["Nghia Lo Uprising—Escape from Nghia Lo"], in *Tran Huy Lieu: Hoi Ky,* 278–344; Tran Tu Binh, "Thoat Nguc Hoa Lo" ["Escape from Hoa Lo Prison"], in *Ha Noi Khoi Nghia* [*Hanoi Uprising*] (Hanoi: NXB Hanoi, 1966).

53. Nguyen Tao, *Chung Toi Vuot Nguc* [*We Escape from Prison*] (Hanoi: NXB Van Hoa, 1977).

54. For an analysis of the composition of the Indochinese penal population during the 1930s, see Zinoman, *The Colonial Bastille,* chaps. 4 and 7.

55. Ibid. The issue is complicated by the fact that political activists were often sentenced for common-law crimes.

56. AOM–Affaires Politiques 7F 1728 Dossier: Mission d'Inspection: Rapport fait par M. Le Gregam, Inspecteur des Colonies sur les îles et les pénitenciers de Poulo Condore, February 23, 1932, 33.

57. Dang Thai Mai placed Huynh Thuc Khang's prison memoirs along with the accounts of Le Van Hien and Cuu Kim Son as a formative influence on the producers of "revolutionary prison memoirs." Dang Thai Mai, *Van Tho Cach Mang Viet Nam Dau The Ky XX*, 123.

58. Huynh Thuc Khang, *Thi Tu Tung Thoai*, 50.

59. For a general treatment of the ICP's literary policies in the 1950s, see Hirohide Kurihara, "Changes in the Literary Policy of the Vietnamese Worker's Party, 1956–1958," in *Indochina in the 1940s and 1950s*, ed. Takashi Shiraishi and Motoo Furuta (Ithaca, N.Y.: Cornell Southeast Asia Program, 1992), 143–64.

60. Phung Quan, *Vuot Con Dao* (1955; reprint, Hue: NXB Thanh Hoa, 1987).

61. Vu Tu Nam, "Mot So Y Kien Tham Gia Ket Thuc Cuoc Tranh Luan: Phe Binh Cuon *Vuot Con Dao*" ["Some Opinions regarding the Debate: A Critique of *Escape from Con Dao*"], *Bao Van Nghe* [*Literature and Arts Newspaper*], July 28, 1955, 3. The same article noted that over one hundred letters commenting on *Vuot Con Dao* had been sent to the journal *Sinh Hoat Van Nghe* [*Literary and Artistic Activities*], some by readers who had served time in colonial prisons.

62. Georges Boudarel, *Cent fleurs écloses dans la nuit du Vietnam: Communisme et dissidence, 1945–1956* (Paris: Jacques Bertoin, 1991), 121–24.

63. After going through four editions in the first half of 1955, *Vuot Con Dao* was pulled from circulation and only republished in 1987. For more on the public criticism of Phung Quan and his novel, see A. T. "Hai Cuoc Thao Luan ve Viet Bac va Vuot Con Dao" ("Two Debates about Viet Bac and Escape from Con Dao"], *Bao Van Nghe*, March 20, 1955.

64. The official attacks against Phung Quan and *Vuot Con Dao* anticipated by almost two years the repression of the northern literary movement known today as Nhan Van Giai Pham. For two cogent accounts of Nhan Van Giai Pham, see Hoang Giang, "La Révolte des intellectuels au Vietnam en 1956," and Georges Boudarel, "Intellectual Dissidence in the 1950s: The 'Nhan Van Giai Pham' Affair," both in *Vietnam Forum*, no. 13, (1990): 144–79.

65. Phan Van Hum, Ta Thu Thau, and Ho Huu Tuong were members of competing Trotskyist factions during the 1930s and 1940s. Nguyen An Ninh was an eclectic radical who combined strains of Marxism, anarchism, Buddhism, and southern Vietnamese secret society traditions.

66. For a characteristic treatment of communist-nationalist conflict behind bars, see Tran Van Giau, *Su Phat Trien cua Tu Tuong o Viet Nam Tu The Ky XIX den Cach Mang Thang Tam* [*Ideological Development in Vietnam from the Nineteenth Century to the August Revolution*], vol. 2 (Hanoi: NXB Khoa Hoc Xa hoi, 1975), 592–600.

67. "Le Duan Recalls Days as Prisoner on Con Son."

68. On the Viet Minh's execution of Ta Thu Thau, see David Marr, *Vietnam 1945: The Quest for Power* (Berkeley and Los Angeles: University of California Press, 1995), 435.

69. For an extended discussion, see Zinoman, *The Colonial Bastille*, chaps. 5 and 6.

70. The classic account in this vein is J. C. Démariaux, *Les Secrets des îles Poulo Condore: Le grand bagne indochinois* (Paris: J. Peyronnet & Cie, 1956).

71. Tran Huy Lieu, *Tinh trong Nguc Toi* [*Love in the Dark Prison*], in Tran Huy Lieu, *Tran Huy Lieu: Hoi ky*, 137.

72. Hoang Dung, ed., *Tho Van Cach Mang 1930–1945* [*Revolutionary Poems and Prose, 1930–1945*] (Hanoi: NXB Van Hoc, 1980), 12.

73. Interview with Vo Van Truc, editor of *Tieng Hat trong Tu,* Hanoi, December 5, 1991.

74. Vo Van Truc, ed., *Tieng Hat trong Tu,* vol. 1 (Hanoi: NXB Thanh Nien, 1972), 193.

75. Ibid., 144.

76. Ty Van Hoa Thong Tin Son La, *Tho Ca Cach Mang Nha Tu Son La 1930–1945* (Son La: NXB Son La, 1980), 7.

77. Ibid.

78. Ibid., 36.

79. As Alexander Woodside points out, "It does not slander the political contributions of one of the most hard-working and resourceful peasantries in all Asia to point out . . . that the Vietnamese revolution was led for the most part by the sons of the traditional intelligentsia, and that this was the section of Vietnamese society which found itself earliest and most often in demeaning circumstances of cultural and political conflict with the colonial power." Woodside, *Community and Revolution in Vietnam*, 303.

80. Bernard Fall, *The Viet Minh Regime,* Data Paper No. 14 (Ithaca, N.Y.: Cornell University Southeast Asia Program, 1954), 74.

81. Hy Van Luong's discussion of the elite origins of the Vietnamese revolutionary leadership is particularly instructive. Hy Van Luong, "Agrarian Unrest from an Anthropological Perspective: The Case of Vietnam," *Comparative Politics* 17, no. 2 (January 1985): 165–70. See also Douglas Pike, *History of Vietnamese Communism, 1925–1976* (Stanford, Calif.: Hoover Institution Press, 1978), 67.

82. On the proletarianization movement, see Gareth Porter, "Proletariat and Peasantry in Early Vietnamese Communism," *Asian Thought and Society* 1, no. 3 (1976): 333–46.

83. Nowhere is this connection between imprisonment and proletarianization more clearly stated than in an interview French writer Andrée Viollis conducted with a former political prisoner in Saigon on October 14, 1931. Describing the significance of his prison experience, the young revolutionary told Viollis: "It was that [prison] which made me a revolutionary, more so because I was not born into the proletarian class." Andrée Viollis, *Indochine S.O.S* (1935; reprint, Paris: Les Editeurs Français Réunis, 1949), 25.

84. For a surprisingly frank discussion of the checkered publishing history of *Nhat Ky trong Tu*, including the suppression of almost two dozen poems in the original manuscript, see Phan Van Cac, "Tu Ban Dich Nam 1960 den Ban Dich Bo Sung va Chinh Ly Nam 1983" ["From 1960 Translation to the Supplemented and Corrected Translation of 1983"], in *Suy Nghi Moi Ve Nhat Ky Trong Tu* [*New Reflections on the Prison Diary*], ed. Nguyen Hue Chi (Hanoi: NXB Khoa Hoc Xa Hoi, 1990).

TWO

"The Fatherland Remembers Your Sacrifice"

Commemorating War Dead in North Vietnam

Shaun Kingsley Malarney

The dead soldier was one of the greatest threats to the legitimacy and authority of the Democratic Republic of Vietnam (DRV) in the first three decades of its existence. Tens of thousands of northern Vietnamese died in military service, first in the French War (1946–54), then in the struggle to unify the country from 1959 to 1975. During these years, the DRV government began to articulate what Hue-Tam Ho Tai refers to in the introduction to this volume as the "official narrative" of war in order to legitimize the war efforts and strengthen the population's will to fight.[1] This narrative, which highlighted Vietnam's history of repelling foreign aggression, also gave extensive attention to dead soldiers so that their deaths would be regarded as noble and meaningful.[2]

This chapter will examine how the experience of warfare and the government agenda to glorify war death affected the social and cultural life of Thinh Liet commune, a northern Vietnamese community located to the south of Hanoi.[3] It will describe the many social and cultural innovations that years of warfare produced, such as the linkages made between past and contemporary struggles, and the creation of new categories of heroes and heroic action. The main objective is to explore the ritual responses to war death that emerged during the American War (1963–75) in Vietnam. As Mark Bradley points out in this volume, the North Vietnamese state employed numerous methods to ennoble war death that included film, war memorials, museums, novels, poetry, and paintings.[4] Among the most important was the government's creation of a new funeral rite, which local officials performed to publicly reiterate the state's gratitude to those who gave their lives. Yet, although residents approved of these rites and were grateful for their performance, they considered them insufficient for addressing one of their most powerful concerns: caring for the souls of the war dead and ultimately integrating them into the benign realm of family ancestors. To this end, residents created a new set of funeral rites. Public acceptance of the official commemorative ceremonies requires us to recognize that the local ceremonies did not imply an act of resistance or opposition to state policies.[5] However, the differences between the responses left the souls and memories of dead soldiers situated in distinct communities of remembrance constructed by different social actors for extremely different reasons.

THE "JUST CAUSE" OF NATIONAL LIBERATION

One of the most important elements in the Vietnamese state's agenda for legitimizing the war attempt was its attempt to draw on the prestige that has historically accrued to those who protected the country from foreign aggression or liberated it from foreign occupation. Over the centuries, the Vietnamese have fought numerous wars, many of which began after outsiders invaded Vietnamese soil. In many of these instances, going into battle and dying to save the nation were portrayed as honorable pursuits. Indeed, fighting for the nation was described in some cases as a "just cause" or "righteous obligation" (*chinh nghia*).[6] The compelling nature of liberating or protecting Vietnam could be seen in the public veneration of military heroes. The Vietnamese pantheon of great historical figures is composed overwhelmingly of men and women who have battled foreign armies. The Trung Sisters, who defeated a Chinese army in A.D. 39, general Tran Hung Dao, who, through a brilliant stratagem, destroyed the fleet of the Mongol invaders in the thirteenth century, or Le Loi, who cast out the Ming and then established the Le dynasty in the fifteenth century, are among the most revered figures in Vietnamese history. While official historiography glorifies these heroes, their importance among the people is equally great. The accomplishments or "meritorious work" (*cong duc*) of some military heroes were such that supernatural qualities have been attributed to them. General Tran Hung Dao is a case in point. Many Vietnamese consider him to have been a "living god" (*than song*) sent to rescue the Vietnamese. He is referred to frequently by his spirit name, Duc Thanh Tran; his powers carried on after his death, and his spirit, propitiated at hundreds of shrines across northern Vietnam, is regarded as one of the most powerful and efficacious in the entire spirit realm. Other military heroes, such as the Trung Sisters (d. 44) and Lady Trieu (d. 248), also have established cults through which the living seek assistance from their spirits. The prestige and efficacy of these figures stemming from their military accomplishments is virtually unmatched in Vietnamese society.

In constructing their narrative of warfare, the Vietnamese Communists highlighted and popularized the historical continuities between their contemporary struggles and Vietnam's earlier struggles. The very first armed military unit formed on December 22, 1944, by the Communists in the caves of Cao Bang Province, a humble group of thirty-four individuals with two revolvers and thirty-one rifles, was called the "Tran Hung Dao Platoon" in honor of the great general.[7] Official propaganda also spoke of the great examples of Vietnam's military heroes and the lessons to be learned from them. General Vo Nguyen Giap, Vietnam's key military strategist during the French War and the mastermind of the victory at Dien Bien Phu, even declared:

> The contemporary ideas of our party, military, and people for the offensive struggle cannot be separated from the traditional military ideas of our people. During our history, all victorious wars of resistance or liberation, whether led by the Trung Sisters [first century], Ly Bon [sixth century], Trieu Quang Phuc [sixth century], Le Loi [fifteenth century], or Nguyen Trai [fifteenth century], have all shared the common characteristic of a continuous offensive aimed at casting off the yoke of feudal domination by foreigners.[8]

Communist leaders also described their struggle as a sacred activity. For example, in an August 1965 speech to an antiaircraft unit in Hanoi, Party General Secretary Le Duan proclaimed, "Saving the nation is a sacred obligation [*nghia vu thieng lieng*] of the people. . . . We are determined to fight and win to keep our independence and freedom, to secure our health and happiness, and to build the nation into a wealthy and beautiful Vietnam."[9] Throughout both wars, the nation and the military necessity of saving and protecting it, were placed in indisputably sacred space. The wars were not simply described as wars (*chien tranh*) in official discourse. The French War was described as a *khoi nghia*, rendered in one dictionary as to "rise up in arms (against an oppressive rule)."[10] The American War was described as the "War of National Salvation Against the Americans" (Chien Tranh Chong My Cuu Nuoc). Dying and suffering in the name of such a cause, which was similar to the great historical struggles of the Vietnamese people, were given noble and transcendent qualities.

ARTICULATING THE NEW VIRTUE

The legitimation of Vietnam's military effort extended far beyond the appropriation of the legacy of resisting foreign occupation. One of the most explicit moves in the ideological realm was the creation and elaboration of a new set of definitions for noble and virtuous actions. Prior to the Revolution, official ideology had emphasized the Confucian virtues of devotion to the emperor and the mandarinate. In the Communist state, the act of devotion remained salient; only the objects changed. According to the new definition, the objects of virtuous action became the fatherland (*to quoc*), the people (*nhan dan*), the party (*dang*), and particularly the Revolution (*cach mang*). Actions carried out in the interest of these four collective entities were virtuous (conversely, actions carried out for the emperor, the mandarinate, or the old order were all stigmatized). The critical element in the construction of the new virtue was the transcendence of self-interest and the selfless devotion to the collectivity. As Le Duan declared, "The revolutionary differs from the nonrevolutionary in that he knows to forget himself for the service of the collectivity, for the common interest. Before all else he always thinks of the Revolution and the collectivity. He always knows to place the interests of the fatherland, the interests of the collectivity, above the interests of the individual."[11] "To relentlessly think of one's self, of one's family," the general secretary commented on another occasion, "is inadequate, selfish."[12]

The revolutionary formulation of selfless virtue was conjoined with the public glorification of death and personal sacrifice to advance the revolutionary cause. The greatest virtue was achieved with death, a transformation that reached its apotheosis in the concept of "sacrifice" (*hi sinh*). The word *hi sinh* predates the Vietnamese Revolution. Semantically, it matched the English-language meaning of sacrifice, that being simply to give up something, usually to gain something else. With the Vietnamese Communists, the semantic domain of *hi sinh* was recast, and sacrifice was associated with, and virtually restricted to, those who died doing the Revolution's bidding. Sacrifice came to connote giving up one's life in a just cause to protect and improve the collectivity. Party officials provided precise definitions of what constituted sacrifice. "Thus sacrifice is to sacrifice what, sacrifice for whom? It is to sacrifice one's being, it is to sacrifice to serve the country, the people, the Revolution."[13] Sacrifice was also the test of true revolutionary mettle and integrity. "Without the virtuous willingness for sacrifice," Le Duan argued, "one is not an authentic revolutionary. If you want to realize the revolutionary ideal, but will not dare to sacrifice yourself, then you are only speaking empty words."[14] The greatest revolutionary virtue could only be achieved in death and sacrifice for the common good.

The willingness to sacrifice was publicly rewarded because a sacrificial death was portrayed as a glorious and noble death, one that further grew in nobility from the willingness and enthusiasm with which it had occurred. It was also a death that was to be eternally remembered and remain an example for those who survived. The glorification of sacrifice was elaborated at the very highest reaches of the party. Discussing the deaths of a number of Party members who were killed or executed by the French, Ho Chi Minh declared, "The blood of the martyrs has made the revolutionary flag dazzlingly red. Their courageous sacrifice has prepared the earth of our nation to bloom into a flower of independence and result in our freedom. Our people must eternally record and remember the meritorious efforts of the martyrs. We must constantly study their courageous spirit to transcend all difficulties and tribulations, and realize the revolutionary work that they have passed on to us."[15] Death by "sacrifice" placed one into a venerable and heroic category, one that transcended the individual's physical annihilation.

The revolutionary elaboration of "sacrifice" has had important linguistic consequences in everyday conversation as well. The verb "to die" in Vietnamese takes multiple forms, with each particular form providing important social information about the deceased. Common people, for example, are generally said to *mat,* "to be lost," or *bi chet,* to "suffer death." Elderly people *qua doi,* or "pass from life." The emperor in prerevolutionary times would *bang ha,* or "pass far below." The deaths of Ho Chi Minh and other high officials are often described with the poetic and respectful expression *tu tran,* "to leave this world." Communist revolutionaries and soldiers killed during the struggle against the enemy can indeed "suffer death," but officially and in everyday parlance, people say that they have been "sacrificed" (*hi sinh*). The death of Hoang Van Thu, a member of the Central Committee of the Indochinese Communist Party who was captured by the French and later executed, provides a fitting example. Thu's death is thus recounted in an official biography: "On May 24, 1944, he was sacrificed at the Tuong Mai Rifle

Figure 2.1. Grave of soldier killed during border war with China, 1979, Tam Nong District Revolutionary Martyrs Cemetery, Phu Tho. Photograph by Natalia Puchalt.

Range (Hanoi), at thirty-eight years of age."[16] Official death certificates for soldiers also use the word *sacrifice* (see later discussion). Unlike the subtle emphasis of difference between the "passing from life" of everyday people and the "passing far below" of an emperor, the expression *hi sinh* applies to all who have fallen for the cause, regardless of rank or position.

The ennoblement of death and sacrifice for the Revolution continued after the death of the individual. Instead of merging them into an anonymous mass of war dead, all those who died carrying out the work of the Revolution were officially grouped into the social category of "martyr" or "revolutionary martyr" (*liet si*) (fig. 2.1). The construction of this category represented an innovation by the state. Like *hi sinh*, the word *liet si* predated the revolutionary era. Party officials, however, recast it semantically to indicate those who had died for the Revolution or fallen in battle with the enemy. Generally speaking, the term in its most common usage applies to soldiers who fell in battle, and anyone who had "been sacrificed" would later be classified as a martyr. The classification, however, required official verification for it to be valid. Many soldiers who died from other causes in the military or noncombatants who died as a result of enemy action were not classified as martyrs. During the American War, thousands of Vietnamese soldiers died from illness and disease while serving in the military. Such soldiers were classified as *tu si,* or "war dead." Large numbers of North Vietnamese civilians were also killed in American bombing raids. These individuals were classified as *nan nhan chien tranh,* or "victims of war." Others were agreed to have been sacrificed but were later denied the honor of being classified as martyrs. Such was the tragic case of Nguyen Ton Duyen, a party official from the village of Giap Tu in Thinh Liet, who was wrongfully executed during the Land Reform campaign (1953–56). After the Correction of Errors campaign, party officials admitted that Duyen's death had been a mistake. They granted that he had sacrificed himself for the Revolution, but they would not allow him to be classified as a martyr, despite his family's protestations. The honor and nobility that inhere in being a martyr are poignantly evident in the fact that Duyen's family, to this day, is still trying to have the decision reversed.

SUPPORTING THE WAR EFFORT

In 1959, the North Vietnamese leadership began the struggle to reunite Vietnam. Over the next five years, the government sent tens of thousands of infiltrators to the South, and combat slowly increased. In February 1965, the United States began its Rolling Thunder bombing campaign against North Vietnam, marking America's definitive commitment to the war in Vietnam. Although many North Vietnamese had died in combat in the years leading up to 1965, their numbers increased significantly afterward. As a result, the government began instituting a number of new policies and practices to prevent its efforts to glorify and ennoble people's sacrifices from seeming hollow and to display its gratitude and appreciation for those who had given their lives in battle.

One of the first steps taken by the government in this period was the modification of the structure of public administration and official policies to make them more responsive to the needs of those who had family members in the military. When the government established the original structure of commune-level rural administration in 1945, one of the five executive committee members was given responsibility for dealing with "social affairs," a charge that included relief for the needy and the delivery of pensions, stipends, or other forms of social assistance to local families. One important group of recipients of state assistance after 1954 was the "policy families" (*gia dinh chinh sach*), a category defined as those families with a member serving in the military or with a member who had been disabled or killed. From the period of the French War, the Vietnamese government had been careful in nurturing links between the state and the families of soldiers, veterans, and war dead. Apparently Ho Chi Minh was the main architect of official policy toward this group. His objective was to make these families "materially content, spiritually happy, and provided with the opportunity to participate in socially beneficial activity."[17] When the American War intensified, and more and more young men went off to fight and die, the burdens on the social affairs officer grew. Faced with the prospect of inattentiveness, the government created a new senior position in the local administration, the social policy officer (*pho ban chinh sach Xa*).[18] This official answered directly to one of the deputy presidents of the commune's People's Committee, usually the village militia commander (*xa doi truong*), and had the exclusive responsibility of assisting the policy families.[19] The addition of this position represented a pragmatic specialization of a previously more general role. Unlike the fomer social affairs officer, who divided his time among a number of tasks, the policy officer's sole responsibility was to assist the policy families and to ensure that they were not ignored by the government.

Government policies toward these families also changed. In the late 1950s and early 1960s, the government had instituted the collectivization of agriculture across the North. Officials recognized that having a child serving in the military represented the loss of a high-quality laborer for the family; therefore, the government instructed local agricultural cooperatives to provide policy families with increased food rations. For many families, the policy family designation ended when their son or husband returned home from the war. For the less fortunate who were killed or maimed while fighting in the military, the designation remained in place, and their family continued to benefit from government support. The families of war dead (*gia dinh liet si*) in particular received a number of special dispensations not available to others. Among benefits that were extremely important in the years before the 1986 introduction of the Renovation (Doi Moi) policy were preferential admissions to hospitals for members of their families, priority status for entering schools and universities for their children, easier access to government jobs, and easier admission to the Communist Party.[20] If a soldier became a martyr while officially residing in his parents' home, his parents would receive a government stipend if the father was over sixty years of age and the mother over fifty-five. They would also receive assistance upon reaching that age if they received no other forms of assistance. If he was married with children, his wife would receive a monthly stipend, as would his children until they reached eighteen. A number of other benefits also accrued at the local level. Families of martyrs always received greater rice allotments than other families. They were given easier work in the agricultural cooperatives and were also given priority for receiving the most prized work assignments. In Thinh Liet commune this entailed membership in the lucrative fishing brigades. When agricultural land was redistributed to the peasantry in 1991–92, the families of martyrs also received the most productive and convenient parcels. To give one example, one of the most desirable pieces of land in the village of Giap Tu, a large fish pond located within the village boundaries, was given to a family that had several members killed during a 1947 battle against the French in the village. A former official in Thinh Liet's administration summed up the situation of the policy families as, "Whatever they do, it's always easier."

Beyond instituting policies that cared for those with relatives in the military, the government also expanded its ceremonial corpus to recognize those who fought and died. As early as 1947, when the government declared July 27 as War Invalids and Martyrs Day (Ngay Thuong Binh Liet Si), the government began publicly commemorating war dead. This holiday, irregularly organized in the late 1950s and early 1960s, became an annual occurrence starting in 1967.[21] On this day, government officials held ceremonies in which they mourned the fallen soldiers and expressed their gratitude, with both speeches and possibly small gifts, for the families of martyrs. The memories of the war dead's singular contributions were also kept alive through the creation of exclusive ceremonies or the delineation of special areas in local cemeteries reserved for war dead. If a martyr's corpse was returned, it was to be buried in this cemetery; in keeping with the revolutionary campaign to simplify funeral rites that had begun in 1954, a small headstone that recorded the deceased's name, rank, and death date was placed on it.[22] Officials mandated that these cemeteries should not be neglected or divorced from everyday social life. Regulations from Ninh Binh Province noted that "everyone has the responsibility to protect and care for the martyrs'

Figure 2.2.   Tam Nong District Revolutionary Martyrs Cemetery, Phu Tho.
The column reads "The Fatherland Remembers Your Sacrifice." Photograph
by Natalia Puchalt.

cemeteries [*nghia trang liet si*] in the cities and communes (fig. 2.2).
People should display their remembrance and express their awareness
of their debt to the heroic martyrs who have carried out their meritorious
work [*cong duc*] for the revolution."[23] The young were also to be taken
to the cemeteries so they could appreciate the martyrs' sacrifices and
learn to care for the graves.[24] In other localities, such as in Nam Ha
Province, officials decreed that when a young couple married, the ceremony was to conclude with their placing a bouquet of flowers on the
war dead monument. Through this act, the couple could express their
debt and appreciation to those who had given their lives for the nation
and revolution.[25]

The most important ceremonial innovation by the government in this
period was the creation of an official memorial service for war dead (*le
truy dieu*). This new ceremony represented an effort by the state to individually recognize the sacrifice of those who died in battle. Its structure
is worth examining in detail. The organizational process for the official
service was set in motion by the receipt of official confirmation of a
soldier's death by the People's Committee of his native commune. Official word was vital because the ceremony could only be performed for
those the military recognized as martyrs. In Thinh Liet, receipt of the

news marked the beginning of a very delicate stage. When official word
of a soldier's death finally arrived, the social policy officer did not immediately inform the family of the death. To help ease the shock of the
news, which, even if expected, had a terrible finality to it, the People's
Committee allowed friends or kin to tell the family that word had arrived and that the social policy officer would be coming to inform them.
After giving the family some time to grieve and then prepare themselves
for the visit, the social policy officer went to make the official announcement and then arranged a date and time for the official memorial ceremony.

The government's memorial ceremony, like regular funerary ceremonies, took place in the home of the fallen soldier. In Thinh Liet commune, it was generally held at two o'clock in the afternoon and lasted
for one hour. Unlike a regular funeral in which mourning attire was
worn, the family and their guests dressed in their normal clothing. The
official presence at the ceremony was extensive. The communal administration was represented by the president of the People's Committee,
the village militia commander and the social policy officer. The agricultural cooperative was represented by the chairman. The party was represented by the secretary of the commune's party cell, the secretary of
the residential cell in which the family resided, and at least one person
from each of the party's mass organizations, such as the Women's Association or the Youth Association. On some occasions every member
of the executive committees of the administration and the party cell were
also in attendance. Beyond the official personnel, the ceremony was also
heavily attended by kin, friends, and co-villagers.

The social policy officer presided over the official ceremony. He
brought a bouquet of white tuberoses (*hoa hue*) to the ceremony (white
is a mourning color in Vietnam, and tuberoses are commonly featured
in funerary ceremonies). When the delegation of officials arrived at the
late soldier's home, the flowers were placed on an altar constructed for
the dead soldier. After one minute of silence, the policy officer began
the eulogy of the fallen soldier. The purpose of his visit, he stated, was
to officially commemorate both the person and the sacrifice of the soldier. The soldier had selflessly sacrificed his life (*hi sinh*) so the war effort
could succeed. The nobility of the soldier's death was reiterated in the
standardized statement the policy officer then read:

> In our people's glorious revolutionary effort against the Americans to rescue
> the nation, Comrade [the soldier's full name] has with his comrades-in-arms
> raised up the spirit of struggle, surpassed all difficulties and hardships to carry

out the responsibilities of his unit, and sacrificed his life on (day, month, year).

The cadres and soldiers of the unit are infinitely sorrowful and proud to have had a person united in will, a comrade-in-arms, who has offered up [*cong hien*] his life in the struggle for an independent and free country; who swore to never stop raising up the will to fight and the strength to eliminate the enemy; who brought forth all his spirit and strength to carry on to victory in the war of national salvation against the Americans and to fulfill all the responsibilities that the party, government, and the people gave him.

Dear family members:

Comrade [soldier's name] has left us. The fatherland and people have lost a loyal and faithful child. His unit has lost a person united in will, a comrade-in-arms. His family has lost a loved one. All of the cadres and soldiers of the unit respectfully send their wishes and ask to "divide the sadness" with the family. They hope that the family will turn its grief into activity for the revolution, strengthen their hatred for the American enemy and their lackeys, and with the rest of the people and soldiers firmly resolve to realize the sacred words from President Ho's will, "Resolve to completely defeat the American enemy," to protect the North, liberate the South, and unite the fatherland.

By organizing the ceremony, the government gave thanks to the family for its sacrifice. The grief of the families was evident during the ceremony. Even though the memorial service often occurred some time after the soldier's death, people wept openly throughout.

Following his speech, the policy officer delivered three items to the soldier's family that formalized the state's recognition of the soldier's sacrifice. The family first received a government-issued "death announcement" (*giay bao tu*). This began with the statement "We very regretfully declare and confirm" and was followed by the soldier's name, rank, and unit. The form also noted if the soldier had been "sacrificed."[26] Other important information included the date of death, place of death, place of burial, and, if it were the case, confirmation that certified the soldier was a revolutionary martyr. Although these categories were helpful, the information on them was sometimes extremely vague. In some cases they noted only that the soldier had died in the South in the struggle against the Americans and that his unit had buried his body near the front. Still, this certificate was necessary for future interactions with the local administration and government bureaucracy. The family was also given a certificate, approximately twelve by fifteen inches, upon which was inscribed in large red lettering, *To Quoc Ghi Cong*, literally rendered as "The Land of the Ancestors Records Your Work," but perhaps more accurately translated as "The Fatherland Remembers Your Sacrifice."[27] This certificate recorded the name, natal commune, and death date of the slain soldier. It was issued for every martyr and definitively marked the deceased's assumption of that status by its placement of the phrase "revolutionary martyr" in large black letters before the deceased's name. It also stated that the soldier had sacrificed his life during the war and included an inscription along the bottom that read, "Eternally remember the moral debt [*on*] to the revolutionary martyrs who have sacrificed their lives for a bright future for the people" (*Doi doi nho on cac liet si da hi sinh cho tuong lai tuoi sang cua dan toc*). The final item given to the family by the policy officer was a sum of money amounting to approximately $150. This sum was a onetime form of immediate assistance for the family. In delivering these three items, the government marked its gratitude to the family for the sacrifice its member had made. At the ceremony's conclusion, a family member stood up and thanked the officials.

The Vietnamese state went to great lengths to ensure that its claims regarding the glory and nobility of suffering and dying for the cause were compelling. It not only glorified those who suffered and died in public discourse but also created a range of new public ceremonies that expressed the honor and nobility of those actions. For many Vietnamese, these ideas and ceremonies were indeed compelling. People described dying for the country as an "honor" (*vinh du*).[28] Relatives of those killed in battle often employ the verb *cong hien*, which in effect means to give something up to something greater than oneself, to describe their family's sacrifice. People gave up their lives to ensure Vietnam's independence and freedom or, as one veteran stated, "to bring back happiness and comfort to the people." Official commemoration, however, was exclusively dedicated to the glorification and ennoblement of the cause. The Democratic Republic of Vietnam was officially an atheist state that rejected any notions of the supernatural; thus nowhere in the ceremonies was there reference to the ultimate fate of the soul or other existential anxieties that war death could produce.

THE DILEMMAS OF WAR DEATH

It is difficult to describe the extent of the trauma and violence experienced by the North Vietnamese during the American War. For both combatants and noncombatants alike, the war was a period of relentless fear and intense anguish. Parents agonized when their sons went off to fight, knowing that they would probably never return, while the soldiers, stuck in the malarial jungles and forests of southern and central Vietnam, with inadequate food and little medicine, watched as their friends and comrades died in staggering numbers throughout the war. Six North Vietnamese soldiers died for every one American. Going off to the front was itself a kind of death. Unlike the Americans, Northern Vietnamese soldiers did not rotate home after a year of duty, nor did they regularly return home on leave. They stayed and fought until death, debilitating injury, or the end of the war. Once at the front, the soldiers were almost completely cut off from their families. The rudimentary transportation and communication system that linked them to home regularly failed in delivering mail back and forth. Many families received no word for years. At war's end, many veterans returned home to wives and families who thought they were dead. Other families finally received official confirmation that their sons had died many years earlier.

In addition to the obvious grief and anguish caused by losing a loved one, the death of soldiers in battle presented a number of powerful cultural dilemmas for the Vietnamese. Death is not a taboo subject in Vietnamese social life. People talk about it openly, sometimes in surprising ways. When an elderly person is about to die, family members often go to the homes of friends, neighbors, and relatives and candidly say, "Grandmother [or grandfather] is about to die," and then invite them to the house to be there when she dies. Nevertheless, local conceptions distinguish between good and bad deaths. A good death has a number of features. Being advanced in years, having many children as survivors, dying quickly and painlessly, having one's corpse complete, and dying at home all constitute a favorable end because they readily facilitate the most important concern following death, the passage of the deceased's soul from this world to what the Vietnamese call the "otherworld" (*the gioi khac*). When a person dies, his or her soul leaves its corporeal form and begins to wander the area near the corpse. The soul is not yet aware that the body is dead (this recognition will not come for several days). If it is in a familiar place, such as its home or near its family's ancestral altar, and has not died in a violent manner, it calmly stays near the scene. After this, family members can begin the funeral rites that will send it on its way to the otherworld. These will be carried out at the family ancestral altar, the portal through which the soul begins its passage. If the rites are correctly performed, the soul will move to the otherworld to become a benevolent family ancestor who will care for the family and reciprocally be cared for by those it left behind.

A bad death includes such factors as dying young, childless, violently, away from home, and/or in such a manner that the corpse is mutilated or incomplete. These factors create the dangerous possibility that the soul will be unable to make its passage to the otherworld to become a benevolent, cared-for ancestor. Instead, it will become a malevolent, wandering, hungry ghost (*con ma*) that is doomed to eternally roam the earth. Each of the different forms of bad death poses its own obstacles to making the passage. Vietnamese, like Chinese, hold that those who die young and childless have an increased potential to become malevolent, wandering spirits.[29] One reason for their malevolence relates to the fact that some spirits are angry for having their lives taken from them early. A more mundane reason lies in the structure of the family ancestral cult. Offerings to care for the ancestors' souls in the otherworld can only be made by those genealogically junior to the deceased. Those who die good deaths have descendants to care for them and essentially placate them so they will remain benevolent in the afterlife. Those who die young are without such sustenance, and so they angrily roam the earth looking for any food or care they can find, often invading the ancestral altars of others to gain their sustenance.[30] Dying in a violent manner frightens and angers a spirit, making it more inclined to take its anger out on the living. Dying away from home is also problematic. The soul, upon exiting and discovering alien surroundings, goes into a frenzied search for familiarity that compounds its terror and frustration. If the soul is distant from the ancestral altar, the task of escorting it to its final resting place is more complicated because the living must first find it and coax it back home to the altar, a difficult and uncertain task that becomes even more so if a long time passes between death and the funerary rites.[31] Finally, a corpse that is missing parts or is otherwise incomplete is theoretically barred from ever making the transition and therefore is doomed to forever roam the earth and never cross to the otherworld.[32] For those who die a bad death, chances are high that they can never cross to the otherworld to become a benevolent ancestor.

The deaths of soldiers in combat often involved every possible dimension of a bad death. Young, childless men died painful, violent deaths, usually hundreds of miles from home. The corpses of many remained intact to be buried by their comrades, but, as the author Bao Ninh describes in his novel of the American conflict, *The Sorrow of War,* others "had been totally vaporised, or blasted into such small pieces that their remains had long been liquidised into mud."[33] Some were buried by their comrades with simple rites, often in makeshift graves with no permanent altars, while others were never buried and had no funerary rites performed for them. All these deaths had the potential to create an army of hungry, wandering souls. Young, heirless soldiers were dying violently and far from their homes, their corpses shattered and incomplete, their souls and deaths unmarked and neglected, left stranded on the earth with no one to nourish them while their passage to the otherworld was barred. For those they left behind, the perils created by battlefield deaths created a great deal of anxiety. The living needed to appropriately honor and care for the deceased soldiers' souls so they were not condemned to wandering the earth but instead could be put to rest with the other ancestors. However, the ritual corpus of prerevolutionary Vietnam and the official ceremonies sponsored by the state were largely inadequate for coping with these concerns. As a result, a set of innovatory ceremonies developed by the people emerged during the American War to cope with the problems that war death presented.[34]

FAMILY COMMEMORATION OF WAR DEAD

When soldiers left their training areas for the front, the prospect of death was immediate. North Vietnamese soldiers generally traveled to the front on foot, trekking several hundred miles through the dangerous trails and malarial jungles of the Central Highlands. This region, known to the Vietnamese as the Truong Son (Long Mountain) range, included in its western salient the Ho Chi Minh Trail. Through this thin, rugged, and sparsely inhabited stretch of central Vietnam and southern Laos, thousands of soldiers and countless tons of war matériel passed, all under the imminent threat of American air strikes devoted to interdicting the flow of human traffic through the region. Beyond the military casualties, soldiers died of disease, accidents, and even attacks by local wildlife. When a soldier was killed, his unit was responsible for reporting the cause of death and burying the corpse. Military units usually had soldiers attached to them who were in charge of the war dead. After they had discharged their duties, the family was then to be informed of the soldier's passing.

Official confirmation that a soldier had been killed while serving in the military was notoriously slow in coming, sometimes taking years to arrive. To give one example, on October 4, 1971, Nguyen Tien Dat of Giap Tu died in an American air strike on the Ho Chi Minh Trail, yet his family did not receive official notification until May 7, 1974. Delays in notification frequently were caused by poor communications within and between military units, and with the rear areas, although some Vietnamese speculate that the party deliberately delayed notification to keep morale high in the rear areas.[35] Soldiers were keenly aware of the possibility of death as well as the delays in notification. To spare their families unnecessary anguish, many who served together made arrangements between themselves for the survivors to either write a letter or pay a visit to the deceased's family to inform them of the date, location, and possibly the circumstances of the soldier's death. A great number of families first learned of a son's or husband's death through this informal system of notification. The information provided by the deceased's comrade helped ease many of the proximate causes of distress inflicted by their loved one's death. Knowledge of the exact date of death helped families organize a proper death anniversary ceremony (*gio*). Many people held that this ceremony was effective only if performed on the true death date; thus families wanted to know the exact date so they could properly fulfill their ritual obligations. When the death date was unknown, families would usually select the day the soldier left, a choice that reflected prerevolutionary practices.[36] Information regarding the location of death was also valued. Unlike the policy of the American military, which attempted to transport home the corpses of all its dead soldiers, the soldiers of the People's Army were basically buried where they fell. Few were transported back to their natal villages for burial. Not having the corpse present complicated the funerary rites and created the possibility that the deceased would become a wandering soul. And though they could not act on it immediately, many families wanted to know the location of death in the hopes that at some future point they could retrieve the corpse and give it a proper burial. Finally, the mere knowledge of the soldier's death allowed the family to immediately conduct some form of funerary rites for the deceased. As mentioned previously, a long period of neglect between death and funeral rites decreased the chances of the soul ever returning to the family altar and increased the chances of it becoming a wandering soul; it also was considered somewhat inhumane. Prompt notification by the deceased's comrades helped to alleviate a small measure of the anguish and suffering caused by a young soldier's death.

The death of a young soldier in battle, in addition to creating a number of anxieties regarding the ultimate disposition of his soul, also complicated the performance of funerary rites for him. Conventional Vietnamese funerary rites, including even the extremely simplified reformed rites propagated by the party after 1954, function under two guiding assumptions: first, that the deceased will generally have surviving children; and second, that the deceased's corpse will be physically present when the funeral is held. A wide range of activities evident at funerals, from the distinctive mourning attire and acts of ritual obeisance that children perform for their parents, to the food prestations and public feasts that accompany funerals, are all linked to these two assumptions. If either condition is not fulfilled, changes are needed in the structure of the rites. The death of a childless individual presents fewer problems than an absent corpse because a regular funeral can still be held. The ceremony will still feature its requisite feast and the transportation of the corpse from the home to the grave. The only difference will be that the parents or other senior kinfolk do not propitiate the lost child, nor do they accompany the casket to the grave site. A funeral without a corpse demands a completely different ceremony. Unlike funerals in which the corpse is present, there is no feast, and kin and co-villagers do not give money, food prestations, or funeral wreaths to the family of the deceased. Nor is any type of symbolic casket carried to the grave. Unlike regular funerals, in which sociality is at a premium and families exchange gifts and debts, funerals in which the corpse is absent are radically simplified.

The deaths of soldiers during the American War necessitated the performance of thousands of funerary rites in which the deceased's corpse was absent. In Thinh Liet, virtually no corpses were returned; this is the main reason that the commune does not have a cemetery for war dead. One common form for these rites in Thinh Liet was a private ceremony arranged by families and known as a *le tu niem* or *le tuong niem*. This type of funeral, which can be glossed as a "remembrance of the dead," was organizationally distinct from the regular funeral held under normal circumstances; its defining characteristic was its modest, familial nature. Funerals typically mobilized people and resources throughout the village; the remembrance ceremony was a family affair in which only a restricted number of family and close kin were present. Funerals also adhered to a lengthy and complex set of rites that began immediately after death. The remembrance ceremony was a simple affair that lasted only a few hours. It was also generally held several days after a family learned of their loved one's death, whereas normal funerary activities began immediately after death. Both events, however, were united in their objective of giving succor to the deceased's soul and helping it make its transition to the otherworld.

When the news of a soldier's death initially arrived, the first task was to set up a funeral altar to commemorate the deceased. These altars were always set up in the home of the deceased's parents and arranged in the

same manner as those of nonwar dead. A table was set in the main room
of the home on the right-hand side of the family's ancestral altar. The
centerpiece of the altar was a framed photograph or drawing of the
deceased. In some cases, the family would place a portrait of the deceased in military uniform. Directly before the portrait was an urn for
incense sticks, and other items, such as candles, flowers, and perhaps a
small oil lamp to light incense, were placed on either side of the portrait.
If family members had been notified within one hundred days of the
soldier's death, they would set a small bowl of glutinous rice upon which
rested a hard-boiled egg held between two chopsticks, pushed straight
down into the bowl, possibly along with other food items as well. These
items were meant to feed the deceased's soul for the first hundred days
after death, but they were not used if death had occurred earlier. The
completed altar would always have a clear area before it to provide the
main location for the performance of all ritual activities.

News that a native son had been killed in the war spread quickly
throughout the village. The ubiquitous kinship ties between co-villagers
facilitated this transmission, but a sense of shared experience, perhaps
even commiseration, in the face of war and its consequences produced
a heightened sense of togetherness that was accentuated when a local
villager was killed. Almost all families had or knew someone serving in
the military, and everyone knew that next time the loss might be theirs.
The news of death therefore disseminated rapidly, and village families
were quick to demonstrate their sympathy for the aggrieved family. Just
as they would in a normal village funeral, kin and co-villagers went to
the house of the deceased to express their condolences and "divide the
sadness" (*chia buon*) of the bereaved family. Upon entering the deceased's home they would light three incense sticks, which they had
brought, say a brief prayer, and place the sticks in the incense urn on
the altar. Their visit gave public expression to their sympathy, simultaneously helping the grieving to cope with their loss and providing a
testament to the dignity and esteem of the deceased and his death. What
was most remarkable about these visits was their singularly affective
nature. Virtually every village family would send at least one representative to visit the family of the deceased soldier to express their condolences. Many sent more. When they arrived, however, they brought no
gifts. They were not reciprocating former debts incurred during their
own family funerals, nor were they sealing a future obligation with a
material prestation. These visits fell beyond the purview of "exchanging
debts through eating and drinking" that characterized all other funerary

practices.[37] What characterized them instead was an unmistakable sense of the tragedy of a life lost, and the common desire to help others cope with an event that could or did happen to them. With their visits, familes asserted their care and concern simply through the act of being there, not through any material items that would form the basis of an exchange relation.

Village families continued to pay visits to the deceased's family for several days after the news first arrived. During these days the home was full of people, but the family's sobbing was still audible in neighboring homes. At about the same time as the number of visitors began to tail off, the family performed the "remembrance of the dead" ceremony, which was always organized in the home of the deceased's family. All immediate family members who could attend were present, as well as a small number of other close relations. The ceremony usually took place in the daytime. Prior to its conduct, family members would go through the normal preparations that preceded family rituals: cleaning the house and the family altar and purchasing any ritual items, such as incense, that would be used in the ceremony. They would also prepare a nice set of clothes for the event. Family members wore their everyday clothing during the ceremony; the elaborate mourning attire of regular funerals, such as gauzy white tunics and peaked cheesecloth caps, was absent. The only items of standard funeral attire visible at the ceremony were the white mourning headbands worn by those junior to the deceased.

All the rites in the remembrance ceremony were carried out before the altar constructed for the deceased. As in other Vietnamese mortuary rites, the purpose of the ceremony was to propitiate the soul of the deceased so it could rest in peace in the otherworld. The ceremony began with the entire family assembled on the floor in front of the altar to say prayers (*khan*) for the deceased's soul. Straw mats had been laid on the floor, and the senior members of the family, with the mother and father placed in the most prized positions nearest the altar, were seated in the front of the group. The task of inviting the deceased's soul back to the home was given to a senior male, usually an uncle or great-uncle, from the deceased's patriline. Standing before the altar, the man repeated the invocations to bring the soul home. Once these were completed, and the soul successfully installed in the altar, the family members individually performed a brief reverence of the spirit. Clasping three incense sticks, each person would stand and kowtow before the altar one, three, or five times. These prayers and obeisances were somewhat nonspecific, yet they were dedicated to ensuring the general well-being of the soul in the otherworld. When the prayers were concluded, each person placed his or her incense sticks in the urn.

The second phase of the ceremony involved the direct propitiation of the soul (*cung*). Apart from the simple act of helping the soul make its transition to the otherworld, the remembrance ceremony was also dedicated to providing specific items, such as food, clothing, or money, that the deceased could use there. Prior to the ceremony, paper votive objects (*hang ma*) that symbolized clothing or money were placed on the altar along with an array of food items.[38] After the initial prayers were said, one person assumed responsibility for propitiating the deceased's soul with the objective of delivering these items to the deceased in the otherworld. A spirit priest (*thay cung*) assumed this role in some households, but since the Revolution endeavored to eliminate all rites performed by spirit priests and placed them under official surveillance, some families instead chose a younger sibling of the deceased. The choice of a younger sibling was linked to the prohibition against genealogically senior family members propitiating their juniors. The propitiator knelt on the floor before the altar and said prayers to entreat the deceased's soul to accept the assembled items. The food items were transmitted through the smoke from the incense burning on the altar. To deliver the money or clothing, family members took the paper items outside and covertly burned them in the family compound, allowing their substance to travel to the otherworld through the smoke. Although this practice was considered "superstitious" and prohibited by the party, many families still burned these items. When these rites concluded, the deceased's soul had been provisioned for life in the otherworld. It had also been installed in the family altar and thenceforth would always be propitiated there.

The prayers and offerings to the deceased's soul usually did not exceed one hour. The remembrance ceremony then concluded with the family members and guests sharing a meal to commemorate the deceased. The foods were simple meat and vegetable dishes, a selection partially determined by wartime scarcity. When the rites were over, the food offered to the deceased was taken off the altar. It was then placed on trays with other dishes, and the assembled group ate the dishes together, usually sitting on the mats laid out on the floor before the altar. This private family meal was the only occasion in which the consumption of food was involved in commemorating the death of a soldier. Unlike funerals, which sometimes featured grand feasts that lasted for days, the remembrance ceremony included no feast. As such, there was neither the public sociality that came with feasts nor the giving of gifts that preceded them. War death engendered a simpler and humbler form of commemoration. Village families still came to the aggrieved family's home to express their sympathy and share their sadness, yet the commemoration of war dead and the assisting of their souls in their migration to the otherworld were largely affairs of the family.

THE COMMEMORATIVE PROJECT TODAY

The reunification of Vietnam in 1975 did not mark the end of official efforts to commemorate war dead. Soon after the war was over, the government began commissioning the construction of monuments for war dead (*dai liet si*) in localities across Vietnam. These monuments are now visible in nearly every commune and district. Often tall spires adorned with a red or gold star at their apex, and the words "The Fatherland Remembers Your Sacrifice" or "Eternally Remember the Debt to the Martyrs" written across the base, they provide continued public testimony to those who gave their lives for the nation. The most spectacular monument for war dead, completed in 1995, now sits directly across from Ho Chi Minh's mausoleum in Hanoi's Ba Dinh Square (fig. 2.3). The irony of this nationwide commemorative effort is the fact that it excludes those who died while serving in the Army of the Republic of Vietnam. Like their North Vietnamese counterparts, thousands of South Vietnamese soldiers died in battle during the war years. Although in the pre-1975 period the southern government constructed its own monuments and cemeteries to commemorate its dead, these were removed after the unification of the country in 1975 (fig. 2.4). As a result, when one sees monuments to war dead in contemporary southern or central Vietnam, they commemorate those who fell fighting the French or fighting for the North. Those who died fighting for the South have effectively disappeared from official discourse. The needs of their family members are no less pressing than those in the North, but the state has not dedicated itself to glorifying or remembering them.

In nearly all northern communes today, the administration organizes a ceremony for the local war dead on War Invalids and Martyrs Day. Led by the president of the commune's People's Committee and assisted by the social policy officer, the party and administration reiterate their thanks and appreciation to those who have sacrificed themselves, and restate the glory and nobility of what they have done. When the speeches are completed, the families of war dead receive a small gift, such as

Figure 2.3. The Ho
Chi Minh Mausoleum
seen through the Shrine
to the Unknown Sol-
dier, Hanoi. Photo-
graph by Natalia
Puchalt.

sugar, condensed milk, sweet biscuits, flowers, fruit, or, as is more common today, a small amount of money. These ceremonies are always well
attended in Thinh Liet. Families still take pride in and are appreciative
of the government's efforts to recognize and ennoble the contributions
of the fallen. This day has also become a second occasion for most
families to organize a modest commemorative ceremony and family
meal. In Thinh Liet, families return home after the ceremony for a gathering of approximately ten to twenty people. They perform a simple
propitiation of the dead soldier's soul—which generally involves lighting
incense sticks, bowing, and placing the incense in an urn on the altar—
and then share a communal meal. The propitiation is significant because
few, if any, people light incense sticks at the war memorial. The act of
commemoration and remembrance at the memorial is clear, yet it has
not become a site to tend to the dead soldier's needs.

Figure 2.4.   ARVN cemetery, Ho Chi-Minh City, razed after 1975. Photograph by Hue-Tam Ho Tai.

The main commemorative ceremony for families remains the soldier's death anniversary. Up until the mid-1980s, wartime scarcities and government regulations prohibiting large-scale death anniversary ceremonies restricted their size.[39] Over the past decade, families have begun to organize ever-larger ceremonies. Today, an average death anniversary ceremony will feature a communal meal for fifty to sixty people. It begins with rites dedicated to caring for the dead soldier's soul, similar to those performed during the commemoration of the dead ceremony. The ceremony is always conducted before the altar in the home of the deceased's parents, the soul is invited back and propitiated, and some votive paper items, such as money or clothes, may be burned for the soul's use in the otherworld. The main participants are also close family members. If the soldier was survived by his widow, she will participate in these rites at her in-laws' home. Almost all widows of war dead in Thinh Liet commune remain in the home of their husband's parents, particularly if they have children, and almost never remarry; doing so is considered an act of infidelity to the late husband. Despite their social importance, in Vietnamese villages, patrilineages have assumed no ritual role in commemorating war dead. The rites remain firmly with the husband's immediate family. Once the rites are concluded, a communal meal is held for the guests, usually friends, neighbors, and relatives who are invited to the ceremony.

In recent years, other methods of commemorating and caring for the souls of war dead have emerged. A number of Thinh Liet families have installed the souls of dead soldiers in the local Buddhist temple. The virtue of installing the soul there is that it receives care and sustenance from all ceremonies conducted in the temple. Such souls are said to "eat of the Buddha's good fortune" (*an may cua Phat*) and will not be left uncared for if there are no more family members to conduct rites. A nun at the temple claims that several dozen families have done this, though the figures are disputed by some local residents and are impossible to verify. Families who perform this rite will later conduct a ceremony at the temple on every death anniversary and will also participate in ceremonies for dead souls at the temple in the first two weeks of the seventh lunar month.[40]

The most remarkable form of commemoration to emerge in Thinh Liet was the dedication of an altar to war dead in the communal house of Giap Tu village. This communal house had been destroyed during a battle with French soldiers in February 1947, producing a great deal of later conflict over which spirits inhabited it. When the house was refurbished in the late 1980s, local men decided it was appropriate for villagers to pay respects to local war dead there. This movement reached its zenith on the eleventh of the first lunar month in 1992, the lunar year anniversary of the aforementioned battle, when local villagers conducted a ceremony to propitiate the souls of eleven local guerrillas who had died that day. The ceremony featured trays of offerings as well as a moving eulogy by the son of one of those killed. The organizers, mostly older men, hoped the ceremony would become an annual event, but resistance mounted, particularly among older women. They felt that while villagers should propitiate war dead, the communal house was not the appropriate venue. As a result, the ceremony was never organized on a large scale again. In early 1996, the altar for war dead in the communal house was rededicated to the spirit of the land (*tho dat*) on which the communal house sits.[41] For a short period afterward, some villagers continued to pay their respects to the war dead in the communal house, particularly on the battle's anniversary, but public rituals stopped. In 1997, the village succeeded in raising enough money to construct a small monument dedicated to the village's war dead. This monument, which records the name of every Giap Tu soldier who died in battle, as well as the names of a number of "Heroic Vietnamese Mothers" ("Ba Me Viet

Nam Anh Hung") who lost several sons in war, sits in the communal house compound and has become the main focus for communal rites dedicated to local war dead.

The problem of war dead in Vietnam persists to this day, especially for those whose loved one's remains have never been recovered. The number of the missing apparently runs into the hundreds of thousands.[42] Many families continue to organize trips to southern and central Vietnam to search for remains. In early 1996, for example, the skeletons of two soldiers were brought back to Thinh Liet commune and buried in the local cemetery near their mothers. Given the widespread practice of secondary burial three years after the initial burial—when the coffin is opened, the bones cleaned and transferred to a large urn, and the urn buried in a different location—the local ritual corpus is well suited to putting the soldiers to their final rest. Concern with finding soldiers' remains is visible in the public media as well. Vietnamese television has broadcast a number of shows that followed both family and military efforts to locate remains. The magazine *The New World* (*The Gioi Moi*) even published an article in October 1996 that described a "new method for finding the burial place of soldiers." This was a form of divination in which a family member placed one chopstick in the ground and tried to balance an egg on top of it. If the egg did not fall, the deceased's remains were directly below. This method was apparently successful in locating the remains of several soldiers, including one who had been missing since December 1946.[43] The Ministry of Labor and War Invalids and the Central Committee for War Veterans also publish *War Veterans of Vietnam* (*Cuu Chien Binh Viet Nam*), a magazine dedicated to circulating information regarding the location of war dead and their graves. Nevertheless, accurate knowledge is often difficult to find, and several trips by Thinh Liet families have been unsuccessful.

CONCLUSION

Anthropological research has shown that mortuary rites in virtually all societies contain the idea that death is transient and that such rites allow the deceased to be reborn into a new community and existence. Drawing on the work of the French sociologist Robert Hertz, Maurice Bloch and Jonathan Parry have concluded that at the end of mortuary rites, "the collectivity emerges triumphant over death" while the soul is transferred "from one social order to another (albeit imaginary) order."[44] What is most distinctive about the death of soldiers in contemporary Thinh Liet

commune is the fact that after death, the dead soldiers were indeed reborn, yet they were reborn into different communities depending on who
performed the rites. In state-sponsored rites, dead soldiers were reborn
into the pantheon of heroes who had suffered and died to protect and
liberate the motherland. The dead soldier became a revolutionary martyr. Despite its professed policy of atheism, the party never challenged
the existence of the soul after death. Playing on this ambiguity, the state
was able to assert that death was not complete annihilation because the
memory of the deceased would live on and be celebrated as a heroic
example for the living. For the soldier's family, mortuary rites also entailed a rebirth, but it was a rebirth into the "otherworld" where the
souls of the dead resided. Through its installation in the family ancestral
altar, the dead soul became a member of the community of family ancestors who care for the living and are reciprocally cared for by the
living. In each case, death itself was a transition to a form of immortality
in a distinct community.

The existence of two distinct communities of remembrance based on
the same subject has a number of historical parallels. After Lenin's death,
the Soviet Communist Party attempted to create a secular cult surrounding his person that would serve to unify the people, yet for many Rus-
sians, Lenin was absorbed into the community of saints and heroes of
Russian history and commemorated as such.[45] The Vietnamese Communist Party attempted to construct a similar cult around the person of
Ho Chi Minh, but in early 1996 it disbanded a cult in a northern province that worshiped Ho as the nineteenth king of Vietnam's mythical
first dynasty, the Hung kings.[46] Conversely, the government in contemporary Japan tries to assert that the commemoration of dead soldiers at
the Yasukuni shrine is a simple act of gratitude for the fallen, whereas
for many right-wing groups and financial supporters, the rites held at
the shrine are a celebration of the Japanese empire. What is notable in
each of these cases is that the deceased and the rituals associated with
them are used to make specific claims about the nature of the social
world, be it the necessity of political unity, the glory of empire, or the
simple need to put the dead to rest.

The existence of two distinct communities of remembrance around
war dead in Thinh Liet does not imply any incommensurability between
the two communities or the popular rejection of the state's assertions.
To return to the language used by Mark Bradley, we do not see in Thinh
Liet the formation of "counter-memory" in these rites. Instead, people

are honored to have their children or family members glorified as heroes of the nation, and state-sponsored forms of commemoration remain popular and well attended. Nevertheless, the Vietnamese state's project could not solve all the problems that war death created. It could lend honor and dignity to a soldier's death, but it was unable to resolve the question of the fate of his soul. As a consequence, when the war dead are remembered in Thinh Liet today, they are remembered as members of a community of brave men who willingly gave their lives for their country, and also as people who died too soon but have still made the transition to the community of ancestors who watch over families. It is in the interlocking web of these two communities that meaning is given to their deaths and comfort is given to the living who had the good fortune to survive the terrible consequences that warfare brought.

NOTES

1. See Hue-Tam Ho Tai, Introduction, this volume.

2. The North Vietnamese state's agenda accords with the actions of other nations. With the rise of the nation-state, the glorification of dead soldiers and war death through tombs of unknown soldiers, military funerals, memorial days, shrines for war dead, and other commemorative sites and activities has grown more elaborate. For examples, see Helen Hardacre, *Shinto and the State, 1868–1988* (Princeton, N.J.: Princeton University Press, 1989); Eric Hobsbawm, "Mass-Producing Traditions: Europe, 1870–1914," in *The Invention of Tradition,* ed. Eric Hobsbawm and Terence Ranger (Cambridge: Cambridge University Press, 1983), 263–307; Bruce Kapferer, *Legends of People, Myths of State* (Washington, D.C.: Smithsonian Institution Press, 1988); George L. Mosse, *Fallen Soldiers: Reshaping the Memory of the World Wars* (Oxford: Oxford University Press, 1990); and Nina Tumarkin, *The Living and the Dead* (New York: Basic Books, 1994).

3. Thinh Liet commune is located approximately ten kilometers south of the center of Hanoi and is composed of the three villages of Giap Nhat, Giap Nhi, and Giap Tu. I conducted field research there from March 1991 to August 1992, from December 1993 to February 1994, and in July 1996 and July 1998.

4. See Mark Bradley, this volume.

5. Elements of resistance to state commemorative rites can be seen in the Vietnamese case in Shaun Kingsley Malarney, "The Limits of 'State Functionalism' and the Reconstruction of Funerary Ritual in Contemporary Northern Vietnam," *American Ethnologist* 23 (August 1996): 540–60; or, in the Chinese case, in Rubie Watson, ed., *Memory, History, and Opposition under State Socialism* (Sante Fe, N.M.: School of American Research Press, 1994).

6. Douglas Pike, *PAVN: People's Army of Vietnam* (New York: Da Capo Press, 1986), 13.

7. Ibid., 28ff.

8. Vietnam, Institute of Philosophy, *Dang Ta Ban Ve Dao Duc* [*Our Party Discusses Ethics*] (Hanoi: Uy Ban Khoa Hoc Xa Hoi Viet Nam, 1973), 269.

9. Ibid., 289.

10. Dang Chan Lieu and Le Kha Ke, *Tu Dien Viet-Anh: Vietnamese-English Dictionary* (Hanoi: NXB Uy Ban Khoa Hoc Xa Hoi, 1971), 371.

11. Vietnam, *Dang Ta*, 275.

12. Ibid., 272.

13. Ibid., 275.

14. Ibid.

15. Ibid.

16. Nguyen Q. Thang and Nguyen Ba The, *Tu Dien Nhan Vat Lich Su Viet Nam* [*Dictionary of Vietnamese Historical Figures*] (Hanoi: NXB Khoa Hoc Xa Hoi, 1991), 269.

17. Ho Chi Minh quoted in Pike, *PAVN*, 313.

18. Translation of the term *pho ban chinh sach xa* is difficult because technically, by designating the official as a "deputy" (*pho*), there would be a corresponding superior. However, this was not the case with this position. Since the position was devoted exclusively to the government's social policies for families with members in the military, I have chosen to translate it as "social policy officer" in order to reduce confusion.

19. The militia commander had a number of important responsibilities during this period, including organizing a local militia composed of men who were not serving in the military, ensuring that young people entered the military, and propagandizing about the honor of military service. It is important to note, however, that at least at the beginning of the American War, the military still enjoyed tremendous prestige. Part of this derived from its defeat of the French, but it had also been augmented by its high profile in postwar reconstruction. Phillip B. Davidson, *Vietnam at War* (New York: Oxford University Press, 1988), 284.

20. See also Pike, *PAVN*, 315.

21. Ibid., 318.

22. For a discussion of the revolutionary reforms of funerals, see Malarney, "The Limits of 'State Functionalism.'"

23. Ninh Binh, Cultural Service, *Cong Tac Xay Dung Nep Song Moi, Con Nguoi Moi va Gia Dinh Tien Tien Chong My, Cuu Nuoc* [*The Task of Building the New Ways, the New Person and the Progressive Family in the War of National Salvation Against the Americans*] (Ninh Binh: Ty Van Hoa Ninh Binh, 1968), 64.

24. Ibid.

25. Government of Vietnam, *Nhung Van Ban ve Viec Cuoi, Viec Tang, Ngay Gio, Ngay Hoi* [*Documents on Weddings, Funerals, Death Anniversary and Public Festivals*] (Hanoi: NXB Van Hoa, 1979), 24.

26. Those who died but were not martyrs would also receive these certificates.

27. Rendering the expression *to quoc* in English is difficult because literally it can be read as the ancestors' land or country, but it can also be fairly translated

as both "motherland" and "fatherland." I have chosen the latter in accordance with its common translation into French as *patrie*.

28. The example of *vinh du* in a Hanoi-published dictionary reads, "*Hi sinh cho To quoc la mot vinh du*: It is an honour to lay down one's life for the fatherland" (Dang and Le, *Tu Dien Viet-Anh*, 762).

29. See Arthur P. Wolf "Gods, Ghosts, and Ancestors," in *Religion and Ritual in Chinese Society*, ed. Arthur P. Wolf (Stanford, Calif.: Stanford University Press, 1974), 131–82.

30. In cases in which a young person dies but is thought to be of particular sacred potency, an altar might be built inside the family home to worship that spirit and bring its blessings onto the family. In Thinh Liet commune, no such altars have been built for dead soldiers. Concern about the depredations of wandering malevolent spirits is evident in the placement of a tray with bowls of rice porridge outside of the home during all funeral rites. This practice feeds the wandering ghosts but keeps them outside of the home and ancestral altar.

31. If a person dies outside of the home, the corpse and casket cannot be brought into the home, and all rites must be conducted in another location. Dying outside the home is such a concern that terminally ill Vietnamese are often granted permission to leave the hospital so they can return home to die.

32. This concern for the wholeness of the corpse is seen in other mortuary rites, such as the obsessive concern shown during the secondary burial ceremony (*cai tang*) to collect the deceased's every bone, including all hand, finger, and toe bones.

33. Bao Ninh, *The Sorrow of War* (London: Secker and Warburg, 1991), 21.

34. One interesting question raised by these innovative rites is why, given Vietnam's long history of warfare, they did not emerge earlier. Given a lack of historical materials on the subject, no answer can be given.

35. The Vietnamese government has never released figures for the number of its soldiers killed in the American War. During the war years, Vietnamese had no precise knowledge of the number of their soldiers killed. Conversely, the government did publish grossly exaggerated figures for the number of Americans killed during the war; such figures were prominently displayed in the Army Museum in Hanoi.

36. See, for example, Toan Anh, *Nep Cu: Tin Nguong Viet Nam*, vol. 1 (Saigon: Hoa Dang, 1969), 62–63.

37. See Malarney "The Limits of 'State Functionalism,'" for a fuller discussion.

38. Paper votive objects were not present in all ceremonies because the government suppressed their production. Some families still used them, despite official regulations. Food items, however, were universally present.

39. See Shaun Kingsley Malarney, "Ritual and Revolution in Viet Nam" (Ph.D. diss., University of Michigan, 1993), 308–59.

40. The fifteenth of the seventh lunar month is the Vietnamese All Soul's Day.

41. Such spirits can also be described with the term *tho dia*, in which the

Sino-Vietnamese term *dia* is substituted for the vernacular *dat*. Thinh Liet residents employed the latter term.

42. One number frequently mentioned is three hundred thousand missing, but this can never be verified.

43. Xuan Cang and Ly Dang Cao, "Tim Mo Liet Si bang Phuong Phap Moi?" ["Discovering the Graves of War Dead by a New Method?"], *The Gioi Moi,* October 1996, 8–11.

44. Maurice Bloch and Jonathan Parry, "Introduction," in *Death and the Regeneration of Life,* ed. Maurice Bloch and Jonathan Parry (Cambridge: Cambridge University Press, 1982), 4.

45. See Nina Tumarkin, *Lenin Lives! The Lenin Cult in Soviet Russia* (Cambridge, Mass.: Harvard University Press, 1983).

46. See Shaun Kingsley Malarney, "The Emergent Cult of Ho Chi Minh? A Report on Religious Innovation in Contemporary Northern Viet Nam," *Asian Cultural Studies* 22 (1996): 121–31.

THREE

Museum-Shrine

Revolution and Its Tutelary Spirit
in the Village of My Hoa Hung

Christoph Giebel

Like Peter Zinoman's and Shaun Malarney's studies in this volume, this chapter focuses on one particular commemorative practice employed by the Communist Party–dominated state in Vietnam to satisfy its need for appropriate self-representation and to shape and control the ways in which the past is remembered. But whereas the commemorative messages in highly selective and stylized prison memoirs analyzed by Zinoman and in official ceremonies for the war dead discussed by Malarney seem, at least superficially, to possess an internal consistency, it is inconsistency in message and form that appears at first sight in the object of this investigation. The commemoration in his native place of Ton Duc Thang (1888–1980), one of Vietnam's most prominent Communist revolutionaries, a southerner who became the country's second president, contains an ostensible paradox. It can be found in the fact that the remembrance by the Party of one of its heroes has taken on openly religious forms since the mid- to late 1980s. Put differently, a paradox suggests itself when, under a self-proclaimed secular, even a-religious political regime, the childhood home of this high-ranking Communist in My Hoa Hung village in the Mekong Delta province of An Giang has been turned into a shrine where popular rituals of hero spirit worship are performed.

Closely tied to the shrine of Ton Duc Thang are several museum exhibits in the south of Vietnam that present versions of the life of this leading public persona. These historical displays not only are

thematically linked to Ton Duc Thang's shrine but actually were conceived and established in conjunction with the altar as integral parts of
one larger commemorative project. My focus here will be on the museum displays in or near Ton Duc Thang's birthplace and in the shrine
itself, and three related concerns of mine will be guiding this inquiry.

First, religious or quasi-religious forms of popular or state-led veneration of revolutionary heroes are by no means a new phenomenon—
one might only mention the widespread talismanic use of renderings of
Mao Zedong's image among Chinese—and have been observed in East
and Southeast Asia, including Vietnam.[1] But especially in the last case,
too little attention has been paid thus far to explaining the social conditions in which these worshiping practices appear, or the ideological-
cultural concepts that undergird them and lend these rituals their meanings (and would steer us away from superficially seeing them as
paradox).

Second, the analytical or theoretical tools of international debates,
for example, in museology, while generally useful, possess certain limitations in describing historical representation and museum projects in
Vietnam.[2] Again, an attempt should be made to understand more from
"within" how local Vietnamese contexts have shaped the specific forms
in which these exhibits have appeared.

Third, with the growing interest in issues such as historical memory,
commemorations, the "invention of tradition" (to refer to Hobsbawm),
public ceremonies, symbols, and the (re)fashioning of historic sites—in
Vietnam and elsewhere—what has tended to become emphasized are
disjunctures, shifts, contestations, and tensions, discursive and otherwise.[3] While these foci certainly can yield important insights and help
undermine long-held assumptions, they have been remarkably weak in
constructing counterarguments of an explanatory inclusiveness. In the
case of the so-called Commemorative Area for Ton Duc Thang in An
Giang, an analysis of the shrine and the adjacent museum can easily—
and legitimately—demonstrate the stark contrast between the two structures, their inherent contradictions vis-à-vis the revolutionary master
script of Marxian provenance, or the multiplicity of contending voices
and signs. In this chapter, however, I want to move beyond the uncov-
ering of tensions and instead propose a view—one view—of the Ton
Duc Thang worship in which its various elements, far from being paradoxical, might merge into a culturally coherent and intelligible message, with the shrine providing the form and the museum exhibit its
contents.

In the end, I will propose that such an integrated commemorative statement, veiled as it might manifest itself at the Ton Duc Thang shrine, needs to be read within its proper regional context. The southern museum-shrine—itself an instrument of official memory construction— seeks to modify and even subtly critique the predominant representations of revolution and war emanating from the North. This last aspect of my argument points to critical differences among the three studies in this volume that are otherwise related in their focus on commemoration by the Communist state. For example, Peter Zinoman does more than Malarney and myself in analyzing the narrative strategies and conventions built into a particular commemorative genre, and how such a customized version of revolution "worked" in the interest of the state leadership. More so than Zinoman and myself, Shaun Malarney is concerned with the popular reception (emendation, supplementation) of such state-initiated practices—a perspective largely absent from this chapter because, as I will argue, Ton Duc Thang's shrine does not target the local population as its primary audience. Rather, my chapter shows that state-organized commemoration in Vietnam is not a unified or uniform project, but that even official interpretations of the commemorated past vary in space and time; that is, they are subject to important regional and generational differences. In this sense, Ton Duc Thang's museum-shrine can be seen as an intervention in a debate where, despite its muted and hidden nature, nothing less is at stake than the self-identity of the revolutionary camp.

In 1887, Ton Duc Thang's parents, Ton Van De (d. 1938) and Nguyen Thi Di (d. 1947), built a house in the hamlet of My An, which belongs to the village of My Hoa Hung. The village is situated on Ong Ho island in the lower Mekong River, just four kilometers from Long Xuyen, the commercial and administrative center of An Giang province. Ton Duc Thang, born in 1888, was the couple's first child. Being a boy, he was tutored, probably from 1897 at the latest to about 1901, by a private teacher in Long Xuyen, who likely had contacts with the famed anti-colonialist Phan Boi Chau (when the latter came to An Giang in 1902 to recruit for his Eastern Travel Movement [Phong Trao Dong Du]) and, later on, with the anti-French conspiracy of 1916 under emperor Duy Tan. Ton Duc Thang's commemorators in An Giang stress the great influence of this fervent anticolonialist teacher on Ton Duc Thang's early politicization. Ton Duc Thang received instruction in the Chinese script and Chinese history and philosophy; afterward, he also learned French in an unidentified "elementary school" in Long Xuyen.[4] Ton Duc Thang lived in his parents' house until 1906, when, at eighteen, he moved to Saigon, the capital of the then-French colony of Cochinchina.

We do not know how frequently Ton Duc Thang returned to his childhood home between 1906 and 1929, the beginning of his sixteen years of imprisonment under the French. In fact, as is the case with many other aspects of his biography, little of a concrete nature can be said at all about this period of his life. From 1906 to 1915, Ton Duc Thang allegedly became a worker in Saigon and was involved in several early protest strikes there. Records show that he was admitted to Indochina's only vocational school, the Saigon School for Asian Mechanics (Ecole des mécaniciens asiatiques de Saïgon), in 1915, but left a year later for metropolitan wartime service at the naval arsenal in the southern French port of Toulon.[5]

His sojourn as a navy mechanic in France lasted from 1916 to 1920. During that time Ton Duc Thang is said to have accomplished his most famous revolutionary deed. In late 1918, France sent a flotilla to the Black Sea as part of the Allied entry into the Russian civil war on the side of "white," counterrevolutionary forces. The anti-Bolshevik intervention collapsed in the spring of 1919 amid widespread mutinies of these French navy units. Ton Duc Thang was *not* among the French expeditionary force in the Black Sea. But since the late 1940s or early 1950s, Vietnamese Communist propagandists and historians have celebrated him for his active and crucial involvement in the Black Sea mutiny as crew member of a French warship. In defense of Soviet Russia, Ton Duc Thang supposedly even raised a red flag on his naval vessel. This fabricated story has become the basis for propagandistically connecting the Russian and Vietnamese revolutions in an act of imagined ancestry.[6]

Back in Saigon, from 1920 to 1929, Ton Duc Thang apparently was active in early efforts to organize workers. In 1925, he claims to have directed a famous strike of navy shipyard workers, which historian Tran Van Giau subsequently called Vietnam's "first political" walkout.[7] In 1926, he joined the newly formed local branch of the Vietnamese Revolutionary Youth League (Viet Nam Thanh Nien Cach Mang Dong Chi Hoi, or, in brief, Thanh Nien), a forerunner to the Vietnamese Communist Party, which had been organized the previous year by Nguyen Ai Quoc (later to become Ho Chi Minh) in Guangzhou in southern China. Ton Duc Thang quickly rose in the ranks of the Vietnamese

Revolutionary Youth League but fell victim to the organization's suppression by the French a few years later.[8]

After his arrest in 1929, Ton Duc Thang would revisit his childhood home only twice. In the wake of the August Revolution of 1945, when the Communist-led Viet Minh, the League for the Independence of Vietnam, seized power, and Ho Chi Minh declared the independence of the Democratic Republic of Vietnam (DRV), Ton Duc Thang was liberated from sixteen years of incarceration on the infamous Con Dao prison islands in the South China Sea. Shortly thereafter, in November 1945, he made his way to My Hoa Hung to see his old mother. But since he was in danger of being captured by the French, who by then had largely retaken control of the South, he stayed only one night, as the story goes, before making his way north to Hanoi to join the DRV government. Subsequently, the French War (1946–54) broke out, followed by Vietnam's division at the seventeenth parallel, massive American intervention in the 1960s and 1970s, and more, drawn-out warfare. And thus Ton Duc Thang's next trip back home would not take place until after the end of the American War, in October 1975, after the de facto unification of the North and the South, when then-president Ton Duc Thang was able to visit his native place one last time.

The thirty years in between those two final visits to his birthplace had seen Ton Duc Thang's rapid rise to political prominence in the DRV, even though his actual influence in the power structure of the Vietnamese Communist Party (VCP) always remained negligible. His leadership of, among others, the National Assembly, the United (later, Fatherland) Front, and the USSR-Vietnam Friendship Association, as well as his vice presidency under Ho Chi Minh after 1960 and his presidency from 1969 to his death in 1980, attest to the representational usefulness of Ton Duc Thang for the Communist Party–led state. This can be explained by his seniority—he surpassed all other party leaders in terms of both age and the length of imprisonment under the French[9]—and his unique symbolic value in multiple capacities: as an undisputed proletarian, anticolonial revolutionary, alleged internationalist activist, and a southerner (reinforcing the DRV's claim to authority over all of Vietnam).

In 1984, four years after his death, the Ministry of Culture, upon the suggestion of local cadres, declared Ton Duc Thang's childhood home a cultural-historic monument. After Ton Duc Thang's brother Ton Duc Nhung (b. 1896) and sister-in-law (b. 1897) both died in 1986, their son's family moved to an adjacent building, and renovations of the original house and the creation of a "commemorative area" (*khu luu niem*)

were begun, with their completion set to coincide with the centennial of
Ton Duc Thang's birth in August 1988. The initiative for these undertakings can be traced to the provincial branch of the VCP, which
planned to use the centennial "to educate the cadres, Party members,
and the people of the province about [Ton Duc Thang's] great example
in struggle, sacrifice, and revolutionary morality."[10] Under the direction
of the VCP's provincial propaganda board and local cadres, the An
Giang departments of construction and culture/information, and the
University of Architecture of Ho Chi Minh City, several projects were
started. These included the actual renovation of Ton Duc Thang's home,
the construction of an exhibition building in the vicinity, the landscaping
of the future commemorative area, the first-ever electrification of My
Hoa Hung, and the building or upgrading of bridges and paved roads
to connect Ong Ho island to the provincial infrastructure in preparation
for the expected visitors. In addition, Lam Binh Tuong, a museologist,
and the An Giang provincial museum in Long Xuyen started gathering
materials and objects for future displays on Ton Duc Thang's life.[11]

In August 1988, in celebration of Ton Duc Thang's hundredth birth-
day, the commemorative area in My Hoa Hung was solemnly inaugurated.

Ton Duc Thang's childhood home is a rather large structure on pillars,
with well over one hundred square meters of living space (fig. 3.1). The
house has at least four bedrooms, the main living room, and a spacious
porch. Some of the walls show elaborate wood carvings, and the interior
is decorated with valuable furniture and several large pieces of lacquer
art. The main item on display, in the center of the house and its living
room, is an altar with Ton Duc Thang's portrait, electric candles, dec-
orative plants, and incense burners. Behind Ton Duc Thang's altar and
standing along a wall is a second altar that can more easily be identified
as a traditional place for ancestral veneration. This function is under-
scored by the display around it of photos of Ton Duc Thang's parents,
brother, and sister-in-law. The neatly kept grave sites of these four relatives, which are equally important in Vietnamese practices of ancestral
worship, are situated behind the building and consciously drawn into
the overall exhibit by way of a well-maintained, well-marked path.[12]

The nearby exhibition building (erected about fifty meters from Ton
Duc Thang's childhood home) is a large, rectangular concrete structure
on pillars standing in water. Its design hardly conveys the impression,

Figure 3.1.   The author and Ton Duc Thang's nephew in front of Ton's childhood home and shrine, My Hoa Hung village, An Giang. Photograph by
Christoph Giebel.

as Dang Kim Quy has written, of "a lotus plant spreading on a pond."
The allusion to a lotus is probably meant to symbolize purity, or perhaps
the socially liberating message of the Communist-led revolution, and is
not the traditional Buddhist "symbol of man's achievement potential."[13]
Inside the building is a large, open exhibition hall with movable partitions on which most of the exhibits (photos, paintings, plates, and panels
with quotes) are hung. Facing its entryway stands a large bust of Ton
Duc Thang on a slightly elevated platform and underneath a ceiling-
high red panel with a gold star—insignia of the state. The bust is framed
by vases that depict a scene from 1958, when Ho Chi Minh conferred
on Ton Duc Thang the DRV's highest order. Adjacent to the exhibition
hall are smaller rooms for guest receptions and a few staff offices.

The exhibit itself consists mainly of pictures tracing Ton Duc Thang's
life in chronological manner: from his native place and family, his vo-
cation as a mechanic in Saigon and France, his alleged role in the Black
Sea mutiny (symbolized by a painting of a warship with a hoisted red
flag), his early revolutionary activities back in Vietnam leading to his
arrest, trial, and imprisonment on Con Dao, to his rise to prominence
at the side of Ho Chi Minh in the newly independent state, and finally

to his own presidency. Furthermore, a few items of everyday use from Ton Duc Thang's possessions are presented in glass cases.

Overall, the commemorative area in My Hoa Hung serves as a destination point for secular pilgrimages. Since 1988, schools and factories have frequently organized tours to My Hoa Hung, and in the short time span until the Eastern European revolutions of 1989, delegations of "fraternal" East bloc countries paid their respects. Photos of these organized visits are displayed in the museum, and a visitors' album further attests to this function of the site. According to museum personnel, especially around nationally symbolic dates—Ho Chi Minh's and Ton Duc Thang's birthdays, Independence Day—the commemorative area hosts youth camps. During my sojourn in My Hoa Hung, however, the education cadre accompanying me from Hanoi and I remained the only visitors, and my companion's worshiping with incense in front of Ton Duc Thang's altar was the only ritual act I witnessed. None of the local people, in particular, came to the compound. Several staff members were at hand, but they seemed to have few duties. I strongly suspect, though cannot prove, that after a flurry of visits and ceremonies during the initial years, in the 1990s the site has become permanently underutilized and, for considerable stretches of time, practically deserted.

Nevertheless, more so than any other memorial place for Ton Duc Thang, including the Ton Duc Thang Museum in Ho Chi Minh City, My Hoa Hung was conceived to provide the official commemoration of the revolutionary with an immediate spatial quality. Ton Duc Thang's childhood home becomes part of several imaginary maps: reaching back in time, it links up with other popular heroic figures of Vietnamese history, one after the other resisting outside aggression. Reaching out into simultaneous time, it becomes one of the places of origin of the modern Vietnamese revolution where revolutionaries all march in unison. Finally, it becomes part of a global map of revolutionary internationalism and humanism to enhance the national prestige of Vietnam.

As noted earlier, the commemorative area is filled with contrasting images and messages, of which I will mention only a few. For example, Ton Duc Thang's veneration results in the partial superseding of the standard biographical script. In his native place, the official claim that he came from a family of *poor* peasants is rejected, and no attempt is made to hide that the family was, in the words of Ton Duc Thang's nephew, "rather rich" (and could, after all, afford a private education for the firstborn son). Further, Ton Duc Thang's childhood home, nicely decorated and built mainly of wood in the traditional style of a peasant home, stands in stark contrast to the adjacent modern museum cast of concrete. While the former is centered on popular ritual and ancestral veneration, and thus looks backward in time, the latter tells a story of heroic struggles and secular successes along Marxist-Leninist interpretive lines and has its eyes set on the future into which time is moving in linear and predictably progressive fashion. But even this narrative, with its emphasis on Ton Duc Thang's proletarian circumstances and class consciousness, is hardly without ambiguity. Its model of a universalist historical materialism is effectively undermined by a strong nativist message about an essentializing spirit of resistance to foreign aggression with which Ton Duc Thang's home region is portrayed as having imbued him from early childhood on.

What, then, can one make of the commemorative area that is apparently so filled with contrasts and contradictions and that in its quasi-religious worship of a Communist leader creates tensions with the state's strictly secular orientation? Is it possible to distill from the commemorative place a unified theme, with a form and contents that fit?

As a first step—one that aims to identify a mold or form for the site— I propose that it is not only ancestral worship rituals with which Ton Duc Thang is venerated. Rather, his childhood home resonates even more with the Vietnamese traditional religious belief in the spiritual properties of the country's landscape and history. Although the building is always referred to only as "President Ton Duc Thang's childhood home," it in fact is meant to be a shrine or temple (*den*) for Ton Duc Thang's hero spirit—a tutelary deity for the locale as well as a figure of national stature that has entered the pantheon of Vietnamese heroic guardian spirits.

By this I do not mean that Ton Duc Thang was made the village patron spirit (*thanh hoang*) of My Hoa Hung. In prerevolutionary Vietnam, the cult of a village patron spirit was always performed in the village's communal hall (*dinh*) and was based on the community's own choice of its guardian deity, which clearly is not the case here.[14] As I will describe later, the local population, which traditionally would enjoy the benevolent acts of its patron spirit, is not really meant to be the recipient of the kind deeds by Ton Duc Thang's spirit; it is thus not the primary audience for the shrine's message. And since veneration takes place at Ton Duc Thang's birthplace—and not at the local communal hall—"origins" of some sort appear as a primary concern to the commemorative project.

I argue, however, that Ton Duc Thang's temple consciously models itself on the religious belief (or state ideology, as Stephen O'Harrow calls it,[15] more problematically perhaps) that bestows superhuman spiritual powers not only on Vietnam's geography—its mountains, earth, and waters[16]—but also on its history, where historical hero figures as guardian deities continue to watch over the nation's affairs and, thus, transcend and tie together past and present. Inclusion into (and exclusion from) the national pantheon was (and still is) an ongoing process, which for long stretches of time entailed a formalized court procedure and which, especially with regard to the question of who among the more prominent cases of historical personae should be "in" and who should be "out," was of an eminently political and self-serving nature. Among the uncontested hero spirits are, for example, leaders who rebelled against Chinese domination or who defended Vietnamese independence against Chinese attacks, like the Trung Sisters (who both died in 43), Ngo Quyen (897–944), Ly Thuong Kiet (1030–1105), Tran Hung Dao (1220s–1300), Le Loi (1384–1433), and Nguyen Trai (1380–1442), who to this day continue to be worshiped in shrines all over Vietnam.

Vietnamese hero spirit tales form a genre with a set of conventional features from which, I will argue, Ton Duc Thang's shrine liberally quotes. To describe their generic makeup, I will briefly turn here to the most prominent collection of such stories of tutelary deities, Ly Te Xuyen's fourteenth-century compilation *Spiritual Powers of the Viet Realm (Viet dien u linh tap)*. Keith Taylor and Oliver Wolters have written detailed studies on the *Spiritual Powers of the Viet Realm,* which, while differing in their approaches and arguments, complement rather than contradict one another.[17] Both Taylor and Wolters argue that the compilation of heroic spirit tales was used for the interests of the court elites. They differ, however, in their interpretations of the spirits' utility to these elites. Taylor traces the tales back to two main concerns: first, to what he terms "Ly dynasty religion," in which royal authority is sanctioned by spiritual powers. Second, at the time of compilation, when dynastic succession was contested and irregular, these spirits functioned as examples of loyalty to rulers. But also highlighting the psychological comfort that the belief in protective deities continued to give later ruling classes in dangerous times, he concludes that the spirit world was a "protective screen" that "was seen by the Vietnamese as a shelter from alien threats and domestic disorder." Further, "by ritually acknowledging these spiritual powers, Vietnamese kings opened legitimizing space for their claims upon the obedience of the people."[18]

Wolters, who mainly works with later versions of the *Spiritual Powers of the Viet Realm,* places his emphasis differently: in the spirit tales he

sees reflections of elite anxieties about village value systems of a potentially rebellious nature as well as concerns over "wild" (animist) village
ritual practices that do not conform with the court's agenda. The hero
spirit tales are used to control and assimilate village customs and are
thus primarily didactic tools to disseminate court concepts of "good
government" and "loyal behavior" among the population. Such do-
mesticated spirits become the ruler's loyal servants and "local surro-
gates." The potentially rebellious energies of the spirits, as well as those
of "villagers of prowess" (i.e., "spirits-to-be"), are harnessed by royal
recognition and employment in the ruler's aid.[19]

Wolters has characterized the tales' often uniform plots in two ways.
First, in instances of outward threats, there is

> the invariably successful relationship between Vietnamese rulers . . . and the
> local spirits but only if the ruler alertly apprehends a spirit's presence, if
> necessary testing it, appoints it to a post of military responsibility, and re-
> wards it for its contribution to victory. The spirit, who always salutes the
> ruler, now joins the entourage. When this procedure is followed, victory is
> "certain."

Second, concerning domestic order, the genre would present

> a spirit's marvelous "manifestations" of spiritual power, its dramatic disclo-
> sure to a ruler . . . , the ruler's wonder and grateful provision of a "shrine,"
> the villagers' "incessant" worship at the shrine, the spirit's "response" to the
> villagers' needs, and the "favours" enjoyed by rulers and villagers alike.[20]

To sum up what is important for my purposes here, guardian spirits
protect the country from external threats and the ruler against internal,
village-level challenges. Their role often is to facilitate a harmonious
relationship between elite and village (sub-) cultures, or between rulers
and the people. Although both sides benefit from the tutelary services
of the deity, the spirit's mediation is not one of equidistance, but one
ultimately done in the ruler's interest. Spirit tales and local temples both
are didactic tools, then, to focus popular allegiance toward the ruler.
Finally, spirits and rulers can come together either through the ruler's
proper apprehension and recognition, or *goi hon,* the "calling up,"[21] of
a worthy spirit, or by way of the spirit announcing (disclosing) itself to
a worthy ruler.

If Ton Duc Thang's childhood home is indeed a guardian spirit shrine—
creating, so to speak, the site's form or mold—and if it were to establish

him as a hero spirit belonging to a greater Vietnamese pantheon, does that not make the commemorative project even more of an oddity because of the exhibition hall's "unfitting" message of Communist revolution? I believe not. Rather, instead of doing the obvious—emphasizing contradictions and incongruences with Communist orthodoxy—an alternative reading of the exhibit on Ton Duc Thang's life is possible that will fit the form (of a guardian spirit shrine) and afford us a way to see the site in its entirety as communicating a uniform theme. To this end, we need to change our interpretive grid from one that focuses on Marxist-Leninist historiographical attitudes and socialist iconography to a more fruitful one that is attentive to Vietnamese cultural-political concepts and the conventions in which they came to be expressed. In order to identify a message suitable to the form, my second step thus is to approach the exhibit hall's display as a didactic text that models itself, if only loosely, on historical texts and political thought of the Vietnamese past.

Again, the works of Oliver Wolters and Keith Taylor are of relevance here. Wolters and Taylor have both undertaken structuralist readings of Vietnamese annals and discerned dominant themes—or what they call "sentences"[22] or "statements"[23]—to shed new light on the histories the annals are concerned with, as well as on their authors and their intentions. Wolters in particular sees such a "sentence" as a signifying system representing the totality of "recurrent 'units,' " that is, words that are syntactically related but do not necessarily always appear with one another; for those portions of the *Complete Historical Records of Dai Viet* (*Dai Viet Su Ky Toan Thu*), annals that were compiled in the mid–fifteenth century, he identifies one such "sentence" as signifying "good government."[24]

Coming back to the exhibit on Ton Duc Thang's life, we will disengage ourselves from a primary concern with the ideological (and museological) master script that makes the commemorative site appear such a paradox. Rather, we will take such an idiom less seriously and see it perhaps only as a required stylistic convention in contemporary Vietnam, where one has to draw from the reservoir of Communist Party–sanctioned political-ideological terminology. Once we focus instead on other "recurrent units," or recurrent expressions, the exhibit can reveal a dominant theme that actually makes sense in conjunction with Ton Duc Thang's hero spirit shrine. I refer here to the museum's repeated and quite prominent emphasis on "simplicity," "sacrifice," "selflessness," "loyalty," and "service"—all, of course, exemplified by and com-

bined in Ton Duc Thang's life. And further following in Wolters's fashion, I would argue that these five terms (or their equivalences
"thriftiness," "unpretentiousness," "faithfulness," etc.) likewise form
the exhibit's "statement." Namely, these words equally fuse into an essential portrayal of "good government"—or, differently phrased, they
are a fundamental commentary on the proper attitudes of the Revolution
vis-à-vis the people, especially after its successful rise to power.

As in the Ton Duc Thang Museum in Ho Chi Minh City, the exhibits
on Ton Duc Thang's life in Long Xuyen and My Hoa Hung indeed pay
particular attention to the characteristic frugality, devotion, and unpretentiousness of this revolutionary and national leader. Ho Chi Minh's
words of praise of Ton Duc Thang to that effect are prominently displayed right in the entrances to both exhibits. And we are reminded of
the concern Ton Duc Thang showed for others throughout his life: for
example, for his own family members, whom he supplied in his youth
with self-made sandals (which are shown in the exhibits), or for his
Vietnamese coworkers, one of them gravely sick, at the Toulon arsenal.
We also meet him loyally caring for his fellow prisoners, even for those
who initially tried to harm him, during the hellish years on Con Dao.
We see him caring for the nation as a whole when, in 1945, he visits his
mother, whom he had not seen since 1929, for only one night because
of "urgent business" awaiting him in the capital. At My Hoa Hung, a
painting of this last scene and a related quote ascribed to Ton Duc Thang
underscore the importance placed on his unselfishness.

The theme of simplicity and selflessness is successfully reproduced
beyond the exhibits. Two examples can illustrate this. First, in 1988, a
symposium on Ton Duc Thang was held in Long Xuyen. The publication in 1989 of the symposium's proceedings then significantly carried
the programmatic title "A Great Ordinary Person"—a phrase coined by
Tran Bach Dang, the former Saigon party chief during the American
War.[25] And second, Dang Kim Quy reports that visitors to the commemorative area are often moved to tears while considering Ton Duc Thang's
"life full of hardship and bitterness, yet pure, loyal, kind-hearted and
simple."[26]

The parts of the exhibits dealing with Ton Duc Thang's life *after* he
became an accomplished national leader focus even more on his thriftiness, self-reliance, commonality with the people, and modesty. Among
the material artifacts presented are his simple presidential clothes and
worn shoes, his bicycle, alarm clock (a gift in 1957 from Vietnamese
embassy personnel in Moscow), table fan, and photo camera—all of

them of basic make—and little gifts from common people that he used in everyday life, such as an ashtray made of a downed US bomber's scrap metal. The only piece of extravagance is a Swiss watch with a portrait of Ho Chi Minh on its face, which Ton Duc Thang is said to have cherished and worn to his end. It was, like most of the other artifacts, given to the museum by Ton Duc Thang's son-in-law Duong Van Phuc. The story goes that Prime Minister Pham Van Dong had seven such watches made for the DRV leadership while he attended the 1954 Geneva conference.[27]

Large black-and-white photos depict Ton Duc Thang's plain attire and rustic furniture in the presidential residence, or his bicycle repair tools, which he is said to have used until old age. The two explanations given are that Ton Duc Thang, even as president, at heart remained a mechanic who loved to tinker, and that he did not want to impose upon his presidential guard to fix his bicycle. Other pictures show him involved in practical, down-to-earth, hands-on, even mundane to trivial activities, like chatting with factory workers, reading to children, and tending his garden plants. Again, it is here that the core of the exhibits' didacticism is to be found. What becomes privileged is clearly *not* his revolutionary struggles, successes, and fame (a focus that is more pronounced in official biographical treatments emanating from the center of Communist Party power)[28] but the fact that power, once achieved, was for Ton Duc Thang not an end in itself but the means to best serve the people—in other words, that power left him humble, committed, and uncorrupted. One plausible reading of the exhibits' statement would thus be about the correct demeanor of those who govern in the name of the Revolution.

How could this kind of ideal revolutionary leadership, of which Ton Duc Thang is portrayed to possess all the essential characteristics, and of which the Communist Party is the legitimate agent, be conceptualized? I have already identified central attributes such as "simplicity," "sacrifice," "selflessness," "loyalty," and "service." They point to an activist government of officials operating under a set of ethics that take as their reference the common good. Its sense of self would be one of idealistic (and at the same time paternalistic) confidence in the righteousness of its initiatives, its unfailing knowledge of "what is best" for the people, and its predictable success. Its continued power and authority would remain an unchallenged given so long as it remained tightly connected to the people, their experiences and circumstances, and in congruence with their "true wishes." Ideally, officials would share the conditions of life of the people and remain immune to the corrupting temptations of power, since, in their altruism, their ultimate reward would be the creation of a just and harmonious society free of exploitation.

Such a concept of *proper rule* extolled in the exhibits' statement is certainly not without historical precedent. Thus, my contention that Ton Duc Thang's museum-shrine produces both in form (hero spirit temple) and in contents (exhibits) a consistent statement must lead us at this point on an argumentative detour into premodern Vietnamese intellectual life. For quite a similar notion of proper rule was once articulated by the great scholar-official Nguyen Trai (1380–1442), and we need to examine his thought here in some detail.

Nguyen Trai lived through the tumultuous decades leading to the fall of the Tran dynasty in 1400, the brief reign of Ho Quy Ly (1400–1407), the harsh occupation of the country by an army of China's Ming dynasty (1407–27), and the subsequent restoration of independence under a new dynasty, the Le. Nguyen Trai himself played an important part in the defeat of the Ming; he joined Le Loi in organizing an anti-Ming resistance—the Lam Son uprising, begun in 1418—and the two men became the movement's key exponents. As emperor (1428–33), Le Loi would retain Nguyen Trai as his chief official; thereafter, their relationship was made a Vietnamese archetype of the fortunate link between a powerful ruler and his able and loyal minister.[29]

Much has been written on Nguyen Trai in scholarly works. Without doubt, the ascent of Confucian axioms for the first time to a commanding position within Vietnamese elite culture is intimately connected to Nguyen Trai and the early Le dynasty. Tran Quoc Vuong actually called it an "irony of history" that the "Confucian bureaucratic-monarchic regime . . . , an exogenous element originating from North China . . . , received a particular boost from the time Dai Viet shook off the Ming yoke."[30] Nevertheless, Nguyen Trai "took . . . seriously the Confucian dictum of serving the state," as John Whitmore has observed, and "strongly believed in an active role" [for scholar-officials]; in his work "service was his dominant theme."[31] Oliver Wolters, for his part, accentuates Nguyen Trai's major contributions differently; according to him, it was from the selfless way peasants rallied against the Ming invaders [that Nguyen Trai] witnessed the people's response when a heroic style of leadership revived. [Therefore, his writings] stressed the ruler's responsibility to the people. . . . The people's well-being now became the test of good government, and the ruler's obligation to use educated officials is confidently formulated.[32]

Finally, Esta Ungar writes that Nguyen Trai's thought

expressed an attachment to traditional Vietnamese values of the ruler as the heroic protector of the people, . . . [onto which] he grafted newer political constructs that . . . enlarged . . . the scope of activity of previous dynastic governments. . . . In his system the people's welfare was the basic concern of the state.[33]

Far from following the inward-looking neo-Confucian interpretation of such central concepts as "humaneness and justice" (ren yi, Vietn. nhan nghia), Nguyen Trai instead believed that nhan nghia obliged a ruler to "calm the people" (an min, Vietn. an dan), in the meaning of "securing the livelihood of the people"—an outwardly looking, activist stance informed by an "ethic of public service."

Significantly, Ungar maintains that Nguyen Trai adapted in such notions the idealistic postulates of the eleventh-century so-called government school of Confucianism, an activist reform movement with strong roots in Mencian thought during the times of China's Northern Song dynasty. She sees a particular affinity to the work of Fan Zhongyan (989–1052),[34] who spearheaded the short-lived early Song reforms. Fan Zhongyan's famous precept that officials should "be the first to become concerned with the world's troubles and the last to rejoice in its happiness"[35] became, in Ungar's words, "an article of faith among fifteenth-century Vietnamese public servants and scholars and was greatly encouraged by Nguyen Trai in his writings and his example."[36] James Liu conceptualized the ultimate vision of officialdom in the policies of Fan Zhongyan and his reform movement as an "ethocracy" based on moral principles and a strict sense of responsibility toward the people. This Confucian idealism with its "practical utilitarian spirit and . . . active political interest,"[37] nicely complemented the emphases on practicality and dynamic leadership in Vietnamese political thought. However, we should keep the important fact in mind that Nguyen Trai adapted, but did not wholly adopt, the positions of early Song reformist Confucianism. Rather, as Ungar argues, he "merged" them with "the traditional Vietnamese leadership ethic,"[38] which envisioned a heroic and just ruler in tune with, and aided by, the spiritual powers of the country.

Nguyen Trai fascinated DRV intellectuals already during the earlier years of the regime's consolidation and resumption of armed struggle. Tran Huy Lieu (1901–69), perhaps the most prominent and influential historian in those days, wrote regularly on Nguyen Trai,[39] and Nguyen Trai's collected works were published in Hanoi in 1969. Two reasons, one external and one internal, may best account for Nguyen Trai's appeal to the DRV. First, he, too, had put his service to the task of expelling foreign occupants (and had ultimately triumphed!). Second, by championing a Vietnamese version of Fan Zhongyan's "government school" of Confucianism (which predated neo-Confucianism), with its model of an "ethocracy," Nguyen Trai spoke directly to the revolutionaries' concern, *now that they were in power,* about building up an efficient bureaucracy with cadres who nevertheless would avoid the corrupting internal dynamics of government and stay selfless and "close to the people."

It is noteworthy that Tran Huy Lieu's revised and final treatment of Nguyen Trai, in 1966, contained an added chapter where Tran Huy Lieu employed "Nguyen Trai in our present endeavor to defeat America and save the country."[40] Patricia Pelley has argued that a strong anxiety among DRV historians about the persistent collaboration with U.S. overlords in the South made Nguyen Trai an even more compelling example, since he, unlike many of his contemporaries, was said to have resisted working with the occupying Ming. While this point is in itself quite convincing—although North-South collaboration patterns were exactly the reverse in the fifteenth century—Pelley's emphasis of Nguyen Trai as a *counterhero,* who is set in contrast to the negative types of foreign occupants and their local collaborators, overlooks Nguyen Trai's *reaffirming* role for the revolution's positive self-image.[41] It is the latter aspect, that is, the revolution's conscious utilization of Northern Song and early Le thought on good government, that I find even more intriguing. Tran Huy Lieu writes that Ho Chi Minh

> often used Pham Trong Yem's [i.e., Fan Zhongyan's] precept to educate the cadres. Communists fight for the happiness of humanity and therefore must "be the first to become concerned with the world's troubles and the last to rejoice in its happiness," and only the communists' "being the first to become concerned with the world's troubles and the last to rejoice in its happiness" is really consequential and complete.[42]

If I were to argue for an affinity between Confucianism and Vietnamese Communism, I would have no better argumentative grounds than those provided by the intellectual links from Fan Zhongyan via Nguyen Trai to Ho Chi Minh. All three stressed the more practical questions of public service and (outward) moral conduct. The neo-Confucian emphasis on political orthodoxy and self-cultivation, however, neither seemed "to relate to Vietnamese considerations" in Nguyen Trai's times[43] nor was much of concern to Vietnamese Communism, with its marked absence of grander ideological designs or contributions. Caution is thus in order lest one neglects the limits to such analogies as well as the long-standing battles fought among and over these two political and intellectual systems. In that respect, David Marr has strongly warned against simplistic comparisons of Confucian and Marxist ethics.[44] And as Nguyen Khac Vien has pointed out, Vietnamese Communism needed to stress its divergence from those "backward" aspects of Confucianism that emphasized, for example, social harmony and hierarchical obligations.[45] But both Marr and Nguyen Khac Vien have also admitted to affinities among revolutionary and Confucian ethical positions. In fact, Nguyen Khac Vien quotes from a VCP handbook that explained "the five revolutionary virtues" to its cadres; these virtues were humanity, a sense of duty, knowledge, courage, and integrity. Fan Zhongyan is, again, very much present (yet unacknowledged) in the handbook's statement that "the cadre who displays [humanity] . . . will not hesitate to be the first to endure hardship and the last to enjoy happiness." Neil Jamieson has perceptively pointed out that "humanity" and "duty" are the "assimilated" terms *nhan* and *nghia* and as such "still core elements of the [VCP] ethical system."[46] All these analyses are helpful, yet, especially in Nguyen Khac Vien's case, they are too general to be more than points of departure.

Thus, much more needs to be done to understand the connections between Confucian idealism/humanism and Vietnamese Communism. For the latter, I suggest that it would be helpful to distinguish between the party in *struggle* and *mobilization* and the party in *leadership* and *power*, as these fundamentally different positions conditioned the revolution's varying judgments of Confucianism either as obstacle and opponent or as (partial) paragon and precursor. Alexander Woodside has hinted at this split perception with regard to the "mandarin" revolutionaries' concern over how to bridge the divide between their elite social backgrounds and the "masses" they were supposed to lead:

> In East Asia, the Confucian gentleman was the universalist concerned with other people's troubles and with the troubles of the universe, the free spirit least bound by the particular concerns of the "petty man." If memories of

the self-serving "feudal" bureaucrat were anathema to the "proletarianized" intellectuals of the 1930s and 1940s, recollections of the classical "gentleman" whose universal humanitarianism recognized no social class boundaries, in its reactions to human misery, were probably far less repellent.[47]

I might add that, to the party in struggle, "self-serving 'feudal' bureaucrats" not only figured in its *memory* but were, as "Confucian" bureaucrats serving the French or Emperor Bao Dai, real-life adversaries. The influence of specific, to varying degrees "Confucian," thinkers like Fan Zhongyan or Nguyen Trai on the twentieth-century revolutionary leadership needs to be studied much more thoroughly. When Ho Chi Minh freely inserted Fan Zhongyan's famous eleventh-century dictum into a "rectification" speech in April 1961, he was not just using "old symbols . . . creatively" and in a calculated and conscious way, as Marr suggests;[48] instead, he revealed a *mind-set* very much familiar with, and receptive to, Confucian humanism (and not just "less repelled" by it, as Woodside would have it), perhaps similar to how Bible-quoting Western politicians reflect a cultural environment suffused with certain strands of Christianity.

Finally, I should note in conclusion of my brief discussion of Nguyen Trai that his retreat on Con Son mountain in Hai Hung Province was turned into a national hero shrine,[49] and that Nguyen Trai became canonized, and continues to be venerated as, among the most important guardian spirits of the Vietnamese realm.

We can now end our detour through Vietnam's intellectual past and return to present-day My Hoa Hung by observing that Nguyen Trai's thought and his precedent as enshrined hero spirit of a national pantheon resonate clearly in the presentation of Ton Duc Thang's own museum-shrine. Although no specific mention is made of Nguyen Trai at the commemorative area for Ton Duc Thang, the exhibits' statement about the proper ways of a revolutionary government bears such resemblance to the particular activist-idealist strand of Confucian ethics espoused by Nguyen Trai (and, as we have just seen, consciously utilized as a guideline for DRV cadres) that it is safe to presume a powerful allusion by the former to the latter.

Ton Duc Thang's commemorators hardly implied the correlation with Nguyen Trai's thought and hero spirit status in an arbitrary or random manner. Rather, the timing of important events likely suggested and reinforced it.[50] The year 1980, in which Ton Duc Thang died, also marked the six-hundredth anniversary of Nguyen Trai's birth. Nguyen Trai's anniversary was widely and prominently observed in Vietnam— not the least because Nguyen Trai's role as heroic defender of the nation against Ming aggression fit neatly with the pervasive anti-Chinese atmosphere just one year after the brief but costly Chinese invasion of northern Vietnam in 1979. A number of conferences on Nguyen Trai were organized, and related publications appeared in subsequent years. Therefore, during the early to mid-1980s, the public celebration of Nguyen Trai as a model advocate of good government and as a protective spirit in the "heroic tradition of resistance" overlapped with, and likely had considerable influence on, the formative stage of the commemoration of Ton Duc Thang.

I have offered ways of reading Ton Duc Thang's museum-shrine against a background of historical allusions and a multitude of cultural quotations and memories. On the one hand, his birthplace shrine establishes Ton Duc Thang as a guardian spirit who has joined the Vietnamese pantheon of historical hero deities. On the other hand, the museum exhibit propagates an ethos of the simple and selflessly devoted cadre, which similarly reaches back in time and connects with certain Confucian concepts espoused by a famous Vietnamese scholar-official.

But are we not dealing here with two quite different and incompatible cultural statements—the markedly non- and pre-Confucian tutelary spirits of the *Spiritual Powers of the Viet Realm,* and Nguyen Trai and his version of Confucian idealist humanism? I would not agree. Esta Ungar has shown how, in Nguyen Trai's thought, Song reformist Confucianism was "merged with," or "grafted onto," established Vietnamese concepts of heroic leadership and the interplay between worldly and spiritual powers. And dynamic relations, not incompatibility, are described by Alexander Woodside when he writes of Vietnamese intellectuals:

> [Their] inclination to [study popular traditions] *accompanied* the Confucianization of Vietnamese intellectual life, was provoked by it, and sometimes collided with its this-worldly sensibilities. . . . The *mixture* of acceptance and rejections varied with each thinker. . . . But it was the *interplay* between Confucian moral theories and the great ancient reservoir of Vietnamese religious and mythical formulations which most decisively shaped Vietnamese views of change before 1860.[51]

I suggest that there is actually a distinct area of commonality in the two concepts. Nguyen Trai was concerned with an "ethocracy" of officials who would aid the ruler for the welfare of the people and social order and harmony. Hero spirits likewise take a mediating position between ruler and ruled: they ensure protection from the top down and loyalty, ideological adherence, and support from the bottom up, as similar guarantors of a stable social order. Both concepts are thus concerned with the harmonious relationship between ruler and the people and emphasize the crucial role of the ruler's agents (or assistants) in bringing it about in a proper way.

It is in this fundamental concern that Ton Duc Thang's spirit temple and museum exhibit finally coalesce in a meaningful way. In its personification by Ton Duc Thang, the statement about an idealistic, selfless, and uncorrupted governing officialdom—an ethos of revolutionary cadres—*itself* is the enshrined spirit of My Hoa Hung. Simple and selfless Communist cadres are the agents (i.e., officials) of an abstract ruler, the Vietnamese Revolution, understood here not simply as the events of August 1945 but as an institutionalized cause or enterprise. Properly called upon and utilized, these officials ensure the ruler's success against outward threats and domestic disorder. Their primary concern with the people's livelihood constitutes the protection that the people expect from the ruler, in exchange for which they recognize the ruler's legitimacy and are loyal.

Instead of tensions, paradox, and subversion, this is, I suggest, the unifying theme that can make sense of the commemorative area. At Ton Duc Thang's birthplace, the uncorrupted cadre, who tirelessly and selflessly works for the benefit of both the Revolution and the people, is venerated as a guardian spirit of the Revolution, and the museum functions as a modern temple inscription announcing the spirit's merit, achievements, and outstanding character.

I have tried here to find an interpretation that would make sense of what appeared to be a highly contradictory commemoration of a Communist leader at his birthplace. Whereas this search has taken me all the way back to the eleventh century, the site's contemporary context, the late 1980s, requires some attention as well. The waning of the Cold War and the decline and ultimate demise of the socialist camp in the 1980s increasingly weakened the external moral authority and political legitimacy that Marxism-Leninism had long afforded the ruling Vietnamese Communist Party. This process opened up space for a popular reembracing of the "traditional"[52] at the same time that the Revolution itself was compelled to seek an alternative model of authority, one that would have to come from within the prerevolutionary Vietnamese range of experiences. Popular reclaiming of ritual practices and the party's need to reaffirm its legitimacy by self-consciously anchoring ("localizing") itself in much more traditional concepts and languages occurred side by side.

While the potentials for posthumous commemoration of Ho Chi Minh and Ton Duc Thang are necessarily greatly different for quite obvious reasons, it is nevertheless interesting that the mid-1970s saw the erection of a monumental mausoleum to Ho Chi Minh in Hanoi, with a structure and a cultic-ritual form outside Vietnamese practices, while spirit shrines-museums resonating with traditional political-cultural concepts appeared in the late 1980s in the countryside.

Commemorative confidence is one aspect that needs to be considered in this context. The Ho Chi Minh mausoleum is one such expression of confidence by the Vietnamese Revolution. It was certainly Vietnamese, but it belonged—on equal terms, as symbolized by the chosen architectural-ritual form—to the larger moral order and authoritative structure of the socialist camp. In the "triumphalist spirit"[53] of the mid-1970s, it felt firmly embedded in a grander historical design, the validity of which had just been proven by the revolution's singular feat of successfully achieving, against great odds, its outward goals of uniting the country and ending foreign domination.[54]

In contrast, at the core of the commemorative effort in My Hoa Hung lies a deep crisis of confidence. Gone were the days of triumphalism and the shelter of a greater outside moral authority that would have provided a familiar choice of commemorative form. The Revolution had lost its sense of purpose, and the split between the trajectory it had prescribed for the country and the material-cultural tendencies of the people widened more and more. Amid the dramatic economic downturn of the mid-1980s, rising social ills, widespread popular dissatisfaction with, or—worse yet—uninterest in, the revolutionary government, rampant corruption and loss of morale among its cadres, and the ominous decline of the global socialist camp, the organizers of Ton Duc Thang's museum-shrine "turned nativist" and (re)discovered in the traditional a new/old source of legitimacy and guidance. In exchange for one historical model of predictability, the now discredited Marxism-Leninism, they tapped into a model within the Vietnamese cultural repertoire that promised an equally predictable course of events, the invincible alliance between Vietnamese worldly and spiritual powers. Instead of the mausoleum, the spirit temple was (re-)created.

But this should not be confused with a change of allegiance, or a turning away from the revolution. Despite the confidence crisis, Ton Duc Thang's commemorators remained committed and fiercely loyal to the Revolution. True to the obligations that their role as cadres entailed, their fundamental concern lay with its survival, and they were anxious to improve the quality of the revolutionary ranks. And so, triggered by the disconcerting changes in the fortunes of the socialist camp, yet another imagined ancestry of Vietnamese Communism was established through Ton Duc Thang. This ancestry was to be found in traditional concepts of authority and order of the country's spiritual and this-worldly realms and in the unbroken sequence of national heroes, who, with the aid of the spirit world to which they themselves would belong after death, had risen to defend the country and reaffirm these concepts. Placing the Communist revolution and Ton Duc Thang (and, of course, Ho Chi Minh) within this continuum reasserted a sense of pride in times of bedeviling self-doubts. But the veneration of guardian spirits also afforded Ton Duc Thang's commemorators with the "safe" and prudent form, and Confucian idealism with a consistent language, to express their warnings about revolutionary decline in the present. In that sense, the site entails more of an act of "talking back" at the state than of lecturing down to the people. Through Ton Duc Thang's museum-shrine, the selfless, activist, and uncorrupted cadre who would ensure harmony between the Revolution and the people was idealized. The nostalgia and criticism in this message only become explicit because of the statement's incompatibility with present times—times that to the commemorators likely appeared "out of joint."[55]

Amid the loud signals of distress is a faint message of hope. To explain this, I should take a brief look at Ton Duc Thang's commemorators. At the same time, the aspect of regionalism will—once again—have to be considered. The museum-shrine in My Hoa Hung and the symposium on Ton Duc Thang's life that coincided with the site's inauguration in 1988 were organized jointly by provincial cadres in Long Xuyen and former Saigon/southern party leaders, who were equally instrumental in establishing the Ton Duc Thang Museum in Ho Chi Minh City: Tran Van Giau, Tran Van Tra, Tran Bach Dang, Luu Phuong Thanh, and others. All of them were critical of the present and tried to foreground the South's contributions to the successes of the Vietnamese Revolution and national reunion. Therefore, what characterized their outlooks was, on the one hand, their deep loyalty to the Revolution they had once helped come to power and, on the other hand, their intense feelings of having been overlooked in the process, pushed aside and marginalized both as idealistic cadres (by careerists) and as southerners (by northerners).

And thus, in the end, the enshrined revolutionary ethos of loyal service at My Hoa Hung can be seen as the commemorators' self-image, and they themselves, along with Ton Duc Thang, come to embody the Revolution's guardian spirits. Just like the tutelary deities, they "announce" their willingness to serve the ruler. Once again, I turn to Oliver Wolters, who has described the attraction between ruler and guardian spirit as "the automatic response of local tutelary spirits to a ruler's presence, *provided that the ruler had already shown signs of achievement and leadership,*" but has also emphasized that spirits can admonish a ruler to "seek and follow *virtus*" (*duc*).[56] Both dynamics, that is, response and admonition, are at work here and undertaken by people who are, on the one hand, loyal to the Revolution and, on the other hand— spurred by their memories of past glories—pained by its present state.

Their hopeful message is that the Revolution can be saved if it is able to refocus on its fundamental purpose, go back to its origins (symbolized by the temple at a prominent revolutionary's birthplace), "clean up its act," and rediscover, accept, and use all the talents available—including those in the South. In a remarkable parallelism to traditional notions of authority and legitimacy, this message further implies that the people, when recognizing such a rejuvenated and reinvigorated rule, would certainly abandon their errant ways and once again follow the revolution. The ease with which this nativist reorientation is undertaken can be explained by the congruence of the two models that provide a sense of historical certainty: success will surely belong to the heroic leadership, aided by ethical and unselfish officials, when it is properly aligned with either the inherent spiritual powers of its domain or the correct forces in the dialectical materialism of the historical process.

In their idealization of the earlier days of the Communist Party–led society, when, supposedly, a revolutionary ethos of service guided the officialdom, and the people and their leaders were in harmony, Ton Duc Thang's commemorators reveal their distress over, and protectiveness of, the Revolution in its present endangered state. *Idealization* and *protectiveness* are thus both at work in this act of "calling the spirits" (*goi hon*): enshrined and *re-called* in the little village of My Hoa Hung are, at once, heady memories of the Revolution's spirit and—awaiting so very anxiously to be *called* to its aid—the Revolution's tutelary spirit.

NOTES

My discussions with Peter Zinoman and his "Declassifying Nguyen Huy Thiep," *positions* 2, no. 2 (fall 1994): 294–317, have helped me to more clearly formulate the concerns expressed in this chapter. In its early phase, this study also profited in many ways from my interactions with Stephen O'Harrow, Keith W. Taylor, and Oliver W. Wolters. The final version owes much to the helpful criticism of Hue-Tam Ho Tai, Keith W. Taylor, Tamara J. Wang, Oliver W. Wolters, and Marilyn B. Young.

   1. For a comprehensive treatment of the post-Tiananmen "craze" of Mao Zedong, see Geremie R. Barmé, *Shades of Mao: The Posthumous Cult of the Great Leader* (Armonk, N.Y.: M. E. Sharpe, 1996). See also the very brief but promising treatment of a Mao Zedong temple in Gushui, Shaanxi, by Begonia Lee, "Houses of the Holy," *Far Eastern Economic Review*, June 6, 1996, 52. Shrines to Ho Chi Minh are mentioned briefly by Hue-Tam Ho Tai, "Monumental Ambiguity: The State Commemoration of Ho Chi Minh," in *Essays into Vietnamese Pasts,* ed. K. W. Taylor and John K. Whitmore, (Ithaca, N.Y.: Cornell University Southeast Asia Program, 1995), 273, 278. For Indonesia and its commemoration of *pahlawan,* see Klaus H. Schreiner, *Politischer Heldenkult in Indonesien: Tradition und Moderne Praxis* [*Political Hero Cult in Indonesia: Tradition and Modern Practice*] (Berlin: Reimer, 1995).

   2. See, e.g., Jo Blatti, ed., *Past Meets Present: Essays about Historic Interpretation and Public Audiences* (Washington, D.C.: Smithsonian, Institution Press, 1987); Eilean Hooper-Greenhill, *Museums and the Shaping of Knowledge* (London: Routledge, 1992); Ivan Karp, Christine Mullen Kreamer, and Steven D. Lavine, eds., *Museums and Communities: The Politics of Public Culture* (Washington, D.C.: Smithsonian Institution Press, 1992); Robert Lumley, ed., *The Museum Time-Machine: Putting Cultures on Display* (London: Routledge, 1988); Susan Pearce, ed., *Objects of Knowledge* (London: Athlone, 1990); Kevin Walsh, *The Representation of the Past: Museums and Heritage in the Postmodern World* (London: Routledge, 1992).

   3. I am, of course, not uninvolved in these matters. See my "Telling Life: An Approach to the Official Biography of Ton Duc Thang," in *Essays into Vietnamese Pasts,* 246–71.

   4. Information provided by Bui Cong Duc and Ngo Quang Lang, cadres of the An Giang Province Culture and Information Department and the provincial VCP Propaganda Board, Long Xuyen, May 4, 1992.

   5. Museum of the Revolution, Ho Chi Minh City: "Ecole des mécaniciens, Registre matricule, commencé le 1er Décembre 1907, terminé le . . . 1918, Thang Ton duc." The matriculation register was given to the museum in 1980.

   6. This point is argued in detail in chapters 1–3 of my dissertation "Ton Duc Thang and the Imagined Ancestries of Vietnamese Communism" (Ph.D. diss., Cornell University, 1996).

7. See ibid., chap. 5, and my forthcoming *Striking Images: Ba Son 1925 – A Case Study of the History and Historiography of Vietnamese Labor* (Ithaca, N.Y.: Cornell University Southeast Asia Program).

8. The French crackdown was triggered by a botched inner–Thanh Nien political murder in Saigon's Rue Barbier that exposed much of the clandestine organization to the French. Not surprisingly, the Rue Barbier case and Ton Duc Thang's significant role in it, remains a taboo subject in Vietnam. Since it is omitted from the commemoration of Ton Duc Thang, it will not concern me here. For details on the case, see my "Telling Life."

9. Huynh Kim Khanh, *Vietnamese Communism, 1925–1945* (Ithaca, N.Y.: Cornell University Press, 1982), 254f. n. 49, discusses the length of incarceration as a "qualification for advancement."

10. An Giang provincial branch of VCP, circular no. 06/TT-TU, Long Xuyen, March 13, 1987 (document no. 39, Ton Duc Thang Museum, Ho Chi Minh City).

11. See Lam Binh Tuong, "Trung Tu Di Tich voi Viec Phuc Hoi Noi That Ngoi Nha cua Chu tich Ton Duc Thang o My Hoa Hung (An Giang)" ["Reconstructing Historic Sites with Interior Renovations of President Ton Duc Thang's house in MHH (An Giang)"], and "Bao Ve Ngoi Nha Luu Niem Chu tich Ton Duc Thang o My Hoa Hung, Tinh Chat Phong Canh va Canh Quan" ["Protecting President Ton Duc Thang's home in My Hoa Hung, the Landscape Character and Beauty"], in Ban tuyen giao Tinh uy An Giang [An Giang Provincial Propaganda Commission], To Thanh Tam, ed., *Mot con Nguoi Binh Thuong – Vi Dai. Ky Yeu Hoi Thao Khoa Hoc ve Chu Tich Ton Duc Thang Nhan Dip Ky Niem 100 Nam Ngay Sinh 20-8-1888–20-8-1988* [*A Great Ordinary Person: Proceedings of the Symposium on President Ton Duc Thang Commemorating the Centennial of His Birth*] (An Giang: Provincial Propaganda Commission, 1989), 59–64. Articles on the constructions in An Giang (July 27, August 5, 12, 1988) (document no. 149, Ton Duc Thang Museum, Ho Chi Minh City). Pamphlet of An Giang Culture/Information Department about the commemoration site, 1988 (document no. 84, Ton Duc Thang Museum, Ho Chi Minh City). Dang Kim Quy, "Ngoi Nha Luu Niem Thoi Nien Thieu Chu tich Ton Duc Thang" ["President TDT's Childhood Home"], *Tap Chi Lich Su Dang* [*Journal of Party History*], no. 5 (1991): 36. Interview with Ton Duc Thang's nephew Ton Duc Hung, My Hoa Hung, May 4, 1992.

12. President Ton Duc Thang himself is buried at Mai Dich state cemetery outside Hanoi, where, in the absence of Ho Chi Minh's remains, his grave occupies the "No. 1" position in the hierarchical layout of the cemetery. His grave's appearance is standardized with those of other state and party leaders; since it is thus obviously not meant as a focal point for rituals, it will not concern me in this discussion.

13. Dang Kim Quy, "Ngoi Nha," 36. I am grateful to Hue-Tam Ho Tai for suggesting to me the former symbolism. Cf. Danny J. Whitfield, *Historical and Cultural Dictionary of Vietnam* (Metuchen, N.J.: Scarecrow Press, 1976), 255.

14. Whitfield, *Historical and Cultural Dictionary*, 275f. See also the helpful, if awkwardly presented, materials in Nguyen Tien Huu, *Dörfliche Kulte im*

traditionellen Vietnam [*Village Cults in Traditional Vietnam*] (Munich: Verlag UNI-Druck, 1970).

15. Stephen O'Harrow, "Men of Hu, Men of Han, Men of the Hundred Man: The Biography of Si Nhiep and the Conceptualization of Early Vietnamese Society," *Bulletin de l'Ecole Française d'Extrême-Orient* 75 (1986): 251.

16. See, with such an emphasis, Yamamoto Tatsuro, "Myths Explaining the Vicissitudes of Political Power in Ancient Vietnam," *Acta Asiatica: Bulletin of the Institute of Eastern Culture* 18 (1970): 70–94.

17. Keith W. Taylor, "Notes on the Viet Dien U Linh Tap," *Vietnam Forum*, no. 8 (1986): 26–59. See also an earlier brief discussion in his *The Birth of Vietnam* (Berkeley and Los Angeles: University of California Press, 1983), 352ff. Oliver W. Wolters, "Preface," in his *Two Essays On Dai-Viet in the Fourteenth Century* (New Haven, Conn.: Yale Southeast Asia Studies, 1988), vii–xi.

18. Taylor, "Notes on the Viet Dien U Linh Tap," 45.

19. Wolters, "Preface," xix, xxviii, xxxv.

20. First quotation: O. W. Wolters, "On Telling a Story of Vietnam in the Thirteenth and Fourteenth Centuries," *Journal of Southeast Asian Studies* 26 (March 1995): 67. Second quotation: Wolters, "Preface," xvi. The differences in perspective of Wolters's two generic sketches are, however, addressed in neither publication.

21. See David G. Marr, *Vietnamese Tradition on Trial, 1920–1945* (Berkeley and Los Angeles: University of California Press, 1981), 263.

22. Oliver W. Wolters, "Possibilities for a Reading of the 1293–1357 Period in the Vietnamese Annals," *Vietnam Forum*, no. 11 (1988): 97.

23. Keith W. Taylor, "Looking Behind the Vietnamese Annals: Ly Phat Ma (1028–54) and Ly Nhat Ton (1054–72) in the *Viet Su Luoc* and the *Toan Thu*," *Vietnam Forum*, no. 7 (1986): 51.

24. Wolters, "Possibilities," 116f.

25. To Thanh Tam, *Mot con Nguoi Binh Thuong—Vi Dai.*

26. Dang Kim Quy, "Ngoi Nha," 36.

27. This happened in 1954, after Stalin's death, but before Khrushchev's denunciation of the Stalin personality cult.

28. See my "Telling Life."

29. The archetypal image persisted despite the fact that, several years after Le Loi's death, Nguyen Trai and almost all his family met with a violent end in a court intrigue.

30. Tran Quoc Vuong, "Traditions, Acculturation, Renovation: The Evolutional Pattern of Vietnamese Culture," in *Southeast Asia in the 9th to 14th Centuries,* ed. David G. Marr and A. C. Milner (Singapore: Institute of Southeast Asian Studies, 1986), 271.

31. John K. Whitmore, "From Classical Scholarship to Confucian Belief in Vietnam," *Vietnam Forum*, no. 9 (1987): 58.

32. Oliver W. Wolters, "Assertions of Cultural Well-Being in Fourteenth-Century Vietnam," in his *Two Essays,* 42.

33. Esta S. Ungar, "Vietnamese Leadership and Order: Dai Viet under the Le Dynasty (1428–1459)" (Ph.D. diss., Cornell University, 1983), 19, 20. The following exposition is based on subsequent passages of the first chapter.

34. Fan Zhongyan; also transcribed Fan Chung-yen in the Wade-Giles system or, in Sino-Vietnamese transcription, Pham Trong Yem.

35. James T. C. Liu, "An Early Sung Reformer: Fan Chung-Yen," in *Chinese Thought and Institutions,* ed. John K. Fairbank, 3d ed. (Chicago: University of Chicago Press, 1964), 111.

36. Ungar, "Vietnamese Leadership and Order," 41.

37. Liu, "An Early Sung Reformer," 108, 131.

38. Ungar, "Vietnamese Leadership and Order," 10.

39. E.g., *Nguyen Trai,* 2d ed. (Hanoi: NXB Khoa Hoc Xa Hoi, 1969). For a very detailed list of Tran Huy Lieu's writings on Nyugen Trai, see Vien Khoa Hoc Xa Hoi Viet Nam, Vien Su Hoc [History Institute of the Social Science Institute of Vietnam], *Hoi ky Tran Huy Lieu* [Memoirs of Tran Huy Lieu], ed. Pham Nhu Thom (Hanoi: NXB Khoa Hoc Xa Hoi, 1991), 495–97. For a more general bibliography of DRV writings on Nguyen Trai between 1956 and 1968, see Patricia Pelley, "Writing Revolution: The New History in Post-colonial Vietnam" (Ph.D. diss., Cornell University, 1993), 207–12, especially notes 65, 75, 77, and 78; and Ungar, "Vietnamese Leadership and Order," 268 nn. 4 and 5.

40. Chapter 11, "Nguyen Trai voi Viec Danh My Cuu Nuoc cua Chung Ta Hien Nay."

41. Pelley, "Writing Revolution," 211f.

42. Tran Huy Lieu, *Nguyen Trai,* 56.

43. Ungar, "Vietnamese Leadership and Order," 34.

44. Marr, *Vietnamese Tradition,* 127–35.

45. Nguyen Khac Vien, *Tradition and Revolution in Vietnam,* ed. David Marr and Jayne Werner (Berkeley, Wash.: Indochina Resource Center, n.d. [1974?]). Here especially his essay "Confucianism and Marxism in Vietnam," 15–52.

46. Nguyen Khac Vien, *Tradition,* 46–51; the quotation is from 48. Neil L. Jamieson, *Understanding Vietnam* (Berkeley and Los Angeles: University of California Press, 1993), 217. See also Marr, *Vietnamese Tradition,* 135.

47. Alexander B. Woodside, *Community and Revolution in Modern Vietnam* (Boston: Houghton Mifflin, 1976), 237. Note the echo from Fan Zhongyan in the first sentence.

48. Marr, *Vietnamese Tradition,* 134; Ho Chi Minh is quoted by Nguyen Khac Vien, *Tradition,* 49f.

49. Whitfield, *Historical and Cultural Dictionary,* 48.

50. I am grateful to Hue-Tam Ho Tai for suggesting this aspect of timing to me.

51. Alexander B. Woodside, "Conceptions of Change and of Human Responsibility for Change in Late Traditional Vietnam," *Vietnam Forum,* no. 6 (1985): 108, emphasis added.

52. See, among others who have observed that phenomenon, Hy Van Luong, "Economic Reform and the Intensification of Rituals in Two Northern Vietnamese Villages, 1980–1990," in *The Challenge of Reform in Indo-China,* ed. Borje Ljunggren and Peter Timmer (Cambridge, Mass.: Harvard University Press, 1993), 259–91. In this essay, however, I am less concerned with the effects of

economic reforms under the policy of Renovation (Doi Moi), begun in 1986, and more interested in the context of the decline of outside models of authority.

53. Hue-Tam Ho Tai, "Monumental Ambiguity," in *Essays into Vietnamese Pasts,* 280.

54. To draw a parallel to premodern times, equal confidence exudes from the Vietnamese tales of heroic guardian spirits and the underlying concept of the spiritual properties of the land, as Oliver Wolters has pointed out with reference to the *Spiritual Powers of the Viet Realm* (Wolters, "On Telling a Story," 67). Challenges to the ruling powers and threats to the country's security—recurrent themes in the Vietnamese experience—had been warded off, as one could very well see in retrospect, whenever ruler and tutelary deity had established a "winning" rapport in the proper manner described by the tales.

55. Wolters, "Possibilities," 129.

56. Oliver W. Wolters, *History, Culture, and Region in Southeast Asian Perspectives* (Singapore: Institute of Southeast Asian Studies, 1982), 102, emphasis added; and Wolters, "Preface," xix.

PART TWO

REPACKAGING THE PAST

FOUR

Framing the National Spirit

Viewing and Reviewing Painting
under the Revolution

Nora A. Taylor

Paintings, like monuments and memorials, serve as sites of commemoration in the form of portrayals of historic events or illustrious war
heroes. In Vietnam, the National Museum of Fine Arts abounds with
paintings depicting legendary battles against Chinese invaders and portraits of soldiers preparing to fight the enemy. Until recently, these paintings, and the artists who painted them, were given more prominence in
exhibition spaces, galleries, and museums than paintings whose subject
matter bore no visible relation to the revolutionary cause. These paintings and their artists were the Vietnamese art world's counterpart to war
memorials and revolutionary heroes described in Shaun Malarney's
chapter in this volume.

This chapter will not dwell on the obvious relationship between these
paintings and commemorative monuments. Rather, it will focus on the
shift that has occurred in art historical memory since the launching of
the Doi Moi reforms in the late 1980s from the art-going public's emphasis on revolutionary period paintings and artists who served the nation in war to artists who did not participate in state politics. In illus-
trating how the politics of memory have penetrated the art world and
how the recent trend toward the marketing of art has informed the way
people think about art in Vietnam, this chapter will join issues raised in
Christoph Giebel's analysis of Ton Duc Thang's commemorative shrine
and Laurel Kennedy and Mary Rose Williams's discussions of the revised
view of Vietnam's past to suit the needs of international tourism.

As in other socialist countries, the government of Vietnam spent much of the second half of the twentieth century promoting artworks that reflected communist ideology. Founded in 1957, the Vietnamese Artists' Association (Hoi Nghe Si Tao Hinh) was aimed at creating a national artistic workforce that would produce art to serve the propaganda needs of the government. Although hardly as large in number of artists or in the creative output as in China and the Soviet Union, the Vietnamese art community grew substantially during the years of hardline Marxist-Leninist policies, between 1954 and 1986. As in the Soviet Union and China, the artists who complied with the criteria set out by the government-sponsored artists' unions were favored in the eyes of the state. In addition to the preferential treatment they received, their works were also made more visible to the public in the form of posters, stamps, calendars, and newspaper illustrations. Likewise, those artists who chose to stay out of the unions or were rejected by the authorities received little attention. And similarly, more recently, as in Russia and China, the Vietnamese artists who have been receiving the greatest amount of attention since the government loosened its control on artistic production and allowed artists to sell their works in the open market are those who never participated in state propaganda campaigns.

Although comparisons with China and Soviet Russia are tempting, it is not the point of this chapter to discuss changes that occur when socialist institutions collapse in favor of the international art market. In Vietnam, the transition from a socialist to a market economy is neither as clear nor as straightforward as in Russia or China. Unlike in Russia, for instance, the socialist institutions set up in the 1950s are still in place; the shift in attitudes toward art and the selection of artists displayed in public exhibitions is not due simply to the transfer from official to nonofficial artists. Unlike in China, the artists now favored in art galleries are not necessarily reacting against their socialist realist predecessors. While China's new artistic stars are denouncing Mao through their paintings, no artist in Vietnam has so far cared to challenge Ho Chi Minh's supremacy in the public eye. In focusing solely on Vietnamese art, this chapter will suggest that this particular situation—although related to what is happening in Russia and China—has more to do with what is going on inside the Vietnamese politics of art historiography and memory than with a transition from socialism to democracy.

The case of a group of painters who have been selected by the new generation of art critics, collectors, and art aficionados as the forerunners of contemporary Vietnamese painting illustrates how memory in the art field is as socially constructed as it is elsewhere in Vietnamese national consciousness. The art-going public, which includes collectors and noncollectors of art, artists, and nonartists, views this select group of painters as enablers of how they "feel" about their country. Their view is in opposition to the one offered by the state, which advocates socialist realism as the "correct" way to represent the nation's feelings. Socialist realism, a movement that originated in Stalinist Russia, was intended to embody the values of Marxist-Leninist-style socialism. It advocated art for the masses and pushed for artists to portray "positive" views of workers and peasants to convey the ideals of the proletarian class. In Vietnam, socialist realism was equated with patriotism, and works that depicted soldiers, farmers, and laborers were considered de facto "patriotic." This equation of art with nationalism is not just formulated by the state. Many Vietnamese have described paintings as beautiful because they display what they consider to be accurate signs of what is "Vietnamese." This would indicate that art has long been considered an appropriate vehicle for nationalism. But the public view of what is "Vietnamese" is different from the state view. The public has in a sense chosen to "forget" the state view and "remember" instead those artists who display none of the state criteria for nationalistic art.

THE CREATION OF A "NATIONAL REVOLUTIONARY PAINTING" TRADITION

Western-style painting, or oil painting on canvas as it is known in the West, first appeared in Vietnam at the turn of the twentieth century, during the French colonial period, when artists came to Indochina from the *métropole* with their easels and palettes to paint the "exotic" Asian landscape. Victor Tardieu (1867–1937), an artist who had won a competition for painting a mural at the Université Indochinoise in Hanoi, decided to establish an art academy in the colony to train local artists and artisans to become professional painters. In 1925, the Ecole des Beaux Arts d'Indochine (EBAI) was founded, and some twenty students enrolled. Most of the students were from local upper-class educated Hanoi families. A couple of students came from Cambodia and Laos, along with a few colonial residents. Classes in composition, anatomy, perspective, painting, and drawing were held in conjunction with a few classes in "indigenous" arts, painting on lacquer and silk.

The EBAI remained open until the 1945 Japanese coup against the French colonial government forced it to close down. Over the course of its twenty years of operation, it graduated 160 students, many of whom continued to paint throughout their lifetime; some became Vietnam's best-known artists. When the school closed in 1945, one of its first graduates and subsequent professors, To Ngoc Van (1906–54, student at the EBAI from 1926 to 1931), decided to reopen it in the hills of Viet Bac, north of Hanoi, at the seat of the revolutionary army. There the school changed its purpose and scope. Young artists were recruited to turn art into a propaganda tool for the revolutionary army. The school became known as the Resistance Class (Khoa Khang Chien). Besides drawing and composition, students studied philosophy, politics, and the fundamentals of Marxism-Leninism. They held daily meetings to discuss art's role in society. Workshops were created for designing posters, stamps, currency, and other visual emblems for the new government.

The painters who followed To Ngoc Van to Viet Bac fell into two groups. In one were those who had already graduated from the EBAI prior to its closing and enlisted in the army out of patriotic duty serving as illustrators and/or revolutionary fighters. The second group consisted of painters who had not yet begun to study painting and, having joined the revolution, decided to study art simultaneously. The students who studied art in Viet Bac for the first time were given a diploma with the emblem of the Khoa Khang Chien.

The new school remained in operation for nine years. In 1954, after the victory over the French at Dien Bien Phu and the establishment of the Democratic Republic of Vietnam, it reopened in Hanoi. From 1954 to 1986, the thirty-some artists who graduated from this class were seen as having contributed some of the most important works of art in the history of Vietnamese modern painting. They were accorded recognition on a par with the soldiers who fought in battle, given certificates of praise, and, in the case of To Ngoc Van himself, awarded the title of "revolutionary hero" (*anh hung*). To Ngoc Van died of injuries he suffered at the battle of Dien Bien Phu and was subsequently honored as a "revolutionary martyr" who sacrificed his life (*hi sinh*) for the revolutionary cause. Concurrently, his contemporaries named him Vietnam's greatest artist. However, the current generation of artists and art critics claim he was given the title not so much for his artistic talent but, rather, for having died fighting for his country.

For nearly four decades, the Resistance Class painters produced paintings of soldiers, combat heroes, women warriors, and the good deeds of the army along with more conventionally patriotic landscapes and rural scenes. These works, intended to be accessible to the masses, were visible everywhere, not only in state art exhibitions, art publications, and journals but also on stamps, posters, and calendars. From 1954 until 1990, these painters were the most well known artists, and virtually all textbooks and art histories of Vietnamese painting until 1990 have focused on them.[1] Such a monopoly on the orientation of painting was connected to the role that artists were given in society and the administrative structure that controlled their livelihood. The Arts Association was founded in 1957 as a subbranch of the Ministry of Culture and ruled by an executive committee elected by members of the association. Any artist could join if he or she fulfilled the requirements of submitting works to a jury and paying a small membership fee. Joining the Arts Association had many advantages. In a society lacking an art market, it provided the desired exposure to other artists' works, possibilities for exhibiting in the national museums—the only outlet for selling a work of art during that time—and abroad. The association seemed to be egalitarian in principle, offering possibilities for all artists to exhibit their work when, in fact, the selection of works was based on predetermined criteria. These criteria became the cause of disputes by the current generation of artists at the 1994 Arts Association congress.

The changes advocated by the current generation of artists in Vietnam are more easily understood if we examine the origins of the criteria created by the National Arts Association for selecting works of art worthy of the label "heroic," "revolutionary," or "national." The selection the artists who were to receive the greatest exposure in the public eye was based primarily on political affiliation or personal participation in the nation's struggles against foreign imperialism. But several thematic and stylistic criteria were also established to determine the acceptability of the works of art to be displayed in public exhibitions. One of these revolved around the question of "national character" (*tinh dan toc*). The term was first used by Ho Chi Minh around the time of the August Revolution in 1945 to define the goals of the cultural policies established by the Democratic Republic of Vietnam. Ho Chi Minh had wanted art and literature to express the spirit of the Vietnamese people. He used the expression *dan toc,* meaning "nationality," "nation," or "national," to describe the people of Vietnam, and the phrases *tinh dan toc* and *van hoa dan toc* to describe the "national character" and the "national culture" of the Vietnamese people.[2] The term was again used in the context of literature to define that which best expressed the qualities that the prevalent political discourse desired to associate with the nation or "Vietnameseness." In the visual arts, it was coined by the Communist

Party in a pamphlet submitted to the second Arts Association congress in 1962, which stated that art must reflect the essence of both the past and present struggles of the people against imperialism and feudalism.[3]

Artists did not always grasp the concept of "national character." Nor did cultural politicians define it in clear terms. Consequently, many artists chose to ignore this issue, leaving it to the viewer or the judges at the national art exhibitions to decide whether their work contained national character. Still, they were obligated to include aspects of what they perceived to be an acceptable theme or style in their work in order to receive recognition from the Arts Association.

In 1962, at the second congress of the Arts Association, an attempt was made to define the components of national character to provide specific guidelines for artists to follow in the making of their artworks. No concise definition was drawn, but the general parameters of the issue were made clear. According to one definition, "national character is the way of life and expression of a community of people who live together over long periods of time."[4] Elsewhere, it was described as the "most natural element that constitutes humankind. So natural, in fact, that it defies all definition."[5] The general understanding of national character was that it exemplified the spirit of the Vietnamese people in their struggle for independence, their daily work, and their ancient historical culture. Daily life, history, and "traditional" culture were the themes that were considered "beautiful" and "true" by the Arts Association and therefore deemed to be most representative of Vietnamese character.[6] The Communist Party's definition of daily life, history, and tradition did not always coincide with artists' understanding of those terms. Often, artists who thought they had displayed national character in their work were surprised to find out that their painting was not accepted by the Arts Association. Le Thi Kim Bach (born in 1938; student at the Hanoi College of Art from 1957 to 1960 and at the Soviet National University of Fine Arts in Kiev from 1961 to 1967) had one of her paintings rejected from a national art exhibition because, she said, the subject of her work, an old peasant woman, seemed overly sad.[7]

Paintings that represented farmers toiling in the fields, soldiers going to the front, or factory workers handling machinery were considered to contain national character, as were paintings that depicted historical figures, war heroes, and legendary independence fighters. But, if there was any suggestion of misery or violence in association with these images, the painting would be dismissed as unpatriotic. In his essay on Marxism and Vietnamese culture, Truong Chinh, secretary-general of the Communist Party from 1941 until 1956, outlined the task of the artist: "to draw from reality what is typical, what people can see at first glance, gather facts, ideas and contradictions into a lively picture, and indicate the right direction leading to the correct future."[8] Portraits were mostly considered trivial exercises in physiognomy and therefore irrelevant to the question of national character, as were still lifes and interiors; therefore, they were not encouraged unless they were representations of important heads of state such as President Ho Chi Minh. Still, none of these topics were strictly forbidden unless they were thought in some way to demean or degrade an aspect of national culture. Nudes and abstraction were the only subjects that were unconditionally banned from public display. Both were seen in official political discourse as "decadent Western bourgeois capitalist" notions to be avoided at all costs.[9] To Truong Chinh, counterrevolutionary art forms such as cubism, impressionism, surrealism, and dadaism were "gaudy mushrooms sprouted from the rotten wood of imperialist culture."[10]

In the early 1960s, the regulations governing Arts Association artists were particularly strict and rigidly enforced. Several incidents involving artists and writers in the late 1950s had caused the Communist Party to pay close attention to the production of paintings and sculpture to ensure that artists were not going against the rules set by the Arts Association for the public display of artworks. The incidents in question involved a group of writers and artists who, at the first meetings of the Writers Association in 1956, had demanded greater freedom of expression and creative rights. These writers and artists were in fact asking to be allowed to produce "art for art's sake," a notion that went against Ho Chi Minh's requirement for artists to follow the Maoist notion of "art for the service of the people."[11] After publishing four issues of two art and literature journals entitled *Humanism* (*Nhan Van*) and *Masterpieces* (*Giai Pham*), several of the contributors were severely punished and sent to prison for "betraying the interests of the Communist Party, the Nation and the people of Vietnam." The painters Nguyen Sy Ngoc (1919–90; student of the EBAI from 1939 to 1944) and Nguyen Sang (1923–88; student of the EBAI from 1940 to 1945) were directly affected by their involvement in this affair. Nguyen Sy Ngoc was sent to a labor camp for two years, and Nguyen Sang was barred from employment with the Arts Association.[12]

The other artists and writers involved were also banned from their previous positions and only gradually reintegrated into the artistic mainstream. The artists and writers involved in the criticism of the

Communist Party's policy toward art and the publication of the *Hu-manism* and *Masterpieces* journals were Communist Party members. Nguyen Sy Ngoc and Nguyen Sang had participated in the resistance movement against the French and had joined the Viet Minh in the mid-1940s. Their criticism of the party came at a time when they thought it was not only safe but also necessary to make changes in the party's cultural policy. Their comrades in China and the Soviet Union had recently admitted to errors in their handling of cultural matters. In China, the Communist Party had introduced a program of liberalization in art and literature known as "Let a Hundred Flowers Bloom" after Zhou Enlai's proclamation to artists: "Let a hundred flowers bloom, let a hundred schools of thought contend."[13] Whereas in China, writers and artists were allowed and even encouraged to speak out against shortcomings in their party's policy, in Vietnam, after months of debate, the party decided to repress any movement toward greater creative freedom. This conservative policy toward the arts greatly affected the morale of artists during the 1960s and 1970s. Many of them felt paralyzed and unable to create. Nguyen Sy Ngoc, for example, was unable to produce more than one painting a year for the remainder of his life and spent most of his time drinking. According to his daughter, "After his years in a labor camp, he was not the same. He ended up spending his days drinking. He basically drank himself to death."[14]

In order to understand the role of "marginality" or "dissent" in the 1960s and 1970s, it is helpful to examine in further detail the differences between works of art that were considered "acceptable" and those that were not. One example of "acceptable" illustrations of "national character" is a painting by Mai Van Hien (born in 1923, student at the EBAI from 1943 to 1945) entitled *Meeting* (*Gap Nhau*, 1954; fig. 4.1). The painting was praised when it was exhibited at the first National Art Exhibition in 1955 because the subject of a soldier meeting a peasant woman illustrates the idea of community and solidarity between the army and the common people. In the painting, a soldier converses with a woman on the Dien Bien Phu Trail who has visibly helped to carry provisions for the soldiers. On her yoke are two camouflaged baskets that she apparently has been carrying for some time, as her bare feet and rolled-up trousers indicate. The mood of the painting is reflected in the artist's simple descriptive style, which lends itself well to its content. The soldier and the woman appear friendly toward each other: the soldier is relaxed, his rifle is casually thrown over his shoulder, far from posing any threat to the woman, and the woman is smiling and con-

Figure 4.1.   Mai Van Hien, *Meeting (Gap Nhau)*, gouache on paper, 1954.
Photograph by Nora A. Taylor, courtesy of the artist.

cealing any physical effort she has endured in transporting goods for the
soldiers. The soldier seems courteous and perhaps even a bit flirtatious.
The scene is fairly straightforward, with no ambiguities either in the
figures' feelings or in the subject matter represented.

In devising the scene of a meeting between a soldier and a peasant
woman, Mai Van Hien was in effect describing the policy of integration
of ethnic minorities and people from the countryside into the Vietnamese
"nation" after independence from French colonialism. The feeling of
camaraderie and equality between soldiers and peasants and between
men and women as suggested in his painting also coincided with the
goals of socialism outlined by the Communist Party to assimilate people
from all classes and create a homogeneous society. *Meeting* was considered to contain "national character" because it illustrated one of the
ideals of socialization and nation-building, which was to create a harmonious community. It also followed what Truong Chinh considered
was "correctly expressing the feelings of the masses that are pure, sincere
and exceedingly warm."[15]

In contrast to Mai Van Hien's painting is a work that was initially
rejected by the Arts Association: *The Enemy Burned My Village (Giac
Dot Lang Toi,* 1954; fig. 4.2) by Nguyen Sang. In this painting, a

Figure 4.2. Nguyen Sang, *The Enemy Burned My Village (Giac Dot Lang Toi)*, oil on canvas, 1954. Photograph by Nora A. Taylor, courtesy of National Museum of Fine Arts, Hanoi.

minority woman, having visibly fled her village with her child at her back and her mother and daughter behind her, solicits the help of a soldier stationed on the roadside. Unlike the friendly atmosphere of Mai Van Hien's painting, the prevailing mood of this scene is one of fear and unease. The soldier's rifle is still slung under his arm in a combat position as if preparing for attack. He looks sternly on the woman coming to seek help. There is no sense of camaraderie or solidarity between the two figures; rather, the painting seems to capture two strangers in a moment of fear.

In another work, *Joining the Communist Party at Dien Bien Phu (Ket Nap Dang trong Tran Dien Bien Phu,* 1963; fig. 4.3), the same artist sets up a conflict between patriotic theme and means of execution. He has used a particularly severe way of representing his figures, drawing them with angular lines, enlarged limbs, and blank features. The composition is centered on the hand of the party officer who reaches out to the soldier seeking admission. Although the gesture seems welcoming, the look on the soldier's face is cold and dispassionate. The wounded soldier appears anxious and lacking in enthusiasm. His expression may betray his doubt or apprehension at joining the party. The soldier behind

Figure 4.3.   Nguyen Sang, *Joining the Communist Party at Dien Bien Phu* (*Ket Nap Dang trong Tran Dien Bien Phu*), lacquer on wood, 1963. Photograph by Nora A. Taylor, courtesy of National Museum of Fine Arts, Hanoi.

him also acts in a less than friendly manner as he prods him past the doorway.

While these two paintings by Nguyen Sang were never criticized directly, they were rejected from national art competitions. Criticism or rejection from national art competitions often meant that the work had been placed before an audience of workers and soldiers who, in the absence of any other formal criterion, were simply asked to decide how closely the subjects of the paintings resembled their habitat, moods, or customs. Sometimes, in lieu of a direct criticism, a humiliation campaign was initiated. Letters from workers and soldiers who found the work in question to be "untruthful" or "inaccurate" were published in newspapers. These letters were aimed at discrediting the author of the work in question, for if the masses did not understand it, then it was considered too "obscure" and therefore unacceptable.[16] Nguyen Sang had painted both of these paintings hoping for a subsidy from the Arts Association, and although the National Museum of Fine Arts eventually purchased the two works, they were not displayed until shortly before his death in 1984. When Nguyen Sang contributed drawings and poems to the *Humanism* and *Masterpieces* journals, his name was put on a black list of artists who were not permitted to exhibit in public. Subsequently, the Arts Association and the Communist Party scrutinized all his works. He was told that they did not contain "national character" because they were too harsh, his figures too severe, his style too "Western."[17]

The rejection and subsequent acceptance of Nguyen Sang's views of history illustrate not only the fluctuations in the definition of "national character" but also the changing attitudes toward war and revolution in recent times. Nguyen Sang's vision is no longer threatening to authorities as they have gradually come to terms with the harsher realities of those years. Whereas in the past, as Mai Van Hien's painting illustrates, virtues of heroism and solidarity were considered the only legitimate representations of the struggle for independence, feelings of pain and apprehension have recently become equally acceptable.

REDEFINING "NATIONAL CHARACTER"
IN THE 1990s

In spite of reforms that had begun to be instituted in other sectors of society at the onset of Doi Moi, the Arts Association was slow in recognizing the need for liberalization in the arts. Nudes and abstraction were forbidden from public view until 1990. And it was not until the 1994 congress that a serious attempt was made to recognize those artists who had been marginalized for not participating in the revolutionary movements of the 1950s through 1970s. At the congress of the Arts Association in December 1994, the fourth since the organization's founding, young art critics advocated replacing the revolutionary guard of painters with the "nonrevolutionary" group of artists who either had been marginalized or had marginalized themselves from art circles for over thirty years. Objections arose over the dismissal of the older generation of painters. For example, the painter To Ngoc Thanh (b. 1940), whose father, To Ngoc Van, mentioned earlier, was considered the greatest of all revolutionary artists, exclaimed: "How can you forget these heroic painters when they sacrificed their lives for their country?" A young critic responded: "But they were such mediocre painters."[18] The debate continued, with one side arguing for revolutionary contributions and the other promoting talent and innovation. Until the congress, one rarely heard such outspoken commentary on artists' positions vis-à-vis the Arts Association. Although none of it was truly scathing— critics called the revolutionary period artists at times "boring," "old-fashioned," "untalented," and "backward"—it was unprecedented to express negative feelings toward such illustrious artists in public.

At the 1994 congress, four artists in particular (Bui Xuan Phai, 1921–88, a student at the EBAI from 1941 to 1945; Nguyen Sang, 1923–88, a student at the EBAI from 1940 to 1945; Duong Bich Lien, 1924–88, a student at the EBAI from 1944 to 1945; and Nguyen Tu Nghiem, born in 1922, a student at the EBAI from 1941 to 1945) were hailed by young art critics and artists active since the mid-1980s as the "masters of Vietnamese modern painting." Clandestine exhibitions and independent publications had been put out in their honor, but it took some time before the Arts Association recognized their contribution to modern Vietnamese art history. Today, works by these artists cover the walls of private galleries that have multiplied in recent years in Hanoi and Ho Chi Minh City and are highly sought after by a new generation of Vietnamese art collectors.

One question that arises from the debate at the congress is why these four particular artists were selected by critics as better representatives of contemporary Vietnamese painting rather than their more conventional colleagues. Where and when did the shift take place? And what kind of criteria was the new generation using to determine what constituted a "great" artist? A closer examination of the four artists' lives and works will reveal that the art-viewing public of the late 1980s identified first and foremost with their personae, their antiestablishment ideas, and their bohemian lifestyles. Second, their works provided them with an interpretation of their own cultural identity that had previously been neglected but that rang truer to their experience than the revolutionary vision supplied by the earlier artists. In sum, what made the four painters the new "modern masters" was not only that time had changed people's perceptions of history and nationalism but also that these artists offered the public a different picture of Vietnamese reality.

Of the four painters, Bui Xuan Phai was best known for his poverty. He has been described as having a "face that reflects the grief of a lifetime"[19] (fig. 4.4). People who remember him recall his gaunt features and how he had to exchange paintings for food.[20] Yet he was also admired for his intellect. Those who knew him recall vividly the hours of stimulating conversation spent in his company. He was well versed in world art history, something of a rarity in a society that had been cut off from the international community since the end of colonialism in 1945. He had studied the works of French painters, often citing Albert Marquet and Georges Rouault among his favorites. He had friends

Figure 4.4.   Portrait of Bui Xuan Phai. Photograph courtesy of Plum Blossoms Gallery, Hong Kong.

among the writers and poets who made up the underground intellectual elite of the 1960s and 1970s and were habitual customers of Nguyen Van Lam's coffeehouse (Café Lam) on 69 Nguyen Huu Hoan street in Hanoi's old quarter. Nguyen Van Lam was a book restorer who collected books but also was fond of painting. Although coffeehouses were banned from the capital from 1959 to 1969, as were all small, private nonproductive enterprises, Lam continued to receive his friends and serve them clandestinely.[21] Most of the writers and artists who frequented Café Lam had little spending money, having to live off food rations distributed by the state, which did not include such luxury goods as coffee. They paid for their accumulated debts with paintings or poems. The often unemployed Bui Xuan Phai was Lam's most loyal customer and subsequently turned Lam into one of the greatest collectors of Bui Xuan Phai's paintings in Hanoi.[22]

Café Lam had the makings of a Paris *café littéraire* of the sort frequented by Pablo Picasso, Henry Miller, and the surrealists in the 1920s. In Europe, this kind of establishment was attractive to people who saw themselves as marginal to the social mainstream. But, while bohemian culture may have a certain romantic appeal in the West, to the officials of a nation that had fought bitterly to rid itself of French occupation

Figure 4.5.   Bui Xuan Phai, *Old Hanoi Street* (*Pho co Ha Noi*), oil on cardboard, 1967. Photograph courtesy of Plum Blossoms Gallery, Hong Kong.

and dismissed all French culture as "bourgeois," an artists' café could seem like a subversive activity. Furthermore, to a government that was trying to promote a working-class ideology, a café where intellectuals met and discussed art and literature at their leisure verged on the counterrevolutionary.

Bui Xuan Phai's "sadness, reflecting a life of misery,"[23] and his passion for painting produced his signature subject matter: scenes of old Hanoi streets (fig. 4.5). While his colleagues, members of the Arts Association, were painting workers, soldiers, and peasants for state art exhibits, Bui Xuan Phai painted the desolate streets of his city, in shades of gray and brown, over and over again, almost obsessively. Although his paintings clearly indicated an attachment to his homeland, it was not the sort of vision that the authorities accepted. His streets were void of life, as if he were mourning the loss of the activities that had filled them in a bygone era.

To art viewers, those who knew him and the many visitors to both his house—for he was a hospitable and generous man—and Café Lam, his street paintings became synonymous with Hanoi during the economic hardships of the 1960s and 1970s. They captured the bleak, desolate, gray atmosphere of the city during that time. When Hanoians

recall the urban atmosphere during those years, their picture often re-
sembles a painting by Bui Xuan Phai. "There was no food sold on the
sidewalk, no transportation, no colorful fabrics hanging outside people's
windows, nothing," is a common way of describing the capital during
those years.[24] Like Hanoi at the time, Bui Xuan Phai's paintings are
empty of colorful markets, street stall vendors, and motorcycles. The
only signs of modernity are his ubiquitous electrical poles that stand at
each street corner as if to mock the government's campaign to develop
industry in the city. In one painting, the only sign above a doorway
reads *nuoc soi,* or "boiled water," as if the artist were reacting against
the heroism of wartime depicted in official art and making a statement
about the deprivation of the population instead.

Bui Xuan Phai's paintings were rarely included in national art exhibitions and were seldom exhibited abroad in traveling exhibitions organized by the Arts Association. In the art history books and brochures
about Vietnamese contemporary painting published before 1986, his
name is never mentioned as an important figure in the Hanoi art scene.
Although he was not accused of undermining Communist Party policy
like Nguyen Sy Ngoc and Nguyen Sang, his family has described how
closely the government watched him and the restrictions that were
placed on him as an artist.[25] The original objection to Bui Xuan Phai by
officials was most likely a response to his eye for the negative realities
of Hanoi life. His view of daily life was contrary to the utopian socialist
vision of community living promoted by the state. His subsequent popularity may have been due to the fact that he dared to show what the
government refused to see, and his popularity among painters today
stems from the fact that he was determined to pursue his own path in
spite of government regulations. Young artists today, trying to break
free from past conventions, are in awe of the fact that Bui Xuan Phai
refused to compromise his artistic ideals for political ones. They, and
the art-viewing public at large, see him and his paintings as encapsulat-
ing the spirit of the nation after the war. Today the war is no longer
remembered for its glory but rather as a negative experience, which is
why Bui Xuan Phai's paintings resonate more strongly with the public.

Bui Xuan Phai's persona is well captured in a 1964 portrait by his
friend Nguyen Sang. In the painting, he is sitting at a table with the café
owner Nguyen Van Lam, facing the viewer and with his chin resting on
the palm of his hand. Mr. Lam, also facing the viewer, sits beside him
with his hands clasped over his knees. Behind them is a sign indicating
the price of a cup of black coffee: thirty cents (*dong*). Both the artist and

the café owner seem calm and nonchalant in this scene, perhaps even slightly bored, and a kind of ennui or emptiness prevails. One is reminded of the portraits of absinthe drinkers in Paris cafés by such French postimpressionist painters as Henri de Toulouse-Lautrec, Edouard Manet, and Pablo Picasso, in which figures often appear afflicted with chronic melancholy or depression.

Art historians in the West have often attributed the affinity of painters at the turn of the century for life in the cafés and the decadence of society at the time to increased interest in "modern life." Modern life in Europe referred to urban development, the increase of traffic in the streets, and consequently the surge in the pace of life. According to Marshall Berman, the swelling speed of daily life generated excitement for everything urban, along with an attraction for the dirt and smoke that it provoked.[26] Artists and writers in Paris became fascinated with the decadence of society in art. The art historian T. J. Clark writes that "modernism can be described as a kind of skepticism, or at least uncertainty, as to the nature of representation in art."[27]

Nguyen Sang's characters seem at home amid the deterioration of Hanoi streets and the degeneration of Vietnamese society as he perceived it. The Communist Party had demanded participation in the revolutionary struggle, but writers and artists such as Bui Xuan Phai and Nguyen Sang were idling away their time in cafés. They were not employed by the state as other artists were, partly out of choice for not wanting to participate in the propaganda campaigns and partly by force for having contradicted the official cultural institutions. Instead of supporting the optimism for the future of the nation as declared in the government-sponsored art campaigns, they represented the cynicism of the people who did not wish to follow the Party. None was more representative of this cynicism than Duong Bich Lien who shunned any exposure to the public and any affiliation with the Arts Association. Although he had taken part in the Revolution, after the restrictions imposed on artists in the 1950s, he deliberately withdrew from the political mainstream. His paintings became legendary for their grace and beauty (fig. 4.6), but he refused to show them to anyone but his friends.[28] Unable to afford new canvas, he often painted over his paintings. His peers admired him for his talent, but he was described as "aloof" and "stubborn" when it came to exposing his work to the public. Today the younger generation considers him one of the "masters of modern art," along with Bui Xuan Phai, Nguyen Sang, and Nguyen Tu Nghiem.

In 1993, the *Portrait of Bui Xuan Phai with Mr. Lam* was sold to a

Figure 4.6.   Duong Bich Lien, *Woman with Flower* (*Tien nu ben Hoa*), oil on canvas, 1980. Photograph by Nora A. Taylor, courtesy of Nguyen Hao Hai.

private collector in France for the highest price ever paid for a modern work of Vietnamese art.[29] Until it was sold, the painting had remained in Mr. Lam's café, never having been displayed in state exhibition halls or the National Museum. Like Bui Xuan Phai's streets and Duong Bich Lien's romantic realist scenes, this and other of Nguyen Sang's portraits, with their singular talent for capturing emotions, have been a source of inspiration for the younger generation of painters who came to Mr. Lam's café yearning for a break from the constraints of socialist Realism.

Ironically, for the post-1986 generation of painters, Bui Xuan Phai and his friends became icons of the rejection of "nationalist"-oriented art. In choosing them as their artistic "heroes," the younger artists and critics were in effect rejecting the concept of national character advocated by the Arts Association. They had realized the limitation of the concept, but at the same time their designation of the three outside unofficial painters as the legitimate rulers of the art world was based on criteria that were not too different from the previous generation's, that is, the need for art to depict the "national soul." This fact only reinforces the plasticity of these conventions. The policy toward the arts after 1945 was one of appropriation or elimination rather than construction. Political discourse was geared toward outlining what was forbidden rather than enabling artists to understand the challenge of creativity. Artists were told what their paintings lacked more often than they were offered suggestions for inclusion of philosophical or spiritual ideas. Negative elements were more easily spotted than positive ones. Confusion surrounding the definition of national character made it easy for artists to make mistakes and for negative feelings to settle in. Furthermore, the imprecise definition of national character accounted for the distorted reaction to it and the fact that it has not been discarded altogether. Unlike in China, there has yet to be an organized collective counterrevolutionary movement in the arts in Vietnam.[30] Many of the movements in reaction to official art in Vietnam took a passive rather than active form.

TRADITION AND MODERNISM

Art historical revisions after 1986 have not been limited to the fluctuations of reputation among artists but are also reflected in the choice of topics. Village and folk art, which had been the main source of artistic production before the colonial era, had been transformed after independence in 1945 to serve the ideals of socialism. Many artisans were forced to join collective labor forces and abandon their family trade. They were brought into the agricultural and industrial sectors, and household workshops that had operated for centuries were turned into cooperatives. As a result, village art virtually died, only to be resurrected at the initiative of descendants of village craftsmen in the late 1980s.[31]

In the early 1990s, two art historians, intent on reviving the "village" aspect of Vietnamese art history, began researching the history of village art from the ninth century, at the end of the Chinese occupation, to the present. They published *My Thuat o Lang* (*Art in the Village*), which became one of the most influential art history books of the early 1990s.[32] The book argued that the origins of Vietnamese art were, in fact, in the village as opposed to the view promoted during colonial times, which held that art originated in royal palaces or was stimulated by religious objects traded from abroad. The idea appealed to the younger generation of artists because it proved that art had a "national" origin yet was not a "state"-oriented production. In other words, village art was given a new interpretation. Instead of serving the state, imperial households, religious, foreign or government decrees, art could be more independent of politics. This gave artists the freedom to express patriotism without risking being interpreted as either "bourgeois" or "socialist" by pretending to avoid politics all together.

When the movement to reincorporate village art into the art historical canon began, artists started to use village motifs such as temple banners, buffalo herders, fish ponds, and folk heroes in their paintings. Some of these motifs, which were potentially sensitive in the 1960s and 1970s, became dominant in paintings since 1986. At first sight, the use of folklore seemed to indicate a break from the worker, peasant, and soldier themes of the previous decades. But, on closer examination, paintings of village festivals and popular legends have become, in effect, redefinitions of national character. By still maintaining elements that are identifiably "Vietnamese," painters seem reluctant to abandon the patriotic ideal in art, even though they claim separation from a particular set of nationalist concerns.

The first artist to experiment with village motifs while maintaining links to "modernism" was the fourth of the "masters" of Vietnamese modern art mentioned earlier, Nguyen Tu Nghiem, born in 1922 and still actively painting. The label "hero" is reserved for the deceased, but Nguyen Tu Nghiem's preoccupation with village art mirrors Bui Xuan Phai's obsession with Hanoi streets. He has spent most of his career painting village folk motifs, making multiple sketches of the carvings that adorn the communal houses (*dinh*) in the villages surrounding Hanoi and transferring them to his canvases (fig. 4.7). He is not interested so much in the content of the sculptures as in their formal aspects. In explaining his work, he likens himself to Picasso, who saw African art as a form of "modernism."[33] Picasso emulated the simple shapes and geometric forms of African art and incorporated them into his experiments with cubism. The "primitive" look of Picasso's work became equated with "modernism."[34] Likewise, Nguyen Tu Nghiem incorporated village folk art into his paintings, giving them a "primitive" look that became equated with "modernism."

In recent art criticism, Nguyen Tu Nghiem has often been described as both "traditional" and "modern."[35] To use village sculpture as a motif in a painting was a very daring act in the early 1980s, when Nguyen Tu Nghiem first revealed his paintings to the public. At first dismissed for lacking national character, he later won a prize at the National Exhibition in 1990 for his representation of the village folk hero Giong.[36] Since abstraction and surrealism were forbidden, artists had not used motifs found in their native culture to express "modern" artistic concepts. Nguyen Tu Nghiem changed that. Furthermore, the

Figure 4.7.   Nguyen Tu Nghiem, *Zodiac,* gouache on paper, 1993. Photograph by Nora A. Taylor, courtesy of the artist.

fact that he used these motifs as symbols of modernism proves how alien they had actually become to contemporary Vietnamese. Like the African sculptures incorporated by European modernists into their works, the village carvings that Nguyen Tu Nghiem employed were removed from their original culture context.[37] He was merely employing what he thought to be their interesting forms, not paying particular attention to the meaning of their content. The younger generation of artists found his idea brilliant. Imitating Nghiem allowed them to experiment with semiabstract shapes without deviating from their indigenous cultural sphere. They could maintain a national identity while still attempting to experiment with other forms. Sustaining "tradition," so to speak, also gave them a guarantee against potential criticism from the Arts Association.

The art critics of the 1980s hailed Nguyen Tu Nghiem's use of village folk art as "Vietnamese modernism." His painting style resembled the European postimpressionist concern for form over content, and yet, iconographically, he was able to retain a semblance of "local tradition." Nguyen Tu Nghiem's and Bui Xuan Phai's work was said to reflect the spirit of the people, but not in the sense that it had been known previously. Far from the heroism of To Ngoc Van's participation in the battle of Dien Bien Phu or Mai Van Hien's warm regard for class solidarity, the national character represented in the works of Nguyen Tu Nghiem or Bui Xuan Phai was one of melancholy, nostalgia, or alienation. These feelings manifested themselves as much in the artists' oeuvre as in their lives. To Ngoc Van sacrificed his life for the nation, while these artists sacrificed their lives for their art.

Naturally, as in post-Communist Russia and to a lesser extent in Deng Xiaoping's China, the market for art has also influenced what artists have chosen to paint. The state no longer being the exclusive patron of the arts, artists have had to cater to a new clientele of international art buyers. Many of the works on display in galleries in Hanoi and Ho Chi Minh City depict scenes of the Vietnamese countryside and village life, not as a political statement against the state nor as a patriotic message, but rather because those images seem to attract foreign buyers. Still, the shift in subject matter is similar to revisions occurring elsewhere as Vietnamese art in general, like the society at large, tries to de-revolutionize itself and move on to a more global perspective.

CONCLUSION

For decades, Vietnamese officials defined national character as expressing the Vietnamese spirit in art and literature, but the basis for its definition was utopian and forced. Politics and aesthetics merged to dictate the criteria for acceptable works of art. Artists who did not display "national character" in their works were discouraged from producing art at all. But, by a turn in historical fortune, those who resisted the pressure were designated heroes in their own right by the generation of artists and art critics who came onto the scene in the late 1980s. They became known for their resistance to these restrictions and for their persistence in the face of strongly discouraging signals to abandon their way of painting.

In spite of revisions in the way artists have been given recognition for their work, political concerns are still at the heart of the selection of Vietnam's so-called master painters. Certainly nationalistic or patriotic concerns are still part of the process of naming which artists best represent the country's "soul." In this way the choices of the late 1980s art critics are similar to those of their mid-1950s counterparts. At least in principle, that is, art is a potential force that could be used to shape consciousness about oneself, one's memory, or collective identity. But it is dramatically different in content. Whereas the state remembers the heroic acts of its people, soldiers, workers, or farmers, and their sacrifices for the good of the nation, the art critics of the post-1986 renovation period remember how the country mourned the loss of their relatives and neighbors to war and poverty. It is as if it had suddenly become politically correct to feel sad after thirty years of being told otherwise.

Bui Xuan Phai, neglected by the official art establishment for wanting to tell the truth, suddenly became Vietnam's greatest painter regardless of whether his paintings showed true mastery of the medium. To Ngoc Van and others of his generation were reduced to mediocrity in popular opinion after having received some of the nation's highest awards in painting simply because the revolution no longer held any significance to the younger generation of artists.

If one looks at "national character" merely as a tool to create propaganda out of art, it is easy to understand why the present post-1986 generation of artists would be so opposed to the concept, considering their desire to distance themselves from revolutionary period policies. Many of them were born too recently to remember their country's struggle for independence. As Vietnam opens its doors to global markets, they are eager to join the international art community. Yet they have not rejected nationalist concerns entirely. In an attempt to forget the past and begin paving the way toward the future, they have instead chosen to remember the past in a new way. In commemorating the three painters who were not part of To Ngoc Van's campaign to revolutionize art, the artists and critics of today are making their own political statement about the role of artists in society.

By embracing artists who had previously been neglected by the Arts Association and spent much of their time in Hanoi cafés, the younger generation is calling for an artistic standard that is not based on socialist ideals. Bui Xuan Phai, Nguyen Sang, Nguyen Tu Nghiem, and Duong Bich Lien were not the most subversive of painters; others, such as Nguyen Sy Ngoc, mentioned earlier, were put into much more strenuous positions vis-à-vis the political mainstream. But, as Bui Xuan Phai's paintings of Hanoi and Nguyen Tu Nghiem's interest in village art reveal, they were nonconformist and unwilling to partake in the "revolutionary" view of art. Perhaps that was precisely why they were chosen. These artists were not politicized and yet were every bit as political. The younger generation has chosen to emulate them in order to be not *anti*revolutionary but simply *non*revolutionary. In doing so, they are trying to rewrite a history where war and revolution do not figure as prominently in the national consciousness.

NOTES

Parts of this chapter were presented at the annual meeting of the Association for Asian Studies in Hawaii, April 1996, as part of a panel entitled "Past Forgetting: War and Revolution in Vietnamese Memory." Some of the ideas formulated here are included in my dissertation, "The Artist and the State: The Politics of Painting and National Identity in Hanoi, Vietnam, 1925–1995" (Ph.D. diss., Cornell University, 1997). Research was conducted between January 1993 and August 1994 and was supported by the Social Science Research Council Southeast Asia Program, through grants from the Andrew W. Mellon Foundation, The Ford Foundation, and Fulbright-Hays. I wish to thank these institutions and the artists, art historians, and friends in Hanoi, too numerous to list, who made my research possible. I also thank Hjorleifur Jonsson, Neil Jamieson, and Hue-Tam Ho Tai for comments on earlier drafts of this chapter.

　　1. Nguyen Quan, *Vietnamese Plastic Arts* (Hanoi: NXB My Thuat, 1987); and Nguyen Quang Phong, *Cac Hoa Si Truong Cao Dang My Thuat Dong Duong [Painters of the Indochina Art School]* (Hanoi: NXB My Thuat, 1991).

　　2. Tran Dinh Tho, "De Co nhung Tac Pham Nghe Thuat Tao Hinh Dam Da Tinh Chat Dan Toc" ["In Order for Works of Art to Have a Warm National Essence"], in *Ve Tinh Dan Toc cua Nghe Thuat Tao Hinh [Concerning National Sentiment in Visual Arts]*, ed. Tran van Can (Hanoi: Culture Publishing House, 1973); see also Patricia Pelley's discussion of the origins of the "national essence" in Vietnamese history in her "Writing Revolution: The New History in Post-colonial Vietnam" (Ph.D. diss., Cornell University, 1993).

　　3. Tran Dinh Tho, "De Co nhung Tac Pham," 6.

　　4. Ha Xuan Truong as quoted by Tran Van Can in *Ve Tinh Dan Toc,* 9.

　　5. Tran Van Can, *Ve Tinh Than Dan Toc,* 11.

　　6. See, for example, Nguyen Do Cung's essay in the same volume cited in note 2.

　　7. Personal communication, conversation with Le Thi Kim Bach, December 1993.

　　8. Truong Chinh, "Marxism and Vietnamese Culture," in *Selected Writings* (Hanoi: Foreign Language Publishing House, 1977).

　　9. Cited in Cu Huy Can, *Culture et politique culturelle en République socialiste du Viet Nam [Culture and Political Culture in the Socialist Republic of Vietnam]* (Paris: UNESCO, 1985); and personal communication, Thai Ba Van, art historian in Hanoi, November 1993.

　　10. Truong Chinh, "Marxism and Vietnamese Culture."

　　11. For more in-depth discussions on the intellectual debate over "art for art's sake," see Georges Boudarel, *Cent fleurs écloses dans la nuit du Vietnam: Communisme et dissidence, 1954–1956* (Paris: Jacques Bertoin, 1991); and Hirohide Kurihara, "Changes in the Literary Policy of the Vietnamese Workers'

Party, 1956–1958," in *Indochina in the 1940s and 1950s,* ed. Takashi Shiraishi and Motoo Furuta (Ithaca, N.Y.: Cornell Southeast Asia Program, 1992).

12. Information on Nguyen Sy Ngoc was given to me by his daughter Nguyen Minh Huong, April 1994.

13. The Chinese "Hundred Flowers" movement was eventually repressed as well. For further discussion on the cultural situation in China during this time, see Julia Andrews, *Painters and Politics in the People's Republic of China, 1949–1979* (Berkeley and Los Angeles: University of California Press, 1994).

14. Personal communication, conversation with Nguyen Minh Huong, April 1994.

15. Truong Chinh, "Marxism and Vietnamese Culture."

16. I am grateful to Duong Tuong for his stories about the process of criticism of artists' works. Truong Chinh, in his "conditions" for the realization of a work of art, mentions that all artists must determine the audience for its creation and test the works by the reaction of the masses. Truong Chinh, "Marxism and Vietnamese Culture."

17. Information on Nguyen Sang was given to me by Phan Cam Thuong, art historian and professor of art history and theory at the Hanoi University of Fine Arts, April 1994.

18. My information on the discussions that took place at the fourth Arts Association congress stem from secondhand sources. As a foreigner, I was not admitted to the meetings. Participants, however, periodically convened outside the assembly hall and reported to me and other uninvited enthusiasts on the debates taking place inside.

19. Jeffrey Hantover, "Bui Xuan Phai," in *Bui Xuan Phai,* ed. Nguyen Quan (Ho Chi Minh City: HCMC Arts Association [Hoi My Thuat T. P. Ho Chi Minh], 1992).

20. I am most grateful to Viet Hai, director of the 7 Hang Khay Street Gallery, for his numerous anecdotes about Bui Xuan Phai during the fall of 1993.

21. There is some discrepancy in the exact dates of the banning of coffeehouses among the people I spoke to during my field research. Nguyen Van Lam himself cites a ten-year period, but others have said that was an exaggeration on his part; the coffeehouses, according to them, were closed for only a few years in the early 1960s. Conversations with Nguyen Van Lam during the summer of 1993 and subsequent conversations with Duong Tuong during the fall of 1993.

22. Nora Taylor, "Masterpieces by the Cup: Top Art Collection Hangs in Streetside Cafe," *Vietnam Investment Review,* no. 129 (March 21–27, 1994): 27.

23. Jeffrey Hantover, *Uncorked Soul: Contemporary Art from Vietnam* (Hong Kong: Plum Blossoms, 1991), 41; and Thai Ba Van in *Bui Xuan Phai in the Collection of Tran Hau Tuan,* ed. Nguyen Quan (Hanoi: Red River Publishing House), 1991.

24. I am particularly grateful to Mai Thuy Ngoc for all her stories about Hanoi during the war and in the years following it.

25. His wife has used the word *criticized* when she mentioned the Arts As-

sociation's objection to Bui Xuan Phai's work, but his acquaintances say he was only "watched." Conversation with Bui Xuan Phai's wife in March 1994.

26. Marshall Berman, *All That Is Solid Melts into Air* (New York: Penguin, 1982).

27. T. J. Clark, *The Painting of Modern Life* (Princeton N.J.: Princeton University Press, 1984), 10.

28. Information on Duong Bich Lien was given to me by his next-door neighbor and close friend, Nguyen Hao Hai, author of several articles on the painter.

29. Information on the price of the painting was given to me by Nguyen Van Lam and confirmed by Viet Hai, director of the 7 Hang Khay Street Gallery in Hanoi, December 1993.

30. For the past several years, Chinese artists have formed a movement in reaction to official art commonly called "cynical realism," or "Mao-pop." The movement is aimed at poking fun at utopian images of Communist Party leaders and commenting on the working class's lack of education. See, for example, Andrew Solomon, "Their Irony, Humor (and Art) Can Save China," *New York Times Magazine,* December 19, 1993.

31. I am grateful to Nguyen Dang Che and Nguyen Dang Dung of Dong Ho village for information on the situation with folk arts.

32. Nguyen Quan and Phan Cam Thuong, *My Thuat o Lang* [*Art in the Village*] (Hanoi: NXB My Thuat, 1991).

33. Personal communication, interview with Nguyen Tu Nghiem, April 1994.

34. See William Rubin, *Primitivism in XXth Century Art: Affinity of the Tribal and the Modern* (New York: Museum of Modern Art, 1984).

35. Hantover, *Uncorked Soul.*

36. Vu Huyen, "Notes on the 1990 National Arts Exhibition," *Vietnamese Studies* 3 (1990): 100–102.

37. Thomas McEvilley's comments on the Museum of Modern Art's *Primitivism in XXth Century Art:* "Doctor, Lawyer, Indian Chief," in his *Art and Otherness: Crisis in Cultural Identity* (New York: Documentext, 1992), 27–56.

FIVE

The Past without the Pain

The Manufacture of Nostalgia
in Vietnam's Tourism Industry

Laurel B. Kennedy and Mary Rose Williams

A remarkable journey occurred in 1996 when a group of ten American veterans of the war in Vietnam returned to the country they had first known as soldiers. Riding Harley-Davidson motorcycles, whose distinctive bass rumble is so loud and overwhelming it is sometimes referred to as "Rolling Thunder," the vets spent eighteen days traveling from Ho Chi Minh City to Hanoi. It is not difficult to imagine that these riders took Vietnam by storm. Even the busiest and noisiest roadways of Vietnam, a quiet country, would have come to a halt as bicyclists, bus drivers, and pedestrians watched the spectacle of American steel, chrome, and leather roaring past. One can wonder why those veterans chose to tour Vietnam on these loudest and most American of motorcycles, and one can wonder what Vietnamese onlookers thought about as the commonplace was disrupted for a few minutes by the American cavalcade. It is not difficult to discern, however, that for the riding veterans, as tourists if not as soldiers twenty-five years earlier, Vietnam was theirs, reclaimed from history and transformed in memory.

Central to this volume is the question of how the past is remembered in Vietnam, and how disparate memories of that past are reconciled, if indeed they can be. While other chapters consider the work of the state in creating an official history, and of oppositional voices in contesting that sanctioned memory, we consider here the operations of the tourist industry, which offers its own narratives of Vietnam. These are often starkly different from those evident in the funerary rituals, the films and artwork, and the museum exhibits described by other works in this collection. Yet tourism's narratives tangle in among the others to form the very complex public history within which both tourists and Vietnamese negotiate their own identities in relationship to each other and to the past.

At first glance, it would appear that the state has just as much control over tourism's image-making as it has over other elements of public memory. After all, tourist development must be approved by the state, and international interests involved in that development are required to work with Vietnamese partners. Yet the narratives used in "selling" Vietnam to potential tourists suggest that the state largely delegated authority for its self-representation to commercial, and usually international, image-makers.

At least in part, the strategy of inviting foreign development of the tourist industry reflected the perception that Vietnam might be a "hard sell" among Western travelers. The belief that the country must be rescripted in the popular consciousness was reinforced in a market analysis of Vietnam's nascent tourism industry, published in 1990 for use by travel industry professionals:

> Vietnam's current travel status (low visitor arrival count and a poor to nonexistent image with potential travelers) is such that even small improvements can represent substantial growth. . . . Vietnam is a country that conjures up many—often contradictory—images. Perhaps the most vivid of these is the overwhelmingly negative picture of the Vietnam War . . . not so much as a result of the communist victory, but rather because the United States was so torn by its defeat. . . . However, the memories and mood of the international community have since softened.[1]

Thus the tourist industry needed to tell a new story of Vietnam to potential travelers. A number of narratives could have been written: Vietnam as a nation of quaint and quiet rural villages; as a nation growing beyond the wounds of conflict; as a nation moving rapidly toward modernity and industrialization.

The construction of Vietnam chosen by the international tourist industry has been of a nation of colonial pleasures, of elephant rides, 1930s Citroens, and afternoon drinks in the shade of the veranda. Evoking the days before the troubles began, the narrative creates a memory in the imagination of a Vietnam wherein there was not hostile resistance to external control, and where today there is neither conflict nor animosity toward former enemies. This Vietnam offers to travelers its Asian exoticism and its mystique, as well as a muted and angerless history.

With this particular narrative, the tourist industry provides a vision of a sweet past that corresponds to Lowenthal's notion of nostalgia: "not so much the past itself as its supposed aspirations, less the memory of what actually was than of what was once thought possible."[2]

Package tour providers rely on a linkage between tourism and nostalgic longing for the feelings—often the greater simplicity—of a past that exists in one's imagination. This brand of nostalgia has produced Williamsburg in the United States, the Raffles Hotel in Singapore, and the son et lumière displays on the twilit walls of French châteaux. Yet in each of these cases, nostalgia can be seen to be a commodity manufactured for sale to tourists. Indeed, a tourist's impressions of the experiences travel will provide are primarily mediated by the tourism industry. The manufacture of nostalgia, then, is a process in which the tourist's memory itself is mediated. As Lowenthal writes, such nostalgia offers "memory with the pain removed."

But the nostalgic memories inscribed in tourist sites are not merely commodities that await purchase by targeted consumers. These narratives interact with and alter the composition of personal memory, of the larger public memory, and of official history. Martha Norkunas describes the development of tourist "attractions" as a process in which social value is conferred to particular reconstructions of both the past and the present, which may or may not correspond to those sanctioned by the state.[3] The process of value conferral—Dean MacCannell calls this "sight sacralization"[4]—occurs through tour organizers' selection of sites, the construction and reconstruction of those sites to meet tourists' (preformed) expectations, through the markers that designate the sites, by the locals who contribute their apparent authenticity, and by the tourists who, by their very attention, confer importance on certain articulations of history. These sites also legitimize the relations of power implicit within them. Other constructions are rendered questionable or in need of correction. This process flattens and suppresses—of necessity, in the eyes of tour organizers—the complexity of history into a "simplified . . . [and] digestible" reconstruction: "Opposed events and ideologies are collapsed into strong statements about the forward movement and rightness of history."[5]

Tourism's narratives interact not only with official history but also with personal memory. Maurice Halbwachs's *On Collective Memory* asserted that individual memory is not permanent and complete, but socially produced, formed and re-formed in interaction with others' conceptions of the past.[6] Thus, as John Urry writes, "Identity almost everywhere has to be produced partly out of images constructed for tourists. . . . [I]t is not just that places are transformed by the arrival or potential arrival of visitors. It is also that . . . people are themselves transformed."[7] Personal conceptions of ethnicity, of gender, of national identity are all negotiated in the context of public culture, including tourism's images.

The strands of official history, of public memory, and of personal memory thus tangle, making true and long-lasting distinctions between them difficult at best.[8] What is perhaps most problematic—and interesting—when considering tourism's narratives among those offered by the state is that while the state is a visible authority whose political objectives are at least usually apparent, the tourist industry's hand is often invisible in the creation of its narratives. Norkunas writes that "the public would accept as 'true' history that is written, exhibited, or otherwise publicly sanctioned."[9] Yet observers may bring at least a little skepticism to reconstructions of the past offered by the (identifiable) state, while accepting more readily narratives whose anonymous authorship does not alert their critical faculties. This makes consideration of tourism's narratives all the more important.

The analysis that follows considers some of the primary narratives offered by the tourist industry in Vietnam, examining both their origins and their thematic nature. The first part of the analysis describes the political economic catalysts to the formation of the Vietnam tourism industry. Because the shape of the industry is determined at least in part by the motives of those involved in the development of tourism, this discussion is concluded with a review of the three participants in the tourist enterprise: the Vietnamese "hosts" who service both tourists and tour operators, the travel industry professionals whose expertise informs the construction of the narratives we are studying, and the tourists most targeted by the industry. It is out of the needs of these three groups that a particular "story" of Vietnam arises. That story is told through two types of tourist "texts," which are analyzed in the following sections of the chapter: the sites being developed for use by tourists, and the travel literature that informs tourists' expectations and, hence, their experience of visiting Vietnam. These texts re-present Vietnam in ways that affect contemporary understanding of the nation, its history, and its political relations to the West not just for Western visitors but potentially for the Vietnamese themselves.

The rapid development of a tourist industry in Vietnam has occurred through a concerted official effort since the late 1980s. Until 1986, visitors entering Vietnam numbered approximately seven thousand; nearly all came from the socialist countries of Europe or from Cuba.[10] These figures began to climb in the late 1980s as Vietnam opened its doors to Western travelers, albeit under heavy registration requirements. In 1986, some ten thousand[11] visitors registered, doubling to twenty thousand in 1987 and to forty thousand in 1988. Despite shortages of hotel accommodations, poor communications infrastructure, and difficult traveling conditions, the tourism industry in 1988 netted some U.S.$57 million. The passage of the 1988 Foreign Investment Law, widely seen as one of the most liberal investment policies in Asia,[12] served as an invitation to the international travel industry both to invest in Vietnam's hotels and ancillary travel services and to add Vietnam as a destination for client travelers. The government declared 1990 "Visit Vietnam Year" and continued its actions to facilitate the expansion of tourism. In 1993, amid rapid refurbishing and construction of hotels and tourist attractions throughout the country,[13] the requirement of police permits for travel to the interior was eliminated and changes were made to expedite the processing of tourist visas. By 1994, over a million overseas tourists visited Vietnam, and by early 1995 the government had signed cooperation agreements for the development of tourism with eight countries and some 170 travel agencies throughout the world.

Few forms of international trade produce such classic economic dependency as tourism. As has been discovered by Cuba, Haiti, and others, natural disasters, political change (or even its threat), or a single season of inclement weather can cause tourist interest to vanish and the economic activity surrounding it to collapse. In assessing the impact of tourism in Vietnam, then, it is useful to consider the motivations that could lead a determinedly socialist nation to re-create itself, within a decade, as an international tourist destination, complete with five-star hotels and golf resorts. The timing of the move suggests that development of a tourist industry was a response to Vietnam's failed economic policies and its increasing economic isolation in the 1980s.

Efforts by the United States to constrict Vietnam's international trade linkages had been initiated in the 1950s, through a trade embargo against North Vietnam under the Trading with the Enemies Act. In 1978, the United States extended the embargo to the whole country following Vietnam's invasion of Cambodia. Until this point, Vietnam had stressed the role of multinational corporations in developing export-oriented industry and had established an attractive international investment climate amid promises of multilateral loans and bilateral aid from

Japan and the West.[14] With the embargo, the United States not only prohibited its own corporations' investment in Vietnam but also blocked most multilateral lending and discouraged its allies, including the world's wealthiest states, from continuing trade relationships. With few major trading partners remaining, and anxious about the expansionist ambitions of neighboring China, Vietnam set out to expand and improve trade and political relations with Eastern bloc countries—whose initial generosity disintegrated within a matter of years, along with the Soviet Union's own economy and political structure.

By the late 1980s, Vietnam found itself with few foreign markets open for the sale of its products, and thus a dire need to generate foreign exchange within its own national borders. These conditions emerged at the same time the number of Asia-bound travelers was beginning to rise, and when Thailand, despite rapid industrialization, was earning the largest share of its foreign exchange through tourism. Further, Southeast Asian entrepreneurs, unbound by the embargo, were interested in and willing to finance the refurbishing of hotels and urban transportation to jump-start the industry. A low-technology industry with comparatively little market research needed to inform planning, tourism offered Vietnam a relatively cheap and easy industry to enter, with the promise of quick foreign exchange earnings.

Given the immediate and financially tangible response to the opening of its borders to tourists, Vietnamese officials moved quickly in the early 1990s to establish the domestic bureaucratic structures and the international liaisons that would encourage rapid development in the industry. With its experience in this industry limited to serving a few thousand Soviet-bloc travelers per year, it is not surprising that Vietnam's emergent tourism administration was characterized by complexity and inefficiency, with three different groups working sometimes in cooperation and sometimes in competition with one another.

In official terms, control over development of the tourist industry lies with the first of these groups, the Vietnam National Administration of Tourism (VNAT). Reporting to the Council of Ministers, this body is charged with coordinating the development of the nation's tourist industry, including research and planning activities, training of personnel to work in the industry, and approval of contracts involving foreign investors (in coordination with the State Committee for Cooperation and Investment). A special unit of VNAT, Vietnamtourism, is responsible for promoting travel to the country and offering actual tours.

VNAT's policies and plans are implemented by some thirty local travel offices, which constitute the second group of state-associated actors. Located in major cities or provincial centers, the local offices take advantage of the poorly defined division of responsibilities they share with VNAT. The local offices often act independently, even competing with Vietnamtourism. Hanoi Tourism and Saigon Tourist in particular have substantial power of their own.

The third group of important players in Vietnam are the People's Committees and the various ministries, which own hotels, control vast amounts of property, and have their own access to official power structures.[15] Acting, like the others, as tour operators, the People's Committees and ministries are also centrally important as potential joint-venture partners for the international tourist industry, or as liaisons between international partners and entrepreneurs in Vietnam's private sector.

While certain aspects of servicing the tourist trade could be handled by Vietnamese "ground operators," the government understood early on that it had neither the investment funds nor the know-how to develop the amenities sought by well-heeled Western tourists. A 1991 government publication, *Vietnam: Investment and Tourism in Prospect,* invited the expertise of international travel agencies. The document noted that the government-operated Saigon Tour had "such relations [with international tourism professionals], but more attention should be paid to attract investment and to attain managerial and professional expertise."[16] Inexperienced but hoping not to be naive, the government required that all tourist developments be approved by the state, and that virtually all major foreign financial investments in the industry be undertaken through domestic-international partnerships. Local partners thus become essential to the international agencies, handling the bureaucratic aspects of operating in the market, arranging local contracts, and facilitating in-country negotiations, albeit generally on the terms set by the tour operators. They also provide other essential components, such as property, local knowledge of exploitable resources, Vietnamese currency, and materials or services needed for the venture. While local, usually quasi-governmental, firms may also play a role in serving tourists, they generally do not compete with their international partners, better endowed as those firms are with both knowledge and financial resources.[17]

For their part, international investors provide foreign currency, certain forms of technical know-how, expertise on the interests and expectations of the tourists being courted, and, perhaps most essential to success, inclusion in the expensive package tours that bring travelers to

Vietnam. The power of the industry rests largely with the tour operators, which are often large, vertically integrated and internationalized Western firms—airlines, hoteliers, and recreational site developers. Acting as broker between travelers and destination hosts, these agencies mediate the promotion of various destinations and oversee the planning of schedules and the selection of stops during the journey.

Development of the tourist industry necessitates more than just providing services, however. The business of attracting and actually delivering tourists—and the right tourists—is difficult. Passengers on cruises, for example, are usually wealthy, but they stay only a short time, and most of their food and lodging is provided on the cruise ship. The wealthy tourists who arrive on elite package tours, or expensive, individualized tours arranged by upscale travel agents, stay longer, spend more, and patronize hotels and local establishments. But attracting these most desirable tourists involves both knowledge of their expectations and of their motives for travel, and the ability to design the right packages—the right narratives—to assure the fulfillment of those expectations.

APPEALING TO TOURISTS

While each traveler's journey is designed with unique motivations in mind, common reasons for travel and types of travelers are known; these inform package tour providers' efforts to attract clients to the destinations they package into tours.[18] Not all types of travelers are likely to voyage to Vietnam: tourists who seek merely a change of venue or a quick getaway would find the very expense and distance of traveling to Vietnam preemptive. And not all types of travelers are desirable clients for the package tours offered by the international tourism agencies discussed here; young Australian backpackers and European "hippie travelers" on shoestring budgets—what Erik Cohen calls "non-institutionalized" tourists[19]—are significant in Vietnam's visitor population but contribute minimally to the tourist economy.

For others, however, it is precisely because Vietnam is costly to visit and relatively unknown as an elite tourist destination that they are attracted. For such travelers, tourism enhances social status by displaying the availability of leisure time and expendable income. For these travelers, the more exotic the destination, the greater the effect—although exoticism need not imply uncomfortable travel conditions. Lenz included Vietnam among the remote and putatively unknown locations that these wealthy "pioneer" tourists have "discovered."[20] It is for such travelers that international class hotels quickly have been built and pre-packaged tours organized, to ensure every creature comfort and minimize uncertainty.

Still others travel to find an "authentic" experience that stands in contradistinction to the modern.[21] Such travelers undertake "pilgrimages" that are not explicitly religious but that nonetheless involve a conversion of the self, or at least the hope that such a transformation will occur. These tourists "seek to see life as it really is, to get in touch with the natives, to enter the intimate space of the other in order to have an experience of real life, an authentic experience."[22] They wish to leave behind the superficiality of modern life as they know it at home; one travel writer who toured Vietnam by train (because "flying seemed entirely too abrupt and antiseptic") described Vietnam as "a place beyond the reach of dollars and the American Express Card"[23]—although both are, of course, very much in circulation. For many in this group, Vietnam's ancient pagodas and temples and the ethnic minorities of the northern highlands provide the requisite mystic exoticism.

For those who once served in Vietnam or for their families, travel to Vietnam also may be about a pilgrimage, but into the past. Not unlike the pilgrimages undertaken after World War I to the battlefields at Flanders and the Menin Gate of Ypres described by George Mosse, such journeys are centered on healing and renewal.[24] Reporter Neil Sheehan worked in Vietnam during the war years and vowed to return to witness it under conditions of peace.[25] Others return to relive that period of their own lives, or the lives of a relative who served in the war.[26] Another group of "pilgrims," albeit with a rather different relationship to Vietnam and its recent history, are the Viet Kieu, or overseas Vietnamese, who represented about one-fifth of Vietnam's travelers between 1993 and 1995.[27] Pilgrimage into Vietnam's most recent war history is also undertaken by those without a personal connection to the period, but with a curiosity about what happened and an expectation that travel in Vietnam will tell them. A large number of study tours of Vietnam have been organized by universities, for example, either for current students or for alumni who seek a combination of leisure and education.

Still other travelers are less interested in the search for "authenticity" or what MacCannell calls the "non-modern,"[28] instead seeking culturally anonymous destinations: beaches and golf resorts and duty-free shopping. Japanese tourists to the beaches of Thailand and Hawaii are often included among this group, and they represent an important market to the travel industry in Vietnam. Interested primarily in leisure and recreation, such travelers usually desire the explicitly modern comforts of air-conditioned high-rise hotels, international cuisine, and well-tended golf courses.

Obtaining these upscale tourists requires the enthusiasm of international travel agents and charter airlines. Travel organizations must invest a great deal of time and money to add new destinations to their existing tour programs, and so must be convinced of the potential of new sites to be both appealing for the clients and profitable for the agencies. Further, there is a great deal of competition for these tourists, particularly in the fast-growing tourist market in Asia. Thus a new destination like Vietnam, attempting to develop a market out of thin air in the early 1990s, had a formidable task before it, and one in which success depended principally upon the international agencies. It is hardly surprising, then, that Vietnam was willing to delegate to these agencies so much authority over the imagery and narratives to be used in luring tourists.

THE FACE OF THE "NEW VIETNAM":
AMENITIES AND ATTRACTIONS

The expertise of the tourism firms lies in their ability to coordinate the logistical aspects of their clients' international journeys, but that can only occur after those travelers have been enticed to the destination by the promise of some desirable experience. As Mowlana notes, it is the task of the tour organizers to "create the experience and image that sells and then proceed to make that the reality for the tourist."[29] Thus tour operators pay close attention both to the sites that potential travelers might visit and to the literature that will familiarize them with those sites in advance. These can be understood, then, as the negotiated product of the needs and interests of the tourism industry, its clients, and the government that signs contracts to facilitate the industry's success. Because the establishment of Vietnam as a tourist destination for Westerners has occurred within a short period of time and through a rather concerted effort, there is some transparency to tourism's development efforts: they can be viewed as explicitly intended to re-create Vietnam to meet the needs and expectations of potential travelers. It is clear that industry planners seek the attention of business travelers and upscale tourists, particularly those on charter packages from Europe, the United States, or Japan. Development has emphasized historical sites that might appeal to these tourists, the refurbishing or new construction of luxury hotels, resorts, and nightclubs, and the provision of infrastructure needed to access ancient temples, pagodas, and other cultural appeals. While visits to sites of Vietnamese antiquity comprise an important appeal of the industry, these have required relatively little new effort or investment as compared to the creation of tourist attractions based in more recent history and the construction or refurbishing of hotels, restaurants, and other tourist services.

The industry anticipated that many of the tourists traveling to the country would be French or American veterans of the war that ended in 1975, returning perhaps to experience Vietnam's beauty in peacetime, to heal the hidden wounds of the war, or to relive certain aspects of that encounter. As one journalist remarked, "Since the end of the Vietnam war, many American films and books have agonized over the meaning of it all. The Vietnamese, who suffered much heavier casualties, . . . take a more practical approach. They are intent on turning the war into a tourist attraction."[30]

Indeed, a considerable amount of energy has been invested in constructing monuments around sites that foreign war veterans might want to revisit, and much of that energy has come from domestic sources. These can be differentiated from sites created for ideological purposes by the Vietnamese Communist Party or local cadres for Vietnamese observers, such as the museum-shrine for Ton Duc Thang described in this volume by Christoph Giebel. Sites prepared for foreign tourists were constructed (or reconstructed) later, usually after the official efforts to develop tourism began, suggesting their rather explicit goal of attracting foreign tourists. Further, they are highly commercialized, with souvenir stands and food stalls. And, unlike monuments and shrines used for political and/or ritual purposes of war commemoration by the families of Vietnamese veterans or organized school groups, these sites do not so much bear witness to the war as "trivialize" it, in the sense that George Mosse used that term, "cutting war down to size so that it would become commonplace instead of awesome and frightening . . . [and] by making it familiar, that which was in one's power to choose and to dominate."[31]

Turning the war into a tourist attraction means retelling, for profit, the story of Vietnam's victory. Since the profit must come from those who lost the war, aspects of the story must be muted and key roles recast to make the story more palatable. In some instances, the actions taken to mediate and moderate history have been unmistakable. There were, for example, attempts to close the American Rooms of the War Crimes

Museum, in which are displayed photographs and artifacts of atrocities carried out by the U.S. military.[32] Although the rooms remain open, the museum was renamed the War Remnants Museum. In an ironic twist of history, most of the Hoa Lo Prison, known to once-resident American prisoners of war as the Hanoi Hilton, was razed to make way for new office towers, the marketing slogan for which read, "Your Ideal Home, Your Dynamic Hub of Business."[33] In Ho Chi Minh City, bars like the "Apocalypse Now" and the "B4–75" opened in the early 1990s, inviting patrons to step into a peculiar re-created past, of the war as experienced by a partying GI. In one of these bars, "the walls are black, and the overhead fan forms the blades of the helicopter painted on the ceiling. Ear-splitting music by the Doors mixes with the pungent aroma of marijuana."[34]

In other cases, historical reconstruction has been more subtle. Perhaps the best-known of the war sites now opened to tourists are the tunnels at Cu Chi, a network of about 125 miles of underground passageways, built as hideouts, meeting places, bomb shelters, and secret travel routes in southern Vietnam. These tunnels were well-known to U.S. soldiers during the war because of the many dangers associated with them: devoid of light, nearly airless with only the occasional tiny ventilation hole, and built narrow and low to make passage difficult for those with large frames, the tunnels were dreaded by many of those ordered to infiltrate them in search of Viet Cong guerrillas. Today the passages have been enlarged to accommodate Western tourists, and at their entrance a lecture hall, video displays, public rest rooms, and a souvenir stand have been built (figs. 5.1 and 5.2). In exchange for a few greenbacks, visitors can purchase miniature Huey gunships fashioned out of American soda cans or engraved Zippo lighters like those used to torch entire villages, or they can pick up an M-16 (or an AK-47) and shoot off a round or two of ammunition without fear of return fire. Operated by the Vietnamese army, the tunnels in 1995 attracted up to five hundred visitors a day, served by female guides in black pajamas and rubber sandals—costumes evocative of the Viet Cong.[35] The peculiar reversal of roles between defeater and defeated is unmistakable.

Tan Bien is another reconstructed war site, but it is its former elusiveness rather than familiarity upon which its developers hoped to capitalize. Known by the U.S. Pentagon as COSVN, this secret headquarters of the Viet Cong persistently defied American efforts at destruction. Now, as tourists, Americans are invited back, their hard currency a compelling incentive to disclosure of the secret site. In 1992, work began on

Figure 5.1. Sign at the entrance to the Cu Chi Tunnel complex, Ho Chi
Minh City. Photograph by Hue-Tam Ho Tai.

Figure 5.2. War Time Souvenir Shop, Cu Chi Tunnel, Ho Chi Minh City.
Photograph by Hue-Tam Ho Tai.

redigging the tunnels surrounding the installation and rebuilding the bamboo huts in which military strategy is said to have been planned. A journalist describing the site in 1992 noted that its design—and profit-making intentions—had far more to do with commerce than with Communism.[36]

Similar efforts were undertaken to restore the remains of the "MacNamara Line," an electronic wall of mines once used to keep Communists from entering South Vietnam. The U.S.$2 million project included reconstruction of the blockhouses and bunkers, the observation towers, and the barbed wire, electronic alarms, and odor detectors used to guard the installation. Undertaken by the Vietnamese Ministry of Defense, the site is actually a monument to American technology, complete with literature describing the history and equipment used at the installation, provided at the courtesy of the U.S. government.[37]

Part of the work of the tourism industry is also, however, to encapsulate the wars of 1945–75 as a single historical moment in the nation's long history and to move tourists' attention along to other images and narratives; hence the slogan "Vietnam: A Country, Not a War." Another significant period in the development of tourism is the French imperialist era, beginning in the middle 1800s. The legacy of French colonial domination is evident in the Impressionist artwork found in Vietnamese museums, in the highland villas built as retreats for colonial officers, and in the architecture of churches, government buildings, and—where tourists would most likely encounter it—in hotels.

In 1990, which was dubbed "Visit Vietnam Year," one of the notable shortcomings of the industry was the lack of hotel accommodations. Ho Chi Minh City had only thirteen hundred international standard beds, and Hanoi had only eight hundred, about half the number needed to meet the national goal for visitors that year.[38] In both cities, however, work had already begun on noteworthy ventures by hoteliers. In Hanoi, a French hotelier began the restoration and renovation of the Reunification (Thong Nhat) Hotel, which during the French colonial era had been the Hotel Métropole. Restoration included not only the classical French colonial architectural motifs of the building and its guest rooms but also the reinstatement of the French name, Hotel Sofitel Métropole, in lieu of the Vietnamese. Once work was completed, an advertisement placed in an English-language publication showed a 1930s-era postcard of the hotel and promised "Charme du Passé . . . Aujourd'hui."

The story of the Reunification Hotel was soon repeated throughout Vietnam. In Ho Chi Minh City, for example, foreign investors renovated

Figure 5.3.   The restoration of the Hotel Continental in the heart of Ho Chi Minh City celebrates Vietnam's colonial legacy. Photograph by Laurel Kennedy.

and restored, at tremendous cost, each of the hotels that would be familiar to pre-1975 travelers in Vietnam (fig. 5.3). Chandeliers and plush carpeting were reinstalled, wicker settees carried back up to the rooftop patio bars, wooden banisters polished back to a glow, and production resumed of porcelain ashtrays of blue oriental designs around Roman-scripted European names. The Cuu Long resumed its former life as the Majestic Hotel, the Ben Thanh as the Rex, the Huu Nghi as the Palace, and the Doc Lap as the Caravelle. Guests at these hotels are invited to enjoy—indeed, to adopt the perspective of—European privilege, the elegance and charm of which belie Vietnam's oppression and armed resistance to imperialism.

For many wealthy travelers to Vietnam, from both the East and the West, the delight of colonial decadence may itself be a somewhat foreign experience. Many travelers seek more explicitly modern, although culturally anonymous, comforts for their travel experiences: air-conditioned suites overlooking expanses of beach, state-of-the-art golf courses and marinas, and the opportunity to shop for souvenirs or duty-free goods. In Ho Chi Minh City, what had formerly been the Four Seasons Hotel on the Australian Great Barrier Reef was relocated by a joint venture of Japanese, Arab, and Australian investors and renamed the Saigon Floating Hotel. In the main cities, discotheques and trendy hangouts like Ho Chi Minh City's funky-but-cosmopolitan, velvet-curtained Q-Bar and Hanoi's art deco Au Lac coffeehouse were designed to offer a familiar refuge to Westerners. Karaoke bars and "hugging bars" had begun to proliferate by the mid-1990s, providing the sexual amenities sought by many international travelers to Asia. Although these types of enterprises were uncommon in traditional Vietnam, the rate at which they were established over a period of just three or four years left little doubt of their necessity in the eyes of industrialized tourism, which would support them financially and/or with referrals to tourists.

The most significant financial investments, however, were in the resort hotels—no more organic to Vietnam than the new discotheques. Outside of Da Nang, in what is once again being called "China Beach," 536 acres of beachfront and a Soviet-built hotel were purchased by an American firm for U.S.$280 million, for development into a tourist complex of hotels, residential housing for expatriates, a shopping "village," and a golf course—one of the scores of anonymous resort hotels that continue to be built. In Hue, a Vietnamese-Malaysian joint venture invested U.S.$408 million in new resorts, the renovation of an older hotel, and a tourist center in the middle of the city. By the mid-1990s, a South Korean company was planning a U.S.$290 million resort complex on the Con Dao Islands, once the site of a French colonial prison; five Singaporean partners were considering a U.S.$300 million tourist complex in Da Lat; and Club Med was negotiating to build a resort near Cam Ranh Bay. These developments and others by the Radisson, Marriott, and Choice hotel chains begged the question of whether Vietnam would soon be actually oversupplied with hotel accommodations, particularly the four- and five-star luxury units intended for the wealthiest tourists.

PACKAGING VIETNAM: THE NARRATIVE OF VIETNAM TRAVEL LITERATURE

With these tourist amenities in place, tourism agencies must still lure visitors to Vietnam, a task complicated by the necessity of creating a new image of the country in the minds of Western travelers. The tourism literature describing travel packages to Indochina is one of the most significant venues in which a re-presentation of Vietnam is offered. While potential travelers to Vietnam can obtain information about the country from a variety of sources, our interest here is with the upscale tourists most actively sought by the tourism industry—those who will arrive on charter tours from the West and who will utilize the newly constructed hotels and restaurants and purchase expensive souvenirs. These tourists rely on organizations like Abercrombie and Kent, Absolute Asia, InnerAsia Expeditions, or Geographic Expeditions, all of which are geared to meeting such travelers' simultaneous desire for the status of novel destinations and the comfort of luxury accommodations.

It is the task of these tourist organizations to create, through travel guides and brochures, a narrative encouraging a potential tourist public to visit Vietnam. Travel brochures, by their very nature, tell the stories of the places tourists will enter into and experience through their various expeditions. These brochures, as narratives, are configurations of "symbolic actions—words and/or deeds—that have consequence and meaning for those who live, create, or interpret them."[39] Thus, the essential human behavior of storytelling serves the rhetorical function of "adjusting ideas to people and people to ideas."[40] The stories in brochures, then, mediate tourists' travel experience even before it has begun.

The narrative analysis of tourism literature for Vietnam that follows is based on catalogs, most of them from 1996, supplied by upscale package-tour providers.[41] The catalogs were richly designed guides with heavy, embossed, full-color covers, artful photographs, and painstakingly worded text. We also examined a guidebook prepared by the travel industry for its own members: *Vietnam: A Travel Agent's Guide,* published in 1994 by the Pacific Asia Travel News. These catalogs and guide use words and images to introduce the "new" Vietnam through a narrative replete with ancient mystery and colonial charm.

The travel brochures employ five tactics to frame Vietnam for the targeted public of wealthy "pioneer" tourists: the establishment of a Europeanized identity; ambiguity in describing the events of the 1945–75 conflicts; depiction of those wars as provincial events; portrayal of U.S. involvement as a social activity; and historical minimization. Through these tactics, would-be tourists who remember the Vietnamese as enemies are provided with re-presentations of Vietnam, which suggest new constructs for remembering the country without its nemesis status. The re-presented landscapes offer Western tourists memories of a past that stabilize and authenticate not the past so much as the tourist's position within it. As Dickinson suggests, memories are "utilized in these sites to create intriguing spaces for [tourists'] consumption."[42]

The tactic of establishing a Europeanized identity permeates the tourist literature. The travel brochures intimate that Vietnam is not really so different from other foreign countries with which America and Europe are on friendly terms. In particular, they seek to establish identification with France, emphasizing the French influence in architecture and ambience. Highlighting Hanoi, for instance, one brochure reads, "Since becoming the capital of Vietnam in the year 1010, Hanoi has undergone numerous changes, but it is the French influence that has always had a special allure for artists and writers." Hanoi, "Paris of the North," also boasts a museum of history that was "built of reinforced concrete and completed in 1932. . . . The History Museum is a unique red structure that was once the French School of the Far East." The "Municipal Theatre is Hanoi's most impressive old French building. Built in 1911, this structure was built to resemble the famous Paris Opera House." The most notable architecture, then, was built under French occupation and is of classical French design.[43]

The French character of Ho Chi Minh City is highlighted as well. Indeed, the same publication that described Hanoi as the "Paris of the North" notes that "during the French occupation, Ho Chi Minh City was known as the 'Paris of the East.' "[44] In the course of its nineteen-day tour of Vietnam, Geographic Expeditions promises "a beautiful overnight at the hill resort of Dalat, redolent with touches of the French colonial past." So as not to completely exclude American travelers from this colonialist experience, InnerAsia Expeditions' brochure describes Dalat's charms as an "old art-decoey French resort favored by Teddy Roosevelt in his post-Presidential hunting days." By establishing identification with France through their tourism literature, the agencies present Vietnam as an ally rather than a former enemy.

A second persuasive tactic employed in the tourist literature to facilitate a different view of Vietnam by Westerners is the ambiguity of references to the wars of the twentieth century. The brochures give little information, for instance, to identify the opponents in the conflict, the length of military engagement, or its final consequences. In the sixty-five-page *Travel Agent's Guide*, for example, the war is not mentioned until nearly halfway through the brochure, and then only briefly, in a description of the Marble Mountains of Danang. The first visual image of the U.S. military presence in the country is presented on page 40 of this brochure. A photograph of an American helicopter is placed next to a paragraph listing the "Old Battlefields" in Ho Chi Minh City that tourists can visit. Weeds and deep grass have grown around the helicopter, suggesting that the Vietnamese give little attention to the remnants of the American military intervention—neither glorifying nor vilifying. With no apparent physical damage to it, the helicopter is void of the connotations of life and death. Where once helicopters could be heard almost constantly in the air, this one sits as a rusting, reassuring testament that the painful conflicts with Vietnam have now been relegated to history. That the Vietnamese lack interest in the past military actions of the Americans is communicated in the copy that accompanies the photograph of the helicopter. While other photos on the same page are accompanied by vivid language—"Ho Chi Minh City pulsates with activity . . ." and the Ben Thanh Market "combines an orderly architectural design with the atmosphere of an oriental bazaar"—the text accompanying the helicopter is devoid of emotive descriptors:

> Many well-known battlefields and locations of the US army are found here, including Da Spring; Tay Ninh, Chon Thanh, Iron Triangle; D Marquis; Hamburger Hill; Khe Sanh Base; Carol; Rockpile Caps; Con Tien; Doc Mieu; Que Son; An Hoa; Bo Bop; Nui Thanh; and Chu Lai.

Unlike the other descriptions on this page, the list of old battlefields contains no discourse that would associate the Vietnamese people and culture with the sites of war. Like the lone helicopter, American military battlefields appear to be dismissed by today's Vietnamese. Abercrombie and Kent offers similar reassurance, opening the description of its "Images of Indochina" tour by noting, "The turbulence of the recent past has faded."

Conspicuously absent from the tourist literature are photographs of males who would have been of military age to fight either with or against Westerners. The majority of the pictures included in the brochures are scenic views of landscapes, shrines and other architectural points of interest, and food. Photos with discernible individuals are unusual and exclusively portray young women and children. With fair, flawless skin, the women are models of loveliness who characterize the Western concept of Asian beauty and pose no threat to Westerners. The children who appear in the photographs seem to be calm and well behaved, and surely too young to remember the hostilities; the TBI Tours brochure includes only one photograph, of a gaggle of schoolchildren giggling and waving to the camera, captioned "A Warm Welcome in Vietnam."

Through an apparent inattention to war-related incidents, areas, and people, this second tactic creates a present-day Vietnam that is distanced from the past both chronologically and conceptually. The recent war history that most Americans would associate with Vietnam is shown to be of little contemporary consequence to the Vietnamese: InnerAsia Expeditions tells potential travelers that names like "Pleiku, Khe Sanh, Quang Tri" will ring a bell for certain old-timers, but as clouds of the war recede—over half of Vietnam's people were born after the Americans left the country—great calm and beauty are revealed. Assured that the Vietnamese have moved on, American tourists can also let go of the past.

Unable to ignore completely the conflict between the United States and Vietnam, the tourism literature employs a third persuasive tactic: depiction of the war as a localized and isolated provincial event. References made to Vietnamese soldiers imply that the fighting involved neither cohesive, organized battalions nor, apparently, any identifiable foreign aggressors. In the Marble Mountains of Danang, for instance, "during the Vietnam War, [the] caves were used by local guerrillas as field hospitals and shelters." Similarly,

> The Cu Chi District, a well-known part of "The Iron Triangle," features the famous Cu Chi Tunnels, an underground network of tunnels constructed by the local guerrillas and militia in 1945 and then expanded during the Vietnam War. Cu Chi is often called an "underground village" because of its labyrinth of interlaced tunnels used by the guerrillas during the Vietnam War. At certain locations, the tunnels' three floors contained rooms large enough for a commando training center, surgical operation, and army supply stations. It was also the birth place of the historic Ho Chi Minh campaign.[45]

In Abercrombie and Kent's description of events occurring on day 10 of an Indochina tour, Cu Chi is offered as "one of the most intriguing battlefields of the Vietnamese War." The copy goes on to explain that "during the height of the conflict, Viet Cong and North Vietnamese forces dug an extensive network of tunnels which served as hiding places, storage halls, medical center and dormitory." In these examples, there is no mention of the enemy against whom the local guerrillas fought. Shaun Malarney notes elsewhere in this volume that Vietnamese historians have generally presented war as sacrificial defense of the motherland against foreign aggressors. In these brochures, those aggressors are rendered not merely anonymous but invisible and unknowable.

Further displacing foreigners from the site of wars in Vietnam is the photograph of the Cu Chi Tunnels that accompanies the copy in the *Travel Agent's Guide.* In this picture, two men squat in front of a shelter that covers the opening to one of the tunnels. One man appears to be a Westerner, perhaps fifty years old. He is dressed in casual clothes and is smiling at the photographer. The other man is Vietnamese; he is dressed in a uniform that could be viewed as military. Weaponless and in sandals, the Vietnamese man appears more like a friendly park ranger than a member of the armed forces.

A final depiction of the war as being "localized" to factions within Vietnam occurs in the description of Vung Tau. In addition to beaches, colonial villas, cafés, religious sites, and other outstanding views, "one can also see some of the spectacular anti-naval guns, a reminder of Vietnam's lengthy territorial struggles."[46] To whom these guns belonged, or the targets at which they were aimed, remains ambiguous, as is the reference to the unspecified "territorial struggles" in which Vietnam has been involved. Foreign tourists may thus exclude themselves from specific military actions that occurred in the region.

On rare occasions when the U.S. military presence is mentioned in these brochures, it is portrayed as part of a fun, social activity—the fourth tactic. In descriptions of Ho Chi Minh City, the Rex Hotel is often said to have served as the U.S. Army's "bachelor officers' quarters." To those without a military background, this allusion conjures images of swinging singles and a life of parties rather than living within a state of war. Further emphasizing the social aspects of the country is a featured attraction, China Beach, "the site where American soldiers used to relax."

The final persuasive tactic that appears in the tourist literature on Vietnam is historical minimization. Interactions between Vietnam, France, and the United States during the nineteenth and twentieth centuries are all but lost in the grand expanse of Vietnam's history, from the ancient to the modern. In this way, even if the contemporary travelers recognize the previous antagonism of the countries, it is presented as a historical moment of comparatively little significance in the context of Vietnam's long and culturally rich past.

Historical minimization is achieved in the tourism literature in two ways: by skipping over details of events during the years the U.S. military was active in Vietnam, and by focusing on the distant past of the culture and country. Few references are made to events in Vietnam between 1945 and 1975. In an article documenting the forty-year history of Vietnam Airlines in the *Travel Agent's Guide*, for instance, there is commentary about its beginnings in 1956; then the chronology of the airline skips to 1975, when unification "brought a boom in air services due to the dramatic increase in economic, political, cultural and social activities." The intervening years simply are not mentioned.

In one brochure, the advertisement for Nha Trang combines both the distant past and more contemporary events. The "Cham Towers of Po Nagar offer a cultural perspective. Built between the 7th and 12th centuries, four of the original eight towers remain. For centuries the towers have withstood the test of time and the upheaval of subsequent kingdoms." Nha Trang also is "filled with notable attractions, including the Pasteur Institute, which was built in 1885. Another famous landmark is the Yersin Museum, where all the scientific data compiled by the French scientist Dr. Yersin (1863–1943) are kept in archives." Absolute Asia's brochure chronicles the history of the Cham people. Events from the late second century through the late 1850s are related, followed by the statement that "Vietnam's recent history is well known, yet few have experienced Vietnam as it lives and breathes today . . . a stunning contrast of traditional rural lifestyles and the modern transformations that have come from an unabashed opening to the west."

Steeped in romance and history, the ruins of the city of Hue ("City of Romance") receive a two-page color spread in one travel brochure, followed by a third page of photographs and copy. Only time seems to have affected this city that, according to the *Travel Agent's Guide*, was "considered the most splendid royal capital in Vietnam from the 1700s to the 1940s." King Khai Dinh's Tomb, built between 1920 and 1930, and the Thien Mu Pagoda, which dates back to 1601, are located near Hue, off the Perfume River. In Danang, My Son Sanctuary, "once the capital of the Kingdom of Champa (from the 5th to the 12th century), was graced with 68 magnificent palaces and temples." Remnants of the temples were excavated earlier this century. With visible ruins a thousand years old or more, Vietnam is promoted as a country whose importance to the world extends far beyond a comparatively insignificant war of the twentieth century.

Through the strategies of establishment of a Europeanized identity, ambiguity in references to the 1945–75 conflict, depiction of that war as a provincial event, portrayal of U.S. involvement as a social activity, and historical minimization, the tourist industry writes a narrative of Vietnam as welcoming, nonthreatening, and steeped in a history that transcends recent animosities.

CONCLUSION: RECOLONIZING THE PAST

Any explanation made by an individual or a group about events of the past or the future is constructed as a story that, as noted earlier, "adjusts" people to ideas. Textbooks, biographies, and even obituaries are a few examples of the pervasiveness of narratives. Understanding how narratives are created, and then interpreting those narratives, provides insights into the processes of adjustment in the public arena. Such an adjustment of Western views of Vietnam, its people, and our shared relationship is thus undertaken by the narratives offered for tourists' consumption.

The meaning of a narrative comes in part from its form. Dichotomies of fact/value, intellect/imagination, and reason/emotion merge in a narrative: "Stories are the enactment of the whole mind in concert with itself."[47] But a narrative also includes, in addition to essential facts, the value system according to which the facts may be evaluated; a narrative tells a story within an ideological and moral construct. Both intellectual and imaginative processes are engaged because the facts are presented in a framework that seems plausible, possible, and imaginable to the participants in the storytelling activity.[48] Providing us with "a way of ordering and presenting a view of the world through a description of a situation involving characters, actions, and settings that changes over time,"[49] narratives become crucially important to how we understand our present—and how we remember our past.

Our analysis of the narratives provided in both tourist sites and certain types of tour brochures suggests that Vietnam's tourist industry sees its commercial success as resting on its ability to transform Vietnam in the minds of the travelers who will visit the country. Over a billion dollars has already been invested in the re-presentation of Vietnam. This process, which it is hoped will be rewarded handsomely by the tourists themselves, provides those tourists with an experience of the country very distant from the experience of the people of Vietnam. It is instead a construction of Vietnam—its history, its culture, its people—designed for Westerners, through their own eyes.

The ideological work done by the tourist sites, the local "hosts" who staff them, the literature that sells them, and the travelers who seek them out is an act of complicity. In a sense, there is a clash of the motives brought by each of these participants, which is resolved through the formulation of a historical narrative that appeases those who hold power. In the case of Vietnam, the objectives of many local people to honor their countrymen in victory and in death and to enlighten foreigners about the Vietnamese experience clash with their even greater need to extract from those foreigners the cash that the travelers will turn over only if the experience makes them feel better. So, rather than an "authentic" experience being offered, something rather different emerges that reflects less an artifactual history than a reordering of the relations between local hosts and foreign guests.

This reordering is evident in the contradictions that exist between the tourist narratives and those offered in Vietnam's official history. A common theme of the tourist industry is its invitation to travelers to view Vietnam through colonial eyes. The refurbishing and renaming of colonial-era hotels, the revival of the excesses of imperialism, and the formulation of Vietnam's identity around the French referent all work to reposition Vietnam in relationship to its own past. Wealthy travelers are invited to assume the position of colonial conqueror, enjoying the fruits offered by the lesser, the conquered. In doing so, the power of Vietnamese resistance to colonialism and its oppression is erased from public memory and substituted with docile submission.

The tourist industry is, in fact, organized around Vietnamese supplication. Offering up their history, their culture, their art to the gaze of the Westerner, the people of Vietnam can be witnessed by tourists as living in the service of foreign visitors. There is no attention, either in the tourist literature or among the sites developed for tourist visits, to the success of Vietnam's industrialization efforts. The very concept of the modern, of a nation building an independent future, is overlooked by the tourist industry—aside from the foreign-built hotels that serve the tourist trade. On the contrary, the tremendous strength and forbearance which permitted the Vietnamese to overcome efforts at foreign domination and to set their own course are largely hidden from view.

While Vietnam's long history is recognized, it is not its history as defender of independence. Rather, it is Vietnam's ancient religious traditions—inaccurately separated from the country's political history— that are celebrated at the temples and pagodas to which tour buses swarm. Treks to the environs of the ethnic minority hill tribes render the traditions of a lost era another type of tourist attraction. With a population that is more young than old, it is venerability and the constancy of enduring religious convictions that are emphasized. There is a double irony in this, for religious freedom and tolerance for ethnic diversity would not be considered hallmarks of the Vietnamese experience, with tens of thousands of Buddhist monks only recently released from re-education camps to return to those admired pagodas,[50] and a history of charges against the Vietnamese government of human rights abuses against ethnic minorities.

If there is a group whose imagery in the travel literature is particularly at odds with Vietnamese experience, it is the country's women. In sharp contrast to the images of Heroic Mother and female guerrilla fighter described in this volume by Hue-Tam Ho Tai, these photographs speak to the Western ideal of obeisant Asian beauty, diminishing the significance of the roles played by Vietnamese women throughout history. Among the most important legends of Vietnam are those describing the strength and cunning of the Trung Sisters in leading a rebellion against Chinese aggression. During the American War, women were no less a part of the Vietnamese resistance than their brothers, husbands, and sons—to the horror and bewilderment of many GIs. Yet the photographs that show them as merely lovely and demure are critical to the work of rescripting Vietnam. In the shaping (or in this case, reshaping) of culture, gender works mythically: male imagery suggests power and virility, while images of women, particularly lovely Asian women, are ornamental and sexual; their faces are round, smiling, unconcealing. A Vietnam characterized by such harmless creatures is safe and unthreatening.

By foregrounding the delights of colonial decadence and backgrounding both the war years and any evidence of modernity; by foregrounding antiquity and backgrounding the vitality of youth; and by foregrounding women and backgrounding men, there is a constancy of effort to minimize the war's significance and to present it as finished business, now available for amusement. Tourists may witness the war in Vietnam with the same detached curiosity as the picnickers who attend reenactments of Civil War battles in the United States. By re-creating as amusement the experiences of the war—the bars, the M-16s, the "R&R" retreats—by showing American military equipment resting in peace, forgotten among the weeds, by offering tranquil French colonial retreats as refuge from the rigors of tourism, the wars with the French and the Americans are shown as resolved, no longer a matter of concern or anxiety. Yet this again belies the experience of some Vietnamese, for whom the divisions between North and South persist.

Far from promoting understanding of the Vietnamese people, their valorous history, their culture and way of life, the tourist industry invites foreigners to experience Vietnam from the position of dominance and control that Westerners appeared to lose forever at Dien Bien Phu in 1954 and in Saigon in 1975. The implications of the tourist industry's re-presentation may extend as well, however, to Vietnam's own political memory and the formulation of its political agenda in the post-Soviet period.

What the foregoing analysis suggests is that Vietnam's past is selectively reconstructed to appeal to Westerners or, perhaps more accurately, to marketers' ideas of Westerners and their interests. When social value is conferred through the selection and development of tourist sites, alternative constructions of the past are devalued, and the political nature of the tourist enterprise is exposed. In this sense, the "new Vietnam" offered by tour operators is peculiarly un-Vietnamese, emphasizing colonial extravagance, GIs' parties, and manicured golf courses. While it is clearly too soon to announce the effects of tourism on the Vietnamese, a central concern of those studying tourism is the ways in which the industry and its appropriations of history and culture challenge the identity of "local hosts." As Lanfant writes, "In this process of manufacture, the identity of the society's population is insidiously induced to recognize itself."[51] After Vietnam has delegated such authority over its own self-image to international commercial interests, the question of whether it can regain control becomes centrally important. The tourism industry may provide to the Vietnamese yet another opportunity for resistance to appropriation, both by individuals who disregard the tourist narrative as pragmatic disingenuity and by officials who press the tourist industry to revise its narratives.

Finally, tourism must be understood as a means of integrating a country into new global systems of power and politics, which must in turn influence the balance of power in a nation's domestic, as well as international, political affairs. Few planned economies have emphasized tourism as a means of generating revenue. As Vietnam continues its novel efforts to develop as a socialist polity with a market-oriented economy, fragile political relations are likely to be strained, and the relative power of private entrepreneurs and the state will surely undergo renegotiation. In international relations, Vietnam's re-presentation offers to the world a warmer and friendlier Vietnam, which may have benefits in a range of political-economic venues. The inherent danger, however, is that the price paid for this nostalgic retelling of quaint colonialism may be a return to it.

NOTES

The authors gratefully acknowledge the comments of John Kirby, Tammy Lewis, and Hue-Tam Ho Tai on early drafts of this chapter.
    1. Murray Bailey, *Travel and Tourism Opportunities in Vietnam: A Blueprint for Development* (Hong Kong: Business International Asia-Pacific, 1990).

2. David Lowenthal, *The Past Is a Foreign Country* (Cambridge: Cambridge University Press, 1985), 8.

3. Martha K. Norkunas, *The Politics of Public Memory: Tourism, History, and Ethnicity in Monterey, California* (Albany: State University of New York Press, 1993).

4. Dean MacCannell, *The Tourist: A New Theory of the Leisure Class* (New York: Schocken Books, 1989), 44–45.

5. Norkunas, *The Politics of Public Memory*, 36.

6. Maurice Halbwachs, *On Collective Memory*, ed. and trans. Lewis A. Coser (Chicago: University of Chicago Press, 1992).

7. John Urry, *Consuming Places* (New York: Routledge, 1995), 165; see also Marie-Françoise Lanfant, John B. Allcock, and Edward M. Bruner, eds., *International Tourism: Identity and Change* (Thousand Oaks, Calif.: Sage, 1995).

8. This point is the subject of debate between those who see history as continuously reconstructed in the present to serve current needs and those who see history as often resistant to such reconstruction. Marita Sturken, *Tangled Memories: The Vietnam War, the AIDS Epidemic, and the Politics of Remembering* (Berkeley and Los Angeles: University of California Press, 1997).

9. Norkunas, *The Politics of Public Memory*, 5.

10. Bailey, *Travel and Tourism Opportunities in Vietnam.*

11. Estimates of tourists entering Vietnam should be understood as approximations rather than precise figures. These statistics sometimes represent travelers entering the country on organized tours, visitors entering through the international airports, or categories including tourists, business travelers, and those visiting friends and relatives. Figures shown here, for example, are the official statistics published by the Vietnam National Administration of Tourism, but they differ from those provided by VNAT to the World Tourism Organization.

12. Among other provisions, the 1988 Foreign Investment Law imposed few requirements on foreign investors, permitted up to 100 percent foreign ownership, permitted imports under joint venture enterprises to be free of duties, and eased repatriation of profits.

13. Murray Hiebert, "Wish You Were Here," *Far Eastern Economic Review,* January 18, 1990, 44–45.

14. Carlyle Thayer, "Dilemmas of Development in Vietnam," *Current History,* December 1978, 221–25.

15. Bailey, *Travel and Tourism Opportunities in Vietnam.*

16. Tre, *Vietnam: Investment and Tourism in Prospect* (Hanoi: Nguyen Minh Hoang Printing House, 1991), 63.

17. For example, Vietnamtourism, the government-run tour agency, provides tours, such as a sixteen-day "Veteran's Tour," as well as side trips that can be used to supplement packaged tours, like the "Humanitarian Side-Trips," which take visitors to a drug rehabilitation center, an orphanage, and a maternity hospital.

18. See, for example, Erik Cohen, "Toward a Sociology of International Tourism," *Social Research* 39 (1972): 164–82; Nelson H. H. Graburn,

"Tourism: The Sacred Journey," in *Hosts and Guests,* ed. Valene L. Smith (Philadelphia: University of Pennsylvania Press, 1989), 21–36.

19. Cohen, "Toward a Sociology of International Tourism."

20. Ralph Lenz, "On Resurrecting Tourism in Vietnam," *Focus,* 43 no.3 (fall 1993): 1–6.

21. Dean MacCannell, "Staged Authenticity: Arrangements of Social Space in Tourist Settings," *American Journal of Sociology* 79 (1973): 589–603.

22. Norkunas, *The Politics of Public Memory,* 2.

23. David Margolick, "To Hanoi by Train, a Journey of 1,000 Miles," *New York Times Magazine,* November 9, 1997, 18, 32.

24. George Mosse, *Fallen Soldiers: Reshaping the Memory of the World Wars* (New York: Oxford University Press, 1990). See also Victor Turner, *Dramas, Fields, and Metaphors: Symbolic Action in Human Society* (Ithaca, N.Y.: Cornell University Press, 1974).

25. Neil Sheehan, *After the War Was Over* (New York: Random House, 1991).

26. Many American veterans of the war in Vietnam have described their travels back to the country either in the mainstream media or, less professionally presented, as postings to the World Wide Web. These travelogues, which often grapple in highly personal terms with the experience of revisiting sites replete with memory and emotion, could be considered a new genre within the literature of the Vietnam-American war. See, for example, Sheehan, *After the War Was Over;* Paul Martin, "Land of the Descending Dragon," *National Geographic Traveler,* May/June 1996, 60–75; Philip Milio, "My Return to Vietnam" (http://grunt.space.swri.edu/pmilio.html, 1996); and Robert Bowley, "Vietnam Visited and Revisited" (http://www.goodnet.com/~rbowley/vietnamstory.html, 1995).

27. Between 150,000 and 260,000 overseas Vietnamese traveled to Vietnam in each of these years. Vietnamtourism, *Tourism* (http://www.vietnamtourism.com/tourist/index.htm, 1998).

28. MacCannell, "Staged Authenticity," 2.

29. Hamid Mowlana, *Global Information and World Communication* (New York: Longman, 1986), 126.

30. "The Profit Hunters," *The Economist,* June 11, 1994, 31.

31. Mosse, *Fallen Soldiers,* 126–27.

32. The Chinese Rooms of the War Crimes Museum were closed after China and Vietnam renewed diplomatic relations. See Steven Erlanger, "Saigon in Transition and in a Hurry," *New York Times Magazine Sophisticated Traveler,* May 17, 1992, 18–19.

33. Completion of the new construction was delayed following efforts by historical preservationists to include a small commemorative museum in the design of the new Hanoi Towers. I thank Hue-Tam Ho Tai for information on the Towers' marketing slogan.

34. Robert S. Greenberger, "Buy Those Zippos, Catch Some Waves, Visit a War Museum," *Wall Street Journal,* January 25, 1993, A8.

35. "War Sites to Bring in Tourist Bucks" *Vietnews* 3, no. 6 (1995): 35–36.

36. Philip Shenon, "Hanoi to Show Tourists Hideout That Eluded US," *New York Times,* December 11, 1992, A4.

37. "War Sites to Bring in Tourist Bucks," 35–36.

38. Murray Hiebert, "Wish You Were Here," *Far Eastern Economic Review,* January 18, 1990, 44–45.

39. Walter Fisher, "Narration as a Human Communication Paradigm: The Case of Public Moral Argument," *Communication Monographs* 51 (March 1984): 2.

40. Donald C. Bryant, "Rhetoric: Its Function and Its Scope," *Quarterly Journal of Speech* 39 (December 1953): 413.

41. We examined the following brochures: Abercrombie and Kent, "The Orient, China and India" (Oak Brook, Ill., 1996); Geographic Expeditions, "Geographic Expeditions" (San Francisco, 1996); InnerAsia Expeditions, "Expeditions" (San Francisco, 1996); TBI Tours, "Orient Spectacular" (New York, 1994–95).

42. Greg Dickinson, "Memories for Sale: Nostalgia and the Construction of Identity in Old Pasadena," *Quarterly Journal of Speech* 83 (1977): 1–27.

43. Pacific-Asia Travel News, *Vietnam: A Travel Agent's Guide* (Phoenix, Ariz.: Americas Publishing, 1994), 14–17.

44. Ibid., 38.

45. Ibid., 30, 42.

46. Ibid., 47.

47. Fisher, "Narration as a Human Communication Paradigm," 10.

48. Gloria E. Blumanhourst, "Coherence: A Narrative Criticism of Two Accounts of Herstory" (master's thesis, Colorado State University, 1986).

49. Sonja K. Foss, *Rhetorical Criticism: Exploration and Practice* (Prospect Heights, Ill.: Waveland Press, 1989), 229.

50. "Faith in Hanoi" *Wall Street Journal,* January 20, 1995, A12.

51. Marie-Françoise Lanfant, "International Tourism, Internationalization and the Challenge to Identity," in *International Tourism: Identity and Change,* 33.

PART THREE

GENDERED MEMORY

SIX

Faces of Remembrance and Forgetting

Hue-Tam Ho Tai

In Greek mythology, Mnemosyne is the goddess of both memory and imagination. In giving her this dual function, the ancient Greeks remind us that memory is about imagining the past. In Vietnam, memory has no name, but it has many faces, and, like that of Mnemosyne, they are faces of women.[1]

The burden of remembering the dead and of imagining war and its place in the collective past has fallen to a postwar population in which women vastly outnumber men. Some are mothers and widows hugging to themselves memories of loss; others are young women deprived by war of the hope of having families of their own, as Da Ngan poignantly reminds us in "The House with No Men."[2] Still others, grown up in peacetime, have little patience with war stories. But memory is not just a matter of who does the remembering; it is also about the types of images that are available for doing so. Indeed, there seems to be little difference between men's and women's use of gender stereotypes.

Photographs of peasant women, their faces lined with age and grief, fill museum exhibits that honor both those who gave their lives to the cause of independence and revolution and the mothers who allowed them to make that supreme sacrifice. Along highways, huge billboards show pictures of smiling young women in flowing tunics (*ao dai*) and conical hats. The billboards beckon foreign investors and tourists with their images of a friendly, peaceful country in which local tradition combines harmoniously with the global economy. Popular magazines, meanwhile, peddle a vision of even younger womanhood enmeshed in a consumer culture that cannibalizes war memorabilia in the quest for throwaway chic.

This varied imagery attests to the importance of the figure of woman in the Vietnamese cultural landscape and to the multiple meanings it inscribes. Mothers, daughters, wives; peasant women and city girls; idle rich and toiling poor; resourceful and powerless; heroic and weak; self-sacrificing and selfish; traditional and cosmopolitan—these are some of the contradictory images of woman that populate the public discourse.

FEMALE CONSTANCY AND MALE ABSENCE

Only by disaggregating the concept of womanhood will we begin to understand how women can symbolize so many conflicting aspects of Vietnamese society and culture and, above all, how they can be made to represent both the power of memory and the fickleness of oblivion, both the debt that is owed to the revolutionary generation and the ingratitude of postwar youth.

If images of women can represent so many different things, it is precisely because woman as a singular conceptual category does not correspond to reality. Gender does not operate on its own but is inflected by age and kinship as well as class. This is especially true in Vietnam, whose language does not recognize the autonomy of the individual but instead enmeshes each and every speaking self in webs of familial and quasi-familial relationships. Images of women thus function in public discourse as a variety of social roles, each a concatenation of attributes and associations. Each image describes a discrete role totally unrelated to others even though, in real life, a woman performs multiple roles, some simultaneously, some successively. Among these, the most often publicly invoked ones are those of daughter, wife, and mother. A woman must negotiate her everyday self among these and many more roles, but in public discourse she is usually portrayed as a young victim of patriarchal oppression or as an admirably competent matron; as a devoted wife or a jealous shrew; as a self-sacrificing mother or a domineering mother-in-law. While one might argue that the necessity of discharging several roles simultaneously is at the origin of both negative and positive images of womanhood, in the symbolic language of public discourse, a woman is seldom described in more than one role at a time.

Some of the contradictions embedded in the different portrayals of women are the result of tensions between kinship and gender ideologies. In the Vietnamese kinship system, men form the core of the patrilineage but women are merely grafted onto it. Paternal relatives are thus called "inside kin" (*noi*), while maternal kin are considered "outside kin" (*ngoai*). In gender ideology, however, these roles are reversed. Women are associated with the inner sanctum, the core of the household; men represent its visible exterior, its public and ritual face. Whereas the women's sphere is the kitchen and their tasks focus on the material well-being of the family, the men's sphere is the front room, where guests are received and ancestors worshiped. In traditional Vietnam, the men's sphere extended to the communal house, where the public life of the community was conducted and from which women were excluded.

Vietnamese child-rearing practices, when combined with traditional segregation of the sexes, further contributed to the reversal of gendered notions of "inner" and "outer." Children of both sexes were cared for in the women's quarters until the age of six or seven. At that point, boys ordinarily transferred to the company of men, while girls remained by their mother's side. It has been argued that, in the Confucian patriarchal family system, the continuity of the male-centered lineage entailed discontinuity and rupture for the women, who had to leave their natal families and were thrust into an alien and often frightening environment upon marriage.[3] Men, however, experienced dislocation and loss at an even earlier age when they were taken from their mothers to begin the process of socialization into the world of males. Thus, despite the Confucian emphasis on the continuity of the male lineage, it is the image of the mother that represents the nostalgic days of childhood and the sense of connectedness with one's personal past. Idealized pictures of young mothers rocking infants in hammocks form a recurrent motif in the visual arts. Countless odes to motherhood have been penned by poets, while popular music, both traditional and modern, abounds in songs with titles such as "Mother's Love," "Mother's Lullaby," and "Mother's Song."

In contrast to this picture of maternal tenderness and constancy, fathers are often portrayed as unreliable creatures, absent emotionally and often physically. This perception is linked to the cultural belief in the relative autonomy of men as beings who are free to "roam the lakes and the streams" (*ho thi tang bong*) while women are tied to their hearth. In 1924, while advocating the partial emancipation of women, Pham Quynh offered a metaphorical distinction between the essential natures of men and women:

Men are like clouds in autumn
Women are like smoke in the hearth.
Though they reach different heights
They are both capable of soaring.[4]

It is the cloudlike nature of men, their lack of restraining bonds,
that frees them and empowers them but also turns them into unreliable patriarchs. The fifteenth-century compilation of folktales *Linh
Nam Chich Quai* (*Wondrous Tales from South of the Passes*) includes the story of "The Rock of the Woman Who Waits for Her
Husband" (Hon Vong Phu). The story concerns a woman who is
abandoned by her husband after he realizes that he has unwittingly
married his own sister. As a child, he had been told that they would
grow up to commit incest, and, wishing to avoid such a fate, he had
tried to kill his sister. He had then fled, leaving her for dead. Upon
finding that the prophecy had been fulfilled after all, he took flight
again. The abandoned wife, ignorant of the exact relationship between herself and her husband or the reason for his abrupt departure, takes their child to the shore to look for him. Slowly, mother
and child turn into a rock as they wait in vain. In the sixteenth-
century folktale "The Woman of Nam Xuong" ("Thieu Phu Nam
Xuong"), a soldier returns home after many years away at war.[5] His
little son, who had not yet been born when he left home, refuses to
acknowledge him and informs him that his father only comes at
dusk. The soldier immediately suspects his wife of infidelity. Dis-
traught, she throws herself into a well. When dusk comes, the father
takes his son to perform the daily ritual of ancestor worship. The little boy then points to the shadow his father casts on the ground and
exclaims: "See, this is my father." Only then does the man realize
that, far from being unfaithful, his wife had tried to keep his memory alive during his long absence. Stories like this, often told to instill
in young girls the importance of female chastity, underline instead
the fearsome unreliability of male power. The twin images of constant mother and unreliable father continue to thrive in the contemporary Vietnamese imagination. In *The Scent of Green Papayas*
(1991), by the expatriate filmmaker Tran Anh Hung, the father is
portrayed as a feckless gambler who absconds with his wife's hard-
earned savings, plunging her, his mother, and his children into near
destitution. His wife, by contrast, exemplifies boundless love, hard
work, and uncomplaining self-sacrifice.

MOTHERS AND SOLDIERS

Given the portrayal of the nation as family-writ-large in Vietnamese culture, it is not surprising that the discourse on the nation teems with images of mothers. Ho Chi Minh took the lead in honoring them: "Our people is grateful to the mothers, of both North and South, who have given birth to and raised all the generations of heroes of our country." Raising heroes for the nation is not the only role a Vietnamese woman performs in either real life or symbolic discourse. Other dimensions of the female condition are also utilized to represent war as well as war losses.

Western war literature largely focuses on the experience of battle and, thus, on the experience of men. In works of scholarship, this focus has only begun to extend beyond the battlefield, making it possible to discuss women's experience. But the face of war, in both fictional and scholarly literature, remains overwhelmingly a masculine one. In *Fallen Soldiers,* George Mosse argues that the advent of the French Revolution linked citizenship to soldiering, while the democratization of the military through universal conscription gave rise to a countercurrent that, by focusing on the largely aristocratic officers' corps, made it possible to associate the military with manliness.[6] Although it emerged in the nineteenth and early twentieth centuries, this celebration of the officers' corps as embodiment of manly virtues is rooted in the medieval chivalric ideal and goes back even further to the Greek and Roman traditions. In what Mosse calls the "Myth of War Experience," combat became the ultimate test of manhood, the experience that separated the men from the boys, as well as the passport to full citizenship. Ironically, this myth was shattered by the Vietnam War. As a result, "the Vietnam War Memorial can stand not only as a monument to the fallen of that war, but also, snatching victory from defeat, as a monument to the death, however provisional, of the Myth of War Experience."[7]

By contrast, only a few works in the Vietnamese language celebrate combat or the feeling of brotherhood forged in battle. Instead of epic poems, praise songs, and ballads, most of the writings penned by the country's heroes are elegiac meditations steeped in the Buddhist belief in the transitory nature of fame and glory, and in the centrality of suffering to the human experience. One of Vietnam's greatest poems, *The Lament of the Soldier's Wife (Chinh Phu Ngam Khuc)*, was written in the mid–eighteenth century by a male author, Dang Tran Con, not to celebrate combat but to express the pain of waiting for the absent soldier.[8] To be sure, the wars of the late eighteenth century, which raged over three decades, also brought forth a number of larger-than-life figures. By and large, however, most historical and fictional accounts of these wars portray the soldiers as undisciplined louts rather than knights in shining armor or gallant officers. In the nineteenth century, the emperors sought to restore order to society by promoting Confucian ideology and elevating civilian officials over military ones. Although officers were valued, military life in general was associated with the lowly. The poorest peasants found their way into the army precisely because they were the most powerless males in society, in no position to object to being drafted.

This tendency to devalue the military was slowly reversed in the late 1920s when anticolonial activists began seeking recruits from among colonial troops, and later, when both sides of the Vietnam War portrayed military service as an honorable and patriotic duty. As Shaun Malarney writes, the North Vietnamese state devised a whole set of commemorative practices to honor the war dead and generate popular support for its cause. This cause was described as a war of national salvation first against the French and later against the Americans. The valorization of the military, however, did not produce a cult of masculinity because it was in keeping with the traditional depiction of war as something forced on the Vietnamese people rather than initiated by them.

This historiographical tradition conveniently ignores the many episodes in which the Vietnamese have acquired territory by annihilating, displacing, or assimilating whole populations such as the people of Champa in what is now central Vietnam in the fifteenth century, and the Khmers of the Mekong Delta since the eighteenth century. It also obfuscates the numerous times when Vietnamese fought against Vietnamese rather than foreigners, during power struggles and episodes of peasant unrest. It highlights instead the experience of fighting in the defense of the homeland.[9] This writing of history as a narrative of patriotic endeavor presents war not as an opportunity for men to test their mettle but as an evil necessity that must be endured by all. It allows heroism to be celebrated without associating it almost exclusively with battlefield combat, as is the case with much Western ideology. Heroism and courage are glossed instead as determination, endurance, the spirit of self-sacrifice, and, above all, the willingness to fight against an invader whatever the odds. It need not be an especially aristocratic or masculine quality.

Indeed, the representation of war as an exercise in patriotic self-defense makes possible its feminization. It makes use of images of the country as victim of oppression and as family whose home is being invaded. These two images are linked to two different conceptions of womanhood. The first, the country as victim, is most closely associated with the figure of the vulnerable young girl at the mercy of cruel fate.[10] Significantly, however, rape and defilement, which is perhaps the most potent metaphor available to describe the invasion of national space by foreigners, is not often used in Vietnam as it has been in the West from the Rape of the Sabine Women to the present. Women who have lost their chastity, whether willingly or not, are utterly stigmatized in traditional Vietnamese culture and thus cannot serve as national symbols.[11] Few anticolonial tracts associate rape with colonial conquest, though appeals to women to join in the liberation of the nation and win their own emancipation in the process were a staple of patriotic rhetoric in the 1920s and 1930s. The most notable exception is Ho Chi Minh's *Le Procès de la colonisation française,* which was written in 1925 with a French rather than a Vietnamese audience in mind and freely describes rape and pillage as colonial crimes.[12]

If the victimization of the country is rendered through the figure of a young and weak girl, patriotic historiography that celebrates the struggle for independence begins with an uprising led by two women. Conventional history normally elides the lives of women, but the Trung Sisters, who led an uprising against Chinese rule in A.D. 39, are the most famous and perhaps the most beloved figures in the Vietnamese pantheon of heroic figures. They have been the subject of countless local cults since their death in A.D. 43, and of a state cult since the twelfth century. Their importance in Vietnamese culture lies not only in the fact that they were the first recorded heroes in centuries of struggle against Chinese domination but also in their gender. They lived in an era when Vietnamese society was characterized by bilateral kinship and uxorilocal marriages; they were descended in the maternal line from the legendary Hung kings and were daughters of a powerful lord. Over the centuries, however, both oral tradition and Confucian historiography turned them into paragons of feminine meekness and modesty. They have been cast as essentially timid women who set aside feminine decorum to avenge the wrongful death of the elder sister's husband and, in the process, overthrow Chinese tyranny. The greater the reserve attributed to them, the more admirable their resolve in overcoming it. The popular depiction of the Trung Sisters stands in marked contrast with that of Lady Trieu, a nineteen-year-old girl who rose up in A.D. 248, also against Chinese rule, but without the similar motive of seeking revenge. Unlike the decorous Trung Sisters of popular culture, whose female soldiers are said to have fled at the sight of naked Chinese males, she "went into battle astride an elephant . . . throwing her yard-long breasts over her shoulders."[13] Lady Trieu is quoted in the history books as having replied to an inquiry about her marriage plans: "I wish to ride a strong wind and tame fierce waves, kill sharks in the Eastern sea, force back the Chinese armies and throw off the chains of slavery; how could I possibly accept to be some man's servant?"[14] It is perhaps her passionate defense of personal (as opposed to national) independence and her lack of an appropriately Confucian motive for throwing herself into battle that makes her unfit for the task of representing a besieged nation.

Stories such as those of the Trung Sisters and Lady Trieu have been used to explain the popular saying "When war comes, even women must fight" (giac den nha, dan ba cung danh), which suggests that women are recruits of last resort into the fight to defend the homeland. Unless war comes so close to them that they have no other alternative, women have no business fighting. As Nguyen Don Phuc reminded advocates of women's emancipation in 1925, "The virtue of the Oriental woman does not lie in quelling revolt in the East or bringing order to the North [danh dong dep bac]; nor does it reside in competing with men for sexual equality or in studying the stars or algebra. Even if they are educated, they should learn only the Four Virtues [tu duc]"[15] It is, however, precisely adherence to the Four Virtues that enables women to contribute to the struggle against invaders. Among these virtues, resourcefulness and good management rank first. Women, after all, are charged with managing their households and protecting the well-being of their families, duties that call for skills worthy of a battle-hardened general. The association between generalship and domestic management is humorously captured in the popular description of the housewife as "general of the interior" (noi tuong).

In Western thought, battle masculinizes the landscape as men organize to defend their homes, their fields, and their women, while the latter retreat to the comparative safety of their homes. As the French national anthem exhorts men, "Citizens, take up arms and form battalions, fight those who would slit the throat of your wives and daughters, and let their impure blood nourish your fields." Lynn Hunt and others have pointed out that the French republican ideal of universal male franchise was linked to a deliberate attempt to rid the public sphere of the corrupting influence of women after the reign of Louis XV, whose various mistresses had often interfered in matters of state.[16] While the French Revolution created France's first national standing army and a republic based on universal suffrage, both were open to men only. French women did not gain the right to vote until after World War II, in 1948.

Working in a different vein, Drew Faust pointed out that the mobilization of Southern men in the Civil War feminized public space in the American South as women assumed tasks hitherto reserved for men.[17] Nina Silber suggests another rationale for the feminization of the Southern landscape, this time focusing on the postbellum period.[18] She argues that the defeat of the agrarian South enabled the more industrial, and above all victorious, North to turn it into an object of romance. In her reading, the feminization of the Southern landscape was largely a postwar phenomenon, a product of its defeat.

In Vietnam, however, war feminizes the Vietnamese symbolic landscape. The transformation happens not because women must move into public spaces left vacant by enlisted men but because the division between private and public becomes blurred. The feminization of the landscape is a sine qua non of the strategy of total mobilization that is necessary to rescue the nation from invasion. It works best when the population can be persuaded that it is under attack, that its home is imperiled. This strategy is based on the tradition of guerrilla warfare, which involves luring the enemy deep onto Vietnamese soil, where it would be surrounded by hostile peasants intent on defending their homes and villages. Guerrilla warfare is not only a strategy appropriate to the technologically inferior; it also has the advantage of not relying on the deployment of standing armies with well-trained officers. Instead, it blurs the distinction between the front line and the rear, between combatants and civilians, between the masculine battlefield and the feminine domestic space. When protecting one's home becomes synonymous with defending the homeland, women, too, can be mobilized, for if they can be portrayed as hapless victims, they are also expected to be resourceful, to behave as "generals of the interior."

The South Vietnamese government ignored this tradition and consistently portrayed the Vietnam War as a civil war arising from ideological conflict; it also employed a high-technology strategy that depended on trained soldiers. Although it tried to generate support among the civilian population, that support was expected to be largely passive. As a result, women were not mobilized either into the army or into greater war-related production. By contrast, the North Vietnamese state successfully mobilized large numbers of women to fight in the War Against the Americans. Its leaders did not argue that guns were unfeminine instruments, or that defending the country was a man's job. Nor did they argue, as some American critics of the deployment of women in the military continue to do, that the presence of women would be deleterious to masculine military morale or that certain tasks were beyond women's capabilities. Women, instead, worked in the fields—as they have always done—with machine guns slung over their shoulders. They risked their lives to bring heavy ammunition to passing military brigades; some even volunteered to fight in the jungles of the Central Highlands. This is not to suggest that women did not encounter male prejudice in the course of fulfilling these many tasks, or that they did not have problems reconciling their images of themselves as women with the tasks they performed. Vietnamese cultural expectations regarding women's proper place and responsibilities were so varied and mutually contradictory as to allow women to assume military duties while holding them to unchanged standards of feminine decorum. Fighting women thus lived under enormous strains.[19]

The importance of women's contribution to the war effort and of noncombat activities such as production work was publicly recognized by the North Vietnamese state during the War Against the Americans with the award of medals to women who had displayed the "Three Competencies" (Ba Dam Dang): competence in replacing men in production work; competence in mobilizing relatives into the army; and competence in fighting if necessary. Women who distinguished themselves in either of these endeavors received a medal that read: "Loyal, courageous and resourceful." Of the three virtues thus recognized, only the second is not traditionally associated with femininity.

In a war of total mobilization in the defense of one's home, war service is not an entitlement to higher social status. With the return of peace, social order is restored as well, and all those who fought are expected to resume their prewar lives. The equation of home and homeland is attenuated, and women's managerial skills are once again confined to their domestic spheres. Women's very real contributions to the war effort in the North did not alter gender relations or their symbolic role in the public discourse.

KEEPERS OF MEMORY

If the invaded country can be associated with the figure of a helpless young girl, and if the country at war can summon up visions of the Trung Sisters and transform women's domestic skills into military ones, postwar remembrance has brought forth another image of women.

Memory is an important aspect of cultural production, a production that the state is eager to control. In the two decades since the war ended, the Vietnamese state has tried to shape collective memory to underline the continuity between the Revolution and the War Against the Americans, on the one hand, and past struggles for national independence, on the other. The year 1995, which marked the twentieth anniversary of the fall of Saigon (April 30) and the fiftieth anniversary of independence (September 2) and the founding of the Vietnamese People's Army (December 19), saw an outpouring of commemorative products, speeches, and rituals. It is customary in Vietnam to honor a man by paying one's respect to his mother. In the same spirit, it is the mother, rather than the wife, who is the cultural vector of grief and memory (fig. 6.1). At the center of commemoration, therefore, was the face of the mother of heroes, full of pride in their deeds and sorrow for their loss.

War commemoration in Vietnam thus is quite different than in the West. In Western literature, war is often treated as a rite of passage that makes men out of callow boys. If a soldier succumbs, his memory is located with his wife or sweetheart. In the words of James Jones, war is a "widow-maker." In Vietnamese commemorations of war, however, the dominant voice belongs to mothers rather than wives. Most soldiers were too young to be married when they went into the army, and thus were deprived of the culturally significant rites of passage that would have granted them entry into the community of adult men: marriage and fatherhood. But marriage in Vietnam does not require that a man "cleave only to his wife"; for him, the key emotional relationship remains with his mother. Even hard-boiled veterans have been known to wax lyrical on the subject of motherhood: "In the life of each of us, our mother is our support, our faith, our sheltering shade, the stuff of life; always nurturing and raising us to become adults; mothers are ready to bear any burden, to sacrifice everything, never asking anything for themselves, except for the ultimate wish that their children should always be faithful to the Homeland and pious toward the people."[20]

The cult of motherhood may account for the abundance of statues,

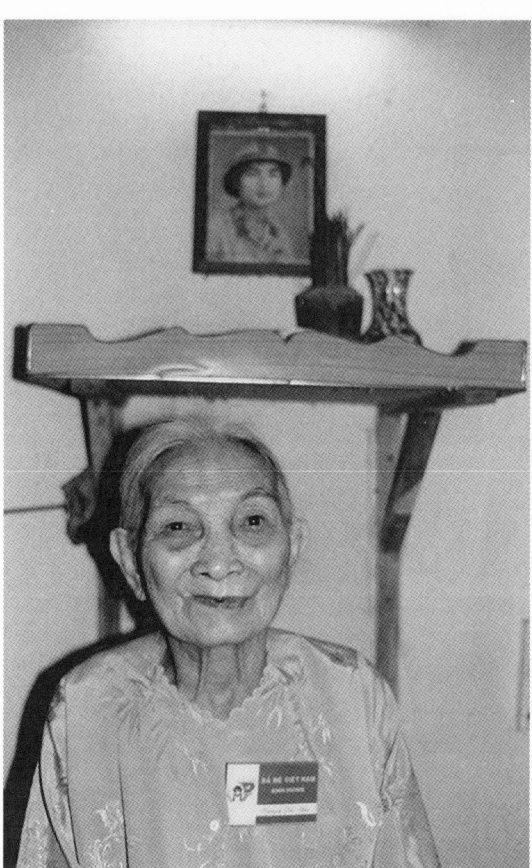

Figure 6.1. A Heroic
Mother poses in front
of her son's altar, Ha-
noi. Photograph by
Natalia Puchalt.

posters, and paintings variously entitled *Mother* or *Mother's Love* in commemorative exhibits. Representations of women-as-mothers vastly outnumber depictions of women's war-related activities. Female soldiers are most often portrayed in off-duty moments: with a rifle over a shoulder but also a child nursing at the breast, a reminder that women took up weapons to defend their young. The equation of women as mothers and of men as their sons is a powerful one. In 1995, the Museum of Women of Ho Chi Minh City staged a special exhibit to celebrate Cu Chi, an area famous for its tradition of rebelliousness long before it became the site of a vast network of underground tunnels that served as headquarters of the guerrillas operating in the Saigon region during the Vietnam War. The exhibit was arranged around two sets of pictures.

One was called "Heroic Mothers," the other "Courageous Sons." At least one of the so-called sons looked to be in his sixties. A poster included in an exhibit mounted at the Museum of Fine Arts in Ho Chi Minh City to commemorate the fiftieth anniversary of the establishment of the Vietnamese People's Army captures the strength of the bond between mother and son. In the foreground is a detachment of resolute young men; above them floats an elderly woman. The caption reads: "We look to Mother; every task we are given, we complete it in order to please Mother." One sculpture on permanent display in various museums throughout the country depicts a soldier eager to be off, while his mother, crouching in front of him, mends a tear in his trouser leg. While this sculpture illustrates the patriotic eagerness of the son and the stoic acceptance of the mother, another mother-son pair captures the joy of reunion in a photograph, also included in numerous museum exhibits, of a released prisoner of war clasping his aged mother in his arms. The Museum of American War Crimes (now renamed War Remnants Museum) in Ho Chi Minh City features a sculpture made entirely of rusted metal recovered from weapons and simply entitled *Mother*. A bronze statue of a woman holding her dead soldier son in her arms stands in the middle of the courtyard of the former American consulate in Da Nang; it is both a symbol of the reoccupation of national space and a tribute to the fallen.

By fixing on the figure of the grieving mother, Vietnamese culture infantilizes the dead soldier. Unlike the Western soldier who has tested his manhood in combat, he remains eternally a child, as a popular song of the South suggests:

> She rocks her child, cradling the bullet that turns his wound red.
> At twenty, her child went away to soldier.
> And having gone, never came back.
> Sleep my child, child of a yellow-skinned mother.
> My god, this body once so slight.
> Which I, your mother, once carried in my womb,
> Which I, your mother, once cradled in my arms,
> Why do you sleep at twenty?[21]

The statues, photographs, and paintings of mothers of soldiers were designed partly in homage to the soldiers, both dead and living, partly as a means of acknowledging the enormous sacrifices of the civilian population. These commemorative productions were functionally equivalent to the military cemeteries in which the soldiers who died during the Revolution and the War Against the Americans are buried. Another way of honoring their survivors was to create the status of "Heroic Mother" (*Me Anh Hung*). This trend had been around for some time, but it reached unprecedented heights in late 1994 with the passage of a resolution in the National Assembly that set criteria for the award of medals to Heroic Mothers. The basic criterion for receiving such a medal was that the woman so honored must have lost at least three children. Although women who had fewer children but had lost them all were also honored, many who received a medal had lost more than three. The resolution received huge press coverage and was enormously popular throughout the country. Most communities organized ceremonies to honor local recipients of the medals, and exhibits were mounted in many places around the theme of Heroic Mothers (fig 6.2).

As the anniversaries succeeded one another in 1995, it became clear that there was growing ambivalence about the past decades of war and revolution. Commemorative events were not only opportunities for the state to inject new vigor into its narrative of national glory and heroic struggle; they also occasioned contrapuntal, subversive questioning of this legacy of struggle. The adoption of the Doi Moi program of economic reforms and engagement in the global economy seemed to undermine the very rationale for war and revolution. In the wake of profound economic difficulties and the worldwide decline of Marxism-Leninism, the triumphalist mood of the immediate postwar period had dissipated and the meaning of victory had become clouded.

Commemoration that was structured not around the celebration of triumph but around the acknowledgment of loss seemed appropriate, and honoring the mothers of dead soldiers was particularly fitted to this purpose. But this was not entirely without risk. Focusing on the extraordinary losses suffered by the Heroic Mothers could—and occasionally did—lead to a questioning of the human cost of war. The combined toll for North and South Vietnam is well over three million, which does not take into account the three hundred thousand North Vietnamese soldiers officially listed as missing in action. In 1991, the playwright Ngo Thao, who had taken part in a major landmark of the 1972 Easter Offensive, the battle of Quang Tri, called that battle "a senseless tragedy."[22] Around that time, two veterans, one male and one female, published novels that captured this feeling of senseless tragedy: Bao Ninh with *The Sorrow of War* and Duong Thu Huong with *Novel without a Name*.[23]

Acknowledgment that the Vietnam War was a civil war came late in

Figure 6.2.   A Heroic Mother poses in front of a list of revolutionary war dead, Ho Chi Minh City. Photograph by Hue-Tam Ho Tai.

the North. By 1995, however, the theme of brothers meeting on the battlefield after a long separation and realizing that they were committed to fight on opposite sides had become a popular trope in literature and television programs.[24] In the South, however, the Vietnam War had been portrayed as a civil war all along, and there, instead of representing women's willingness to make personal sacrifices for a just cause, maternal images symbolized national grief. The image of Mother Vietnam weeping for all her children was popular in southern poems and songs written during the war. As the songwriter Trinh Cong Son put it in his "Mother's Legacy" (Gia Tai Cua Me) in 1969, "One thousand years of being enslaved by the Chinese; one hundred years of being colonized by the French; twenty years of civil war, day in day out. This is mother's legacy: a forest of dry bones, mountains covered with burial mounds."[25]

Heroic Mothers include only those whose sons and daughters died in the cause of the Revolution and the War Against the Americans. There are countless other mothers whose sons died fighting in the South Vietnamese army, and whose grief goes officially unacknowledged. Photographs of wrinkled women who are said to have lost three, five, or nine children blend into the collective figure of Mother Vietnam who loves her children unconditionally and mourns them equally, whatever side they fought on. They remind many southern viewers of the war losses they suffered but that have been erased from public memory.[26]

MANAGING PEACE

This commemorative silence is striking in light of what some scholars have called the "southernization" of Vietnam under Doi Moi, that is, its conversion into a replica of the pre-1975 South. In both the nostalgic recollections of disaffected southerners and the wishful projections of envious northerners, this pre-1975 South is not marked by war, chaos, or corruption, but represents an era of abundant consumer goods and relative freedom. Yet those who died so that the South could remain what the country as a whole is now becoming continue to be publicly unmourned.

The transformation of Vietnam along "southern" lines makes difficult comparisons between postwar Vietnam and postbellum America. Still, there are some similarities between the Vietnamese South and the American South. Both, unlike their northern counterparts, were heavily agrarian; both were defeated in a civil war; and both have been feminized in the cultural memory of their respective societies. The association of femininity with the Vietnamese South actually predates Communist victory. The lack of strong allegiance to Confucian ideology among southerners, their greater interest in making money rather than in acquiring diplomas or joining the bureaucracy—all these fed into a set of gender stereotypes in which women were associated with economic activities and lack of access to formal education and public life. Even the popularity of Buddhism in the South could be taken as a sign of femininity, since women were its greatest source of support. The North, however, with its stronger Confucian legacy and its role as a source of bureaucratic and political manpower, was cast as more masculine. Other regional differences were also described in gendered terms: southerners, living in the fertile Mekong Delta, were indolent and hedonistic in comparison with the rest of their compatriots.

The very qualities that seemed to explain southern defeat at war, however, may explain southern success in peacetime. With Doi Moi, postwar reconstruction has been cast in economic terms. The two heavily masculine sectors, the bureaucracy and the army, are retrenching while the private trading sector, a traditional feminine domain, is expanding. The social transformation of Vietnam since Doi Moi has gen-

Figure 6.3.   Billboard, Ho Chi Minh City. Photograph by Hue-
Tam Ho Tai.

erated much ambivalence, not to mention regional tensions. This ambivalence focuses on two sets of issues, both of which have found
expression in gender symbolism: the first involves the shifting status of
those involved in economic activities and those engaged in intellectual
and political pursuits; the second concerns memory and forgetting. The
shift from political status to economic power is dramatized through the
image of the "general of the interior," while youthful fickleness seems
embodied by the nubile fashion plates who decorate magazine covers
and billboards (fig. 6.3).

The year after Doi Moi was launched, the film *How to Behave* (*Cau
Chuyen Tu Te*) by Tran Van Thuy was released in Hanoi.[27] The film's
theme was the search for the meaning of the term *tu te*, which can mean
roughly "decency," "kindness," or "appropriateness." As the filmmaker
looked, mostly in vain, for people who lived according to this principle,
he came across war veterans whose medals had been earned in battles
from Dien Bien Phu (1954) to Khe Sanh (1968) but were now reduced
to eking out a living driving pedicabs, repairing bicycles, or peddling
vegetables by the roadside. Meanwhile, rich and idle young Vietnamese
pursued the good life, which consisted of surrounding themselves with

consumer goods. The most revealing moments of the film involve two women. One, who in the filmmaker's eyes best represents the meaning of "decency," is a peasant who was abandoned by her husband and hounded out of her village after she contracted leprosy. Wishing to provide shelter for her small boy in case she died, she had built a house brick by brick with her bare hands, even as her flesh was being eaten away by disease. This is the idealized self-sacrificing mother of popular culture, just as her feckless spouse represents the unreliable male. The film also provides her with an opposite, the grasping wife, who has equally strong roots in popular culture. She is represented by a self-confident, well-to-do urban woman in designer glasses who declares: "In practical terms, kindness nowadays means someone doing you a favor by using either political influence or material wealth. Kindness is an old-fashioned idea that only older people talk about. Today, people are far too busy to discuss outmoded concepts like that."

This self-regarding young woman has her literary counterpart in the short story "The General Retires" (Tuong Ve Huu) by Nguyen Huy Thiep.[28] In this story, which created a stir when it was published in 1988, Nguyen Huy Thiep pits a retired general against his daughter-in-law. Their confrontation is narrated in an affectless voice by the general's son, who is supposed to be the head of the family yet does not feel entirely responsible for the welfare of his household. The general symbolizes all the old virtues of the revolution but also its limitations. He clings to the spirit of egalitarianism in the face of growing social stratification. Coming from humble peasant stock, he is uncomfortable among the paraphernalia of middle-class aspirations his son and daughter-in-law are accumulating. He is more at ease with the peasant couple who care for his aged mother than with his own children and grandchildren, who despise his lack of education. Above all, he is made to feel superfluous and he eventually retreats from the domestic battlefield and rejoins his old regiment. The story ends with his son's laconic report that his father has died in battle, presumably in Cambodia.

The old general has been routed from his home (from which he had been absent for decades) by his daughter-in-law, who well deserves the popular nickname of "general of the interior." She is the epitome of the competent housewife who knows to the last penny how much should be spent on wedding festivities: enough to cut a dash, not so much as to cause financial difficulties. Like her husband, she is well educated and thus a symbol of the postwar preference for knowledge over revolutionary virtue. She is also an urban icon. Employed full-time as a physician in a maternity clinic, she augments the family's income by raising German dogs for sale to the nouveaux riches of northern Vietnam who, for the first time in decades, have possessions to protect. Her father-in-law, however, discovers to his horror that she feeds her dogs with aborted fetuses from the clinic. In northern Vietnam, where restaurants selling dog meat are spreading everywhere in the wake of Doi Moi, readers will recognize this as a metaphor for the topsy-turvy state of postwar society, which allows dogs to eat human flesh. Once her father-in-law has expressed revulsion, the wife is forced to stop making use of fetuses as free dog food. She also has to stop raising dogs, since the loss of free food makes this sideline unprofitable. While the old general sym-bolizes revolutionary morality and the link with the heroic and simpler past, his daughter-in-law embodies the amorality of the market. Yet, like the grieving old women who have been honored by the state, she, too, is a mother. Her children, however, are alive, not dead, and it is her duty to see to their welfare. Popular images of postwar women as ruth-less "generals of the interior" obfuscate the responsibilities that a male-dominated culture has assigned to them as mothers yet are difficult to fulfill on civil servants' salaries.

The loss of status and income of males in the public sector is captured in the short story "The Waltz of the Chamber Pot" ("Vu Dieu cai Bo") by Nguyen Quang Than.[29] The author sets up a humorous but sharp contrast between the poverty-stricken and ineffectual intellectual, the still powerful but obstructive party cadre, and the prosperous and pro-ductive (female) entrepreneur with whom both are involved. Although the intellectual is nominally on the payroll of a research institute, there is no money to fund his research, so he has to seek employment in the private sector. He is hired by the woman entrepreneur, supposedly to teach her little boy English, but in reality to be his nursemaid. The cham-ber pot is thus the symbol of his loss of status and of his fall into a demeaning, feminine occupation. The woman keeps in the good graces of the party cadre because of his remaining political clout but has little use for him personally because he is sexually impotent. Indeed, the only man capable of satisfying this cheerfully hedonistic woman is another (male) entrepreneur who breezes in and out of the story, bringing with him both news of the world outside Vietnam and funds of dubious prov-enance. The postwar economy, the story seems to imply, has reversed traditional equations between gender and power and has emasculated once powerful males.

WOMEN IN THE MUSEUM

The multifaceted role of women in society and cultural memory has found expression in the split personalities of the two museums dedicated to women, one in Ho Chi Minh City and the other in Hanoi. The Ho Chi Minh City Museum of Women tries to negotiate the multiplicity of roles that Vietnamese society assigns to women by embracing an all-inclusive definition of their identity. Thus, visitors are greeted by a large wall poster that details feminine qualities through the ages:

> The Vietnamese women have the tradition of being "heroic, unsubmissive, faithful and competent: which are materialized in various fields of activity: the Vietnamese women fight off the enemy for national salvation. . . . When it was necessary, Vietnamese women also knew how to rule the country. South Vietnamese women are not only talented producers, creating well-known articles, but are also competent housekeepers, experts in family management, tailoring, embroidery, in cooking tasty meals, making cakes and jams—thus embellishing the life of the family and society.[30]

The Ho Chi Minh City Museum of Women opened its doors to the public on April 4, 1985, in time to coincide with the tenth anniversary of the fall of Saigon. Established before Doi Moi, it devotes far more space to showcasing women's wartime contributions than does its counterpart in Hanoi, which was inaugurated a full decade later. An official of the Hanoi Museum said, "We think that the Museum of Women of Ho Chi Minh City pays too much attention to war. We want to focus on the role of women in peace."[31] By the time the Hanoi Museum of Women opened in November 1995, the great wave of commemoration had largely ebbed, and public interest was refocusing on the present. In the lobby of the museum stands a bronze statue—the winning design in a competition that attracted over fifty entries—of a young mother holding a child aloft on her shoulder. In the words of the museum guide,

> The statue is designed to represent the most valuable attributes of womanhood. She is shown with one hand forcing down the forces of disturbance. Her face is full of resolve, her breasts jut out to part the ocean waves. They are full of life-giving milk. On her shoulder is perched a young child, for it is the responsibility of women to nurture future generations, their most sacred task. The child looks forward to the future, his arms stretched out to embrace all the challenges of life.

Over the statue is a huge chandelier whose lights are "in the shape of milk drops," reminding spectators once again of the nurturing role of mothers (fig. 6.4). A mural will be created as a backdrop for the statue

Figure 6.4.   Mother and child statue, Museum of Women, Hanoi. Photograph by Hue-Tam Ho Tai.

when more funds are available. It will show "the river that is formed from the thousands of drops of milk from the mother." The mural will illustrate not only motherhood but also the popular saying "When drinking water, remember its source" (*uong nuoc nho nguon*). This popular saying has been widely appropriated by the state to remind the population of its debt toward the revolutionary generation for the sacrifices it made to safeguard independence. In the context of the museum, however, that saying seems stripped of its political message and serves merely as a reminder of the debt owed to mothers in all circumstances.

Instead of trying to integrate women's multiple roles into a single identity, the Hanoi Museum of Women spreads them over three floors. The exhibits begin on the ground floor with celebrations of Vietnamese motherhood inspired by religious cults, folk myths, and history. The second floor is devoted to the history of women during the Revolution and the War Against the Americans and to the achievements of the Women's Union to whom the museum belongs. The third floor is given over to women's clothing. Although many of the costumes featured are those of ethnic minorities and thus can be said to have documentary value, the main aim of the exhibits apparently is to catch the eye. Indeed, other exhibits are purely about current fashions. Such is the case of the revolving display that features *ao dai* by one of Hanoi's top designers and provides the end point of the exhibit. Thus, as one progresses from floor to floor, the image of Vietnamese womanhood shifts from mother, to mature young woman, to young girl; from traditional, self-sacrificing, hardworking, thrifty mother, to courageous peasant guerrilla defending the homeland in wartime, to fashion-conscious, big-spending, urban young woman.

In Ho Chi Minh City, the message inside the museum is somewhat more consistent and, as the Hanoi official suggested, more focused on women's revolutionary contributions, in keeping with the state's narrative. Outside, however, the commemorative concerns of the state are being undermined by those of private individuals. Although the museum is open free of charge, it has few visitors and a very small budget. As in other sister institutions in the South, the staff stretches the museum's income by allowing weddings to be held on its lawns and catering banquets. An annex is also used for meetings and dances. When the museum mounted a photographic exhibit in honor of Heroic Mothers in 1995, it flanked the lawn with temporary partitions upon which were affixed photographs of recipients of medals. They were women in their seventies or older, their faces etched with lines of sorrow, and they were invariably clad in drab peasant pajamas. On weekends, wedding parties would assemble in front of the museum for collective photographs. The bride was usually attired in a Victorian dress and the groom in a tuxedo. The pictures of old women who had lost their sons in the war formed a disregarded backdrop for the recording of the bride's passage into marriage and motherhood and the couple's affirmation of their membership in the rising urban, Westernized middle class. In southern towns and villages where museums are unavailable for this purpose, cemeteries to revolutionary martyrs have become a favorite spot for taking bridal pictures. Sites that are meant to commemorate war are thus used as backdrops for the reaffirmation of life and of social continuity. But the life and society they celebrate are very different from the ones that the Revolution sought to bring about and that the War Against the Americans was fought to preserve.

CONSUMING OBLIVION

While the state wished to honor those women who had given more than three sons to the revolutionary cause, it was also seeking to enforce its birth control policy, which limited to two the number of children each family was permitted to have. At the beginning of the campaign, the state had emphasized the need to limit population growth in order to create "a stable society and a prosperous country." By 1996, that patriotic slogan had been replaced by a less public-minded appeal: "Limit yourselves to two children in order to raise them and educate them well." Such an appeal bespeaks the end of the wartime ethos personified by the Heroic Mothers and the ascendancy of the middle-class culture represented by fictional females and fashion models. It also signifies the declining power of the official epic narrative of glorious war and revolution to inspire.

In *Fable for the Year 2000,* a play written in 1991 by Le Hung, a young Vietnamese competes with an older man over the right to pass over a bridge. While the old man claims that the privilege of age and the enormous sacrifices his generation has made give him the right of way, the younger man retorts, "What legacy have you left us but dire poverty?"[32] Discussions of postwar greed and selfishness form a strange contrast to 1920s debates about the collusion between the patriarchal family and colonial rule. In the 1920s, it was young people who, using the image of young girls to represent their own sense of powerlessness, attacked the family as oppressive. Their rebellion combined desire for personal emancipation and commitment to a cause that was both larger and nobler than the family: the liberation of the entire nation. In the 1990s, the tables have turned. Old soldiers, like the retired general of Nguyen Huy Thiep's short story, represent the revolutionary cause and the larger community, while the young mother who is unwilling to subordinate the good of her family to that of the nation represents the current retreat from public-mindedness.

Although *Fable for the Year 2000* appears to pit revolutionary memory against postwar oblivion, forgetting comes from many sources and in many guises. It is not simple ingratitude, nor solely a matter of generational differences. For some, it can be a rejection of the epic narrative of national glory bought at the price of immense sacrifice which is at the heart of the state's commemorative project. For others, it can be a refusal to falsify the past by internalizing a narrative that is at odds with one's own experience. Public memory, for them, is not a place of respite from official history, but its handmaid.

Forgetting can also be an attempt to keep the past from damaging the present. Memory may be socially constructed.[33] It may be shaped collectively, but it also defines the nature and boundaries of community on the basis of shared experience and shared sentiment. It is usually evoked, even constructed, in communal settings such as weddings, funerals, or death anniversaries. These are events in which ties of kinship and community are ordinarily reaffirmed through the recitation of personal anecdotes as much as by participation in common rituals. Yet, the divisiveness engendered by war and revolution confronts many Vietnamese with the impossibility of using memory to reinforce family feelings. In the North, the wounds left by the Land Reform program of the 1950s have not completely healed. Novels such as Duong Thu Huong's *Paradise of the Blind* expose the rifts it caused in individual families.[34] In the South, both war and revolution are behind the suppression of memory. The difficulty of remembering failure and defeat is only one factor in this suppression.[35] Whereas many overseas Vietnamese mark April 30 as the Day of Shame (Ngay Quoc Han), in counterpoint to the Vietnamese state's celebration of victory and reunification, those who remain in Vietnam but fought against Communism do not have the luxury of publicly holding their own rites of remembrance. But southern forgetting is not merely a case of individual memory collapsing under the weight of state suppression. Practically every southern family has members who fought on different sides of the Vietnam War and whose sufferings are therefore blamed on different agents. Every memory calls forth a countermemory: stories of imprisonment under the South Vietnamese regime are countered by narratives of experience in reeducation camps under the new Communist one. Anecdotes celebrating heroic deeds in guerrilla bases are met with tales of tragic death on the high seas while trying to escape the country. Some extended families have members who bear the scars of torture and others who have been accused of inflicting torture on prisoners. Satisfaction at the outcome of the War Against the Americans (as its supporters call it) clashes with nostalgia for the prosperity and freedom of the pre-Communist era as others remember it. Sometimes the division of war is not spread across a large extended family but has to be accommodated within a single individual. Some mothers who have been honored because their sons died in the revolutionary cause had others sons who fought in the Armed Forces of the Republic of Vietnam, and died in the war or suffered in its aftermath. While those who fought against the French, the Americans, or the South Vietnamese government are interred in cemeteries devoted to revolutionary heroes, the remains of those who fought on the other side in the Armed Forces of the Republic of Vietnam had to be taken away when its military cemetery was razed after 1975. Only the suppression of memories such as these makes possible the continuation of family life, family sentiment, and even personal sanity.

Thus, for the sake of family harmony, southern dead, absent from national commemoration, often go unmentioned in the collective narratives of their extended families. Condemned to the shadows, they refuse, however, to remain unmourned. Their demand to be recognized, however, threatens the peace of the community at the level of family, community, and nation. The destruction of the cemetery has fed popular stories of ghosts who wander along the highway where it used to be located and disturb the living, as do the wandering ghosts of popular culture who must be appeased by rituals of remembrance in the seventh month.

Bequests sometimes carry with them bitter memories. As the narrator of *Paradise of the Blind* recognizes, "Forgive me my aunt: I'm going to sell this house and leave all this behind. We can honor the wishes of the dead with a few flowers on a grave somewhere. I can't squander my life tending these faded flowers, these shadows, the legacy of past crimes."[36] New acquisitions, by contrast, come without the burden of memory. It is this dimension that makes them so desirable as building blocks in a new family narrative that is not made up of loss, grief, and divisive bitterness.

The consumer culture is stripping many symbols of war service of their commemorative shadows. The magazine *Phu Nu* (*Women*), which is published by the Ho Chi Minh City Women's Union, is full of articles about fashion. In June 1995, when commemorative activities were at their height, it ran an article on hats. The magazine cover featured a model who was too young to have been born while the War Against the Americans was being fought. She was wearing a black sleeveless silk top with a mandarin collar and frog closings, which managed to be reminiscent all at once of the black pajamas worn by peasants and guerrillas and of the Western fashion fad known as "Indo-chic." On her head was a pith helmet. Colored green to provide jungle camouflage, this had once been a useful piece of military attire. Repainted shocking pink to attract attention, it had become a frivolous item of feminine decoration. It was an eye-catching illustration of the ability of the market to transform war memorabilia into transient fashion.

The complexity of women's representational roles in Vietnamese public culture should not obscure the fact that women have real lives that are infinitely more complex, and that women's images and women's lives are sometimes in conflict. Political liberalization made possible more open discussion of war and of women's experiences in war; it accompanied the transition to a market economy in which many women, especially the peasant women who contributed the most to the war effort, are losing ground. Thanks to the new openness, the picture of wartime gender equality is being modified.[37] Meanwhile, their postwar circumstances are leading some women to rethink their sacrifices. The Heroic Mothers, icons of revolutionary memory, are often forgotten as real individuals. At the end of 1995, a published survey disclosed that half a million women were living alone without children to support them. Because this coincided with the tail end of the festivities honoring Heroic Mothers, it led to discussions in the press of the plight of women whose children had died in the war and were now destitute. It was disclosed that some women, including war veterans, were opting to have children outside marriage because they had little or no hope of finding a husband, yet wanted to experience motherhood and to provide a modicum of security for their old age.[38] And while fictional female entrepreneurs seemed to be gaining in power and status in the new market-driven society, the press was also full of articles concerning young peasant women who had been lured into the cities by prospects of jobs in the private sector only to fall into prostitution.

Winners and losers in the market economy, young and old, grieving and forward-looking, self-sacrificing and hedonistic, icons of memory, symbols of forgetting; women embody the dilemmas and contradictions that are involved in making sense of war and postwar, revolution and counterrevolution in Vietnam.

NOTES

This chapter is a revised version of a paper presented at the annual meeting of the Association for Asian Studies in Honolulu, March 1996.

1. The Vietnamese term for commemoration, *tuong niem*, combines "imagining" (*tuong*) with "remembering" (*niem*).

2. Da Ngan, "Nha Khong Co Dan Ong" ["The House with No Men"] (1990), in *Literature News: Nine Stories from the Vietnam Writers' Union*

Newspaper, Bao Van Nghe, selected and translated with introduction and illustrations by Rosemary Nguyen (New Haven, Conn: Council on Southeast Asia Studies, 1997), 38–53.

3. Margery Wolf, *Women and the Family in Rural Taiwan* (Stanford, Calif.: Stanford University Press, 1972), 32–41. Her argument, which has already been questioned in the case of China, needs to be considered in the context of the Vietnamese tradition of village endogamy, which substantively modifies the effects of virilocal residence on women.

4. Pham Quynh, "Dia Vi Nguoi Dan Ba trong Xa Hoi Nuoc Ta" ["The Position of Women in Our Society"], *Nam Phong [Southern Wind]* 82 (April 1924); quoted in Hue-Tam Ho Tai, *Radicalism and the Origins of the Vietnamese Revolution* (Cambridge, Mass.: Harvard University Press, 1992), 98.

5. It would appear that the tale is based on a real event that took place in the fourteenth century. See Nguyen Nam, "Luoc Dich Quoc Ngu Cuoi The Ky XIX ["Translations into the Romanized Script in the Nineteenth Century"] in *Tap Chi Han Nom [Han Nom Journal]* 1, no. 34 (1998): 20–31 n. 13.

6. George L. Mosse, *Fallen Soldiers: Reshaping Memory of the World Wars* (New York: Oxford University Press, 1990).

7. Ibid., 225.

8. For a translation into English, see Huynh Sanh Thong, *An Anthology of Vietnamese Poems from the Eleventh through the Twentieth Centuries* (New Haven, Conn.: Yale University Press, 1996), 401–18.

9. See Patricia Pelley, "The History of Resistance and the Resistance to History in Post-colonial Constructions of the Past," in *Essays into Vietnamese Pasts,* ed. K. W. Taylor and John K. Whitmore (Ithaca, N.Y.: Cornell Southeast Asia Program, 1995).

10. This figure was prevalent in the cultural debates of the 1920s. See Hue-Tam Ho Tai, *Radicalism and the Origins of the Vietnamese Revolution,* chap. 3 ("Daughters of Annam").

11. Vietnamese discomfort with the equation of rape and invasion suggests a reason behind the discrepancy between Chinese accounts of the capture of the Trung Sisters in A.D. 43 and Vietnamese oral tradition, according to which they met their death when they threw themselves into the Hat River to elude capture.

12. Ho Chi Minh, *Le Procès de la colonisation française* (Paris: Librairie du Travail, 1925). It has been suggested that Nguyen The Truyen actually wrote this book, since Ho, at the time, was either in China or on his way there from Moscow.

13. Keith W. Taylor, *The Birth of Vietnam* (Berkeley and Los Angeles: University of California Press, 1983), 91.

14. Quoted in Phan Huy Le et al., *Lich Su Viet Nam [History of Vietnam],* vol. 1 (Hanoi: NXB Dai Hoc va Giao Duc Chuyen Nghiep, 1991), 225.

15. Nguyen Don Phuc, "Dan Ba Dong Phuong" ["Oriental Women"], *Nam Phong* 101 (December 1925); quoted in Hue-Tam Ho Tai, *Radicalism and the Origins of the Vietnamese Revolution,* 99. The Four Virtues are *cong* (good management), *dung* (decorous comportment), *ngon* (harmonious speech), and *hanh* (appropriate behavior).

16. See Lynn Hunt, *The Family Romance of the French Revolution* (Berkeley

and Los Angeles: University of California Press, 1994); Sara Maza, "The Diamond Necklace Affair Revisited (1785–1786): The Case of the Disappearing Queen," in *Eroticism and the Body Politic,* ed. Lynn Hunt, (Baltimore: Johns Hopkins University Press, 1991).

17. Drew Faust, *Mothers of Invention: Women of the Slaveholding South in the American Civil War* (Chapel Hill: University of North Carolina Press, 1996).

18. Nina Silber, *The Romance of Reunion: Northerners and the South, 1865–1900* (Chapel Hill: University of North Carolina Press, 1993).

19. This is vividly captured in Karen Gottschang Turner with Phan Thanh Hao, *Even the Women Must Fight: Memories of War From North Vietnam* (New York: Wiley, 1998).

20. The entire speech was printed in *Saigon Giai Phong [Liberated Saigon],* January 11, 1995.

21. Trinh Cong Son, "Ngu Di Con" ["Sleep, My Child"], 1969, author's translation.

22. David Ignatius, "Vietnamese Begin to Question If War Was Worth Sacrifices," *Washington Post,* November 2, 1991.

23. Bao Ninh, *The Sorrow of War;* English version by Frank Palmos based on the translation from the Vietnamese by Vo Bang Thanh and Phan Thanh Hao with Katerina Pierce (New York: Pantheon, 1995); Duong Thu Huong, *Novel without a Name,* trans. by Phan Huy Duong and Nina McPherson (New York: Morrow, 1995). *Novel Wilhout a Name* was originally written in 1989.

24. This is based not on personal observation but on a private communication from a Hanoi intellectual.

25. Trinh Cong Son, *Gia Tai cua Me [Mother's Legacy],* 1969.

26. Mona Ouzouf, "Le Panthéon: L'Ecole Normale des morts," in *Lieux de mémoire,* vol. 1, ed. Pierre Nora (Paris: Gallimard, 1984), 157

27. Tran Van Thuy, *How to Behave (Cau Chuyen Tu Te),* 1988; distributed in the United States by First Films: Icarus.

28. Nguyen Huy Thiep, "The General Retires," in *The General Retires and Other Stories,* translated with an introduction by Greg Lockhart (Kuala Lumpur: Oxford in Asia, 1991).

29. Nguyen Quang Than, "The Waltz of the Chamber Pot" ["*Vu Dieu cai Bo*"] (1991), in *Literature News: Nine Stories from the Vietnam Writers' Union Newspaper,* Bao Van Nghe, 6–37.

30. This is a verbatim extract from the English-language portion of the wall poster.

31. Communication with author, January 1996.

32. Reported in *Far Eastern Economic Review,* May 11, 1992.

33. Since the appearance of Maurice Halbwachs's pioneering work, *Les Cadres sociaux de la mémoire,* scholarly attention has focused on the social construction of memory. Less attention has been paid to social amnesia, although it is a theme that reverberates in societies that have undergone divisive episodes such as Indonesia in 1965 and Cambodia under the Khmer Rouge. In both cases, it is reported, it is memory, if publicly verbalized, that threatens community.

34. Duong Thu Huong, *Paradise of the Blind* (1988), trans. Phan Huy Duong and Nina McPherson (New York: Morrow, 1991).

35. On the link between failure and forgetting, see Michel Bozon and Anne Marie Thiesse, "The Collapse of Memory: The Case of the Farm Workers (French Vexin, Pays de France)" in *Between History and Memory,* ed. Marie Noelle Bourguet, Lucette Valensi, and Nathan Wachtel (Chur: Harwood Academic Publishers, 1990).

36. Duong Thu Huong, *Paradise of the Blind,* 258.

37. See in particular the accounts in Karen Gottschang Turner with Phan Thanh Hao, *Even the Women Must Fight.*

38. See, for example, ibid., 157–63. Also Ngo Ngoc Boi, "The Blanket of Scraps," in *Literature News: Nine Stories from the Vietnam Writers' Union Newspaper,* Bao Van Nghe, 96–123.

SEVEN

Contests of Memory

*Remembering and Forgetting War
in the Contemporary Vietnamese Cinema*

Mark Philip Bradley

In a modest house in a residential quarter of Hanoi, an elderly mother says good-bye to the guests attending the rituals surrounding the death anniversary (*ngay gio*) for her son who was killed in the American War. After the last guests depart, she collapses onto the floor crying and calls out for her family to assemble around her. Reminding her children that their brother's bones are still lying in a military cemetery in the South, she implores them to bring his remains home so that she can lie next to him when she dies. Her son agrees, adding, "Thank heaven my sister has so many connections." His observation prompts an increasingly acrimonious exchange between his sister and his wife:

SISTER:	Shouldn't we all help? I'm busy with my husband's business trip to Singapore. You both have never seen Saigon. You could combine business with a little sight-seeing.
WIFE:	My husband is busy with the shop, and I'm taking care of mother. You have more time.
SISTER:	I'll talk straight. You joined this family. Help take care of it. You got my brother's room because he died.
WIFE:	And you got some of mother's gold. We don't get paid for taking care of her.
SISTER:	I had to borrow that gold to grease a few wheels.
WIFE:	Our family has special status because our brother got killed. That's why they let you pass your exam and get a job in Hanoi.

> SISTER: You're wrong. I got that another way. But it is through family status that they don't close your store!
>
> WIFE: Look at my husband. He can't go. I don't know my way around the South. How could we exhume the bones?
>
> SISTER: You think I'm good at it? It is hard enough to take care of my husband and his family. It's expensive to transport bones. Where would I get the money?
>
> MOTHER (CRYING): Stop it! All of you. You're so ungrateful to the dead. But you were quick enough to use our new family status. My son, if only you hadn't died in the South. Let me try to find the bones! If I die trying, none of you will care. As for the money, are these packets enough? If not, let's sell the furniture, the house. But I must bring my son's remains home.

Offering a solution to this impasse, the sister suggests that her husband's brother, an unemployed veteran, could use the money and go on behalf of the family. The veteran agrees but refuses the money. The sister tells him, "Stop living in the clouds. No one is like you now—doing something for nothing." The veteran replies, "Your brother died asking for nothing."

This painful symbolic representation of the tensions between remembering and forgetting the American War in contemporary northern Vietnamese society, which formed the core of Tran Vu and Nguyen Huu Luyen's 1987 film, *Brothers and Relations (Anh va Em),* was a sharp and highly unusual challenge to the official memories of war carefully constructed by the Vietnamese state throughout the wars against the French and the Americans and in their aftermath. The official narrative of sacred war (*chien tranh than thanh*) celebrated the heroic resistance of soldiers, workers, and peasants in an effort to infuse a larger meaning onto the suffering and death caused by war and to legitimate the state's twin goals of national liberation and socialist revolution. Many of the archetypal figures in the state cults of remembrance are present in *Brothers and Relations.* The sanctified memory of the fallen soldier, the probity of the simple veteran, and the self-sacrificing heroic mother all occupy a central place in the official pantheon of revolutionary heroes as symbols of selfless patriotic and socialist virtue. But in *Brothers and Relations* they function quite differently, standing in sharp contrast to the self-seeking daughter and her family intent upon using for their own advancement the special privileges granted by the state because of their brother's death in battle. For the filmmakers, the family's unwillingness to honor their brother's memory comes to represent the wider ingratitude, inequity, selfishness, and immorality they attribute to post-war Vietnamese society, in which the state's wartime promises of socialist revolution remain unfulfilled.

Brothers and Relations is one of a number of revisionist films released in the mid-1980s that transformed the shape and content of historical memory in contemporary northern Vietnam. The Vietnamese state had employed film, with its power to capture a particularly broad audience, along with such popular cultural forms of remembrance as war memorials and museums, novels, poetry, paintings, and commemorative rituals honoring the war dead and their families to disseminate its construction of war. In appropriating one of these key mediums, the revisionist films of the 1980s articulated a form of what Michel Foucault termed "counter-memory,"[1] the residual or resistant strains of remembrance embedded in popular consciousness that withstand official constructions of the historical past.

The films appeared in a period that favored the advancement of a contrapuntal representation of war in Vietnam. The embrace of market economic reforms at the Sixth Party Congress of the Vietnamese Communist Party in 1986 brought with it a significant loosening of state control in the cultural realm. As one scholar of this period has argued, the policy of Renovation (Doi Moi) in the arts allowed intellectuals to work with a degree of freedom unknown since the Popular Front period in colonial Vietnam in the late 1930s.[2] But if official censorship relaxed somewhat, so, too, did the state subsidies for the arts that had provided the single source of funding for the Vietnamese film industry. The demands of the market economy put new pressures on filmmakers to ensure that the content of the films they produced resonated with potential filmgoers.[3]

Emboldened by this new climate of artistic freedom and market incentives, the works of revisionist filmmakers mounted a powerful, if sometimes oblique, narrative challenge to official memories of the Vietnamese experience of the war and attracted large, appreciative audiences.[4] They posed several far-reaching questions that undermined the central premises on which the state's memorializing project had rested. Who rightfully possesses the memory of fallen soldiers? Whose wartime sacrifice is deserving of commemoration? And what are the real legacies of war? In framing their responses, filmmakers consciously rejected the prevailing aesthetics of socialist realism that had governed Vietnamese cinema and given shape to the state's heroic narrative of war. In its place they made use of a diverse repertoire of rich visual imagery that reached back to ritual forms of family and village life long suppressed by the state, the metaphorical and subversive uses of gender in traditional literary idioms, and the discursive strategies of anticolonial political discourse familiar to much of their intended audience. Reversing and supplanting many of the symbolic meanings the state ascribed to war, the revisionist films of the 1980s reveal the contours of the contested articulation of war remembrance in contemporary northern Vietnam.[5]

WHO RIGHTFULLY POSSESSES THE MEMORY OF FALLEN SOLDIERS?

The fallen soldier is perhaps the most potent symbol of official efforts to commemorate and legitimate the national experience of war. As George Mosse argues in his seminal account of state memorializing practices in Europe in the aftermath of World War I, the body of the soldier killed in battle came to transcend death and was increasingly linked to the highest aspirations of patriotic nationalism. Images of the fallen soldier in the arms of Christ, Mosse asserts, "projected the traditional belief in martyrdom and resurrection onto the nation as an all-encompassing civic religion."[6] Central to the European state-sponsored cult of the fallen soldier was the construction of war monuments and military cemeteries that functioned both as shrines of national worship and as physical symbols of the superior claims made by the state on the memories of those who died in battle.

The development of memorial holidays and specially designed cemeteries by the Vietnamese state to render the death of soldiers as symbols of national revolutionary martyrdom mirrors key aspects of these interwar European practices. Like its counterparts in Europe, the Vietnamese state sought to own the memory of its war dead, an effort most starkly revealed in the official memorial services organized by local party cadres. Here a fallen solder's sacrifice for the state and revolution, rather than this relationship to his lineage or village, served to exclusively define the meaning of his life and death.[7]

Fallen soldiers occupy a central place in the symbolic vocabulary of many of the revisionist films of the 1980s, but they are used to subvert rather than affirm the scaffolding of official memories erected by the state and to stake a claim for the primacy of individuals and civil society as the rightful heirs to memories of the war dead.[8] *Brothers and Relations* places the remains of the fallen soldier at the center of its withering critique of an amnesic postwar Vietnamese society (fig. 7.1). At the end of the film, the veteran encounters his brother and his wife in the parking lot of the airport outside of Hanoi as he returns from his trip to recover

Figure 7.1. The Truong Son Cemetery on the Ho Chi Minh Trail contains
the graves of nineteen thousand North Vietnamese soldiers. Photograph by
Hue-Tam Ho Tai.

her brother's remains. Before he can speak, the wife giddily informs him
they are off to Singapore for their much-anticipated business trip. When
he tells her that the small box he is carrying contains the remains of her
brother, she absentmindedly nods and quickly asks their driver to pull
away because they are late for their flight. The scene shifts to a crude
hand-marked grave in a rocky grotto near a rushing stream. Against the
accompaniment of swelling traditional music, the veteran's voice ad-
dresses the fallen soldier: "Your sisters are busy. I won't take you back
to them. Your mother will be sad, but she will understand. Stay here.
This new place is your home." In a society indifferent to the memories
of fallen soldiers, the filmmakers suggest, the monopolizing claims of
state commemorative practices no longer hold significance. Only on the
marginal bounds of civil society can they be infused with a new, more
private and resonant meaning.

Nguyen Xuan Son's 1987 film, *Fairy Tale for Seventeen-Year-Olds*
(*Truyen Co Tich cho Tuoi 17*), appropriates official memories of the
fallen soldier in gentler but nonetheless subversive ways. The film tells
the story of a young student, An, who falls in love with a soldier when
she sees his picture and hears his mother read from his letters written
from the front. An and the soldier never meet, but their tender relationship emerges through letters they exchange with each other and in a
series of dream sequences in which the young girl encounters the spectral
figures of the soldier and his regiment, who appear to be taking shelter
from the war in a dark cave. An's love for the soldier meets severe official
disapproval as a violation of the wartime imperative of collective self-
sacrifice. In an early scene, her teacher asks An's class to prepare an

essay on a poem "depicting the image of a revolutionary you like best." When An offers an appreciation of a poem about a revolutionary's love for a young girl, her teacher gives her a low mark, telling her she should have discussed a poem that portrayed his revolutionary determination. Later, when the teacher realizes that An herself is in love with a young soldier, she holds a "self-criticism" session in which she and An's class-mates tell An that her behavior is inappropriate and disruptive to the spirit of her class.

In contrast to these official judgments, *Fairy Tale for Seventeen-Year-Olds* concentrates on the approving support An receives for her love of the soldier from her father and the soldier's mother. For both of them, the war has taken a deeply personal toll. Her father is a veteran of the French war whose wife died of grief after going years without word of the fate of their son, who apparently died in battle. He tells An her relationship with the soldier is a "fairy tale" but indulgently advises her to continue it as she is too young to know the "realities of war." The soldier's mother, Mrs. Thu, a political cadre whose own husband was killed in battle during the war against the French, also affirms An's love for her son, sharing his letters with her and urging An to write to him in return.

The film ends on the day of Hanoi's victory in the American War. Just before Mrs. Thu is to give a victory day speech in the courtyard of An's school, she receives a telegram with the news that her son was killed in one of the war's final battles. As she gives her speech celebrating "the heroic sacrifices that won us victory from the American imperialists," the pain in her face betrays the more personal meaning of her son's death and the memory of her husband. She tells An's father later, "I never thought I would experience such grief on this day of our victory," to which he replies, "We've won independence at the cost of young lives." In its focus on the human dimension of a soldier's life and death, *Fairy Tale for Seventeen-Year-Olds* suggests the necessity of a more intimate interpretation of the memory of fallen soldiers than the one put forward through the state's commemorative practices to provide essential con-solations for the private sacrifices of war. As the young girl An says in the final frames of the film after she comes to know of her lover's death, "My love made me happy. I want to retain that happiness . . . to know nothing but my beautiful fairy tale."

Perhaps the most complex exploration of the question of who right-fully possesses the memory of fallen soldiers emerged in Dang Nhat Minh's 1984 film, *When the Tenth Month Comes (Bao Gio cho den*

Thang Muoi), the first of the revisionist films to be released in Vietnam. Dang Nhat Minh, one of the most popular and influential filmmakers in Vietnam, set the film during the Vietnamese invasion of Pol Pot's Cambodia in 1979. This decision may have reflected the skeptical response of a war-weary population to the state's efforts to render the Vietnamese invasion and subsequent occupation of Cambodia (1979–89) within the official narrative of war as patriotic self-sacrifice, particularly when the state appeared unable to find employment in the civilian sector for demobilized veterans returning from the Cambodian campaigns. It is likely that the Cambodian setting of the film, which was released two years before the rise of the Renovation agenda eased state controls on filmmakers, also provided Dang Nhat Minh with a thinly disguised parable to advance his critique of state memorializing practices in a manner that implicated but did not directly challenge the more sacrosanct claims of official narratives of the French and American Wars.

When the Tenth Month Comes tells the story of the decision of a young woman named Duyen to keep the news that her husband was killed in battle hidden from her husband's family and village. By the end of the film Duyen comes to know that her behavior is improper. Kneeling next to the deathbed of her husband's father, she cries out, "I haven't told the truth. . . . I've done wrong." From the state's perspective, the nature of Duyen's error would have been obvious: she prevented her husband's memory from fulfilling its officially sanctioned commemorative purposes. At points the film does acknowledge the legitimacy of state claims on the fallen soldier's memory. Early in the film the father of Duyen's husband calls the death of his elder son during the American War a "patriotic sacrifice for the advancement of the national liberation movement and the socialist revolution." Similarly, the final scene of the film after the dead soldier's family and village have come to know of his wife's deception appears to suggest the official order has been restored. As martial music swells, Duyen's son and his teacher, surrounded by children carrying party banners, gaze admiringly upward at the yellow star and red background of the Vietnamese flag snapping purposefully in the wind. But these rather perfunctory scenes are oddly disconnected from the larger narrative of the film, better reflecting a bow to the very real concerns of continuing state censorship rather than a full embrace of official commemorative practices.

The film concentrates on the impact of the war on the interior lives of Duyen and her husband's family. When the state intrudes on their experiences, it is often represented in highly critical ways that undermine its memorializing pretensions. The least sympathetic characters in the film are two local party cadres, a sister of Duyen's husband and her husband. From their first appearance, arriving late for the death anniversary of the sister's mother in a serious breach of traditional filial etiquette, they are portrayed as vain, self-important, and grasping for power and position. Later the sister tells the heroine she should get her brother out of the army because she could find him a safer civilian position. "You two," she adds patronizingly, "just don't know how to get ahead." The film offers a more indirect critique of the state through the character of the village schoolteacher who aids Duyen in her deceptions by drawing a revealing parallel between the teacher's efforts to help the heroine hold on to her husband's memory and a radical shift in meaning of the poem he writes that gives the film its title. In an early scene the schoolteacher reads the first few lines of the poem to a friend—"When the Ten Month comes / The rice will be harvested in the fields / A full five tons rich in yield"—and says that *Literature and Arts (Van Nghe),* the leading literary journal in Hanoi, has promised to publish it with some changes. "Isn't it good enough as it is?" the friend asks. "Not quite realistic enough," he replies. "Productivity is up to seven or eight tons now." By the end of the film the schoolteacher has redrafted the poem, but instead of a socialist realist paean to rice production, it deals with how an individual can mediate the sorrow and pain of a loved one's death.

By contrast with the film's portrayal of the state, its depiction of Duyen's multiple social roles as wife, opera singer, and widow lends her character a surprisingly sympathetic form despite the evident disapproval of her actions. Duyen's relationship to her husband's family and village is clearly that of an outsider. Within Vietnamese patrilineal familial custom an in-law is "outside" (*ngoai*), a term used to describe nonpatrilineal kin and suggestive of the secondary role a wife occupies in her husband's family. As an opera singer and a former member of a traveling theatrical troupe, Duyen is also connected to a social group viewed with some ignominy in northern Vietnamese society as an alien presence that should properly remain apart from the closed formal structures of village life.[9]

In part Duyen's marginal and vulnerable position in her husband's family and village provides Dang Nhat Minh with a more impressionable and less dangerous agent for launching his critique of state claims on the memory of fallen soldiers than if he had chosen to center the film on one of the exemplary and resolute heroes and heroines of official memories of war. Duyen's social position as an outsider in her husband's family also allows her to occupy a symbolic role that is familiar to Vietnamese audiences and particularly well suited to the film's exploration of the more intimate and localized meanings of a soldier's death; the wife who brings dissension to her husband's family serves as a universally recognized trope in traditional Vietnamese folktales and literature for the competitive dangers conjugal relations can pose to the natural primacy of blood ties. The respect the film accords to Duyen's unfathomable grief as a widow mourning the death of her husband, however, ultimately lifts her character above these familiar social types. Its compassionate portrayal of Duyen's predicament emerges most affectingly in a scene of a village opera performance. Singing of the plight of a soldier's wife and her devotion to her husband, Duyen collapses on stage, overcome by the emotional parallels to her own situation.

But if the narrative of *When the Tenth Month Comes* at times accords Duyen an empathetic place, its broader focus remains a critical examination of the transgressions Duyen acknowledges at the end of the film and the path through which she comes to know her behavior is wrong. The film concentrates on Duyen's failure to fulfill her filial duties to her husband's family and his lineage and her moral obligations to his village in a manner that subtly undermines the state's monopolizing claims on the memory of her dead husband. It articulates its disapproval of Duyen's actions in a crucial scene in which the family of her husband observe the death anniversary of her husband's mother. At the culminating feast marking the anniversary, one family member reads a letter full of filial devotion purportedly written by the heroine's husband. The letter, however, is actually a fabricated one, written at Duyen's request by the village schoolteacher as a way of convincing the family that her husband remains alive.

When Duyen uses a death anniversary at which the soul of the departed ancestor is believed to be present to advance her deception, her actions emerge as a particularly egregious violation of traditional Vietnamese practices of remembering and propitiating the memory of the dead. The rites of the death anniversary, one leading scholar of these practices argues, are essential to affirming the primary familial obligations of filial piety (*hieu*), "symbolically joining the living, dead and yet to be born members of the family . . . in an intimate relationship of mutual dependency."[10] The visual dynamics of the scene sharpen the contrast between Duyen's serious breach of familial norms and the proper behavior of the people who surround her. As Duyen cowers in the shadowy corners of the frame, seemingly both fearful that the letter will not be believed and ashamed of what she has done, her husband's family demonstrate their respectful attitude toward the soul of the mother by dutifully undertaking the ritual practices that make up the formal observations of a death anniversary.

The film's particular concentration on the feasting component of the death anniversary also reinforces its focus on the claims of family and village, rather than the state, on the memory of Duyen's husband. The feast marking the death anniversary, in which a family traditionally invited its neighbors in the village to share, was among the central targets of a sustained campaign by the state against superstitious practices in northern Vietnam after its rise to power in 1945. For the state, the elaborate network of social exchange promoted through the feast both incurred wasted expenditure better used for collective economic purposes and represented undesirable feudal customs that promoted social inequality and status competition. In its place, the state promoted a simple didactic ceremony among the immediate family of the deceased that focused on the departed ancestor's contribution to the rise of a new revolutionary society. Dang Nhat Minh's inclusion of the feast in his depiction of the rites of the death anniversary, which reflects the very real return of such traditional ritual practices in northern Vietnamese society in the 1980s, pointedly places the memory of the dead within the world of the village community and suggests that Duyen's deceptions most importantly violate familial and village rather than state norms.[11]

Significantly, *When the Tenth Month Comes* guides Duyen toward the self-knowledge that her deception injures her husband's family and village through a series of conversations with the spirit world. This marks another conscious break with the state's insistence on empirically verifiable solutions to human problems rather than recourse to the metaphysical realm that was at the core of its campaigns against superstitious practices. In one of several dream sequences, which draw upon a common traditional belief that the spirits of the ancestors can appear in dreams to warn of approaching calamities, Duyen meets the village guardian spirit (*thanh hoang*), who tells her he is "a husband like yours who followed a famous king to repel the Mongol invaders from the North," a reference to the thirteenth-century Mongol invasion of Vietnam. While the state consciously sought to appropriate these ubiquitous village cults to legitimize its prosecution of the wars against the French and the Americans within what it termed the "timeless tradition of patriotic resistance against foreign aggression," the guardian spirit in the film speaks to a more localized meaning of the cults as a symbolic protector of village welfare and the focal point for village ritual life.[12] He tells Duyen her husband now lives in the "heart of the village," which gives his spirit power and meaning. Only by sharing the memory of her husband with the village, he suggests, will she find peace.

Later the films uses an encounter with the spirit of Duyen's husband to provide the vehicle through which she comes to appreciate the significance of his family's claims on his memory and her obligation to them. The meeting takes place at what the film calls the "Day of Buddha's Forgiveness," an event Duyen's grandmother recalls as a practice from the "olden days" in which "the dead could meet the living in a midsummer market." Coming upon her husband, she notes his sadness and asks, "Is there something that needs atonement?" Her husband tells her: "I've done my duty. The living should make each other happy." "Father thinks you will still return," Duyen tells him. "Let him be peaceful in his own mind," he replies. "He and I will meet again." Her husband's gentle rebuke serves as a reminder of the spiritual dilemmas that Duyen's transgression of filial norms poses for his family. Without the knowledge that their son has died, they are of course unable to properly honor his memory. But an unpropitiated death, according to traditional Vietnamese beliefs, can threaten the family in a number of ways, turning the dead family member into a restless and potentially malignant spirit who can bring ill fortune to the family. Duyen's encounter with her husband at the Day of Buddha's Forgiveness, a loosely fictionalized version of the Buddhist Feast of Wandering Souls (Ngay Xa Toi Vong Hon), in which village communities traditionally sought to pacify the souls of those who had no one to remember them, suggests her actions have wrongfully placed her husband's spirit in a potentially dangerous sacred space. In urging Duyen to give his father peace, a request approvingly rendered by the film, Duyen's husband reminds her of the primary ties of kinship and the urgency of restoring the proper order of familial remembrance for the dead.

This narrative unfolding of Duyen's journey toward self-knowledge through the spirit world is punctuated by the frequent appearance of a small paper kite, which in the end serves as the film's most potent symbol of her husband's ties to his family and village community and the transcendent claims they make on his memory. The kite makes its first appearance in an early scene in which Duyen recalls a visit she and her husband made to the shrine of the village guardian spirit shortly before he left to join the army. At the shrine her husband burns a paper kite as an offering to the guardian spirit in a further inversion of state-sanctioned practices that banned the burning of paper votive items (*hang ma*) to propitiate the spirit world. Throughout the rest of the film, the kite is linked to Duyen's husband, whose father proudly claims that his son was the "best kite flyer in the village." Kite flying occupied a particular ritual significance during the tenth month or harvest season, which provides the setting for the film, as a representation of the sun. The kite's oppositional movements to and fro mimicked the sun's movements in the sky and formed a part of traditional agricultural rites that sought to bring the rain and sun necessary for a full rice harvest.[13] Within this context, the acknowledged kite-flying prowess of Duyen's husband suggests the high esteem in which he was held by his family and the essential role he played in the ritual lives of the village.

Shortly before the end of the film, and the approaching harvest, Duyen and her young son appear on a hillside joyfully flying a paper kite like the one her husband had offered to the village guardian spirit. In that single image—the kite sweeping and arching over the landscape but tethered to the earth by the string the boy holds—the film depicts the soaring spirit of Duyen's husband, whose relationship to the world below gains its meaning through the inviolable bonds of family and community. If fears of continuing state censorship may have prompted Dang Nhat Minh to formally close his film with a reprise of socialist realist imagery that supports official claims on Duyen's husband, *When the Tenth Month Comes* suggests that at the very least the state must share the memory of the fallen soldier with his widow, his family, and his village.[14]

WHOSE WARTIME SACRIFICES DESERVE COMMEMORATION?

Along with their sweeping challenge to official claims on the memory of fallen soldiers, the revisionist films of the 1980s also focused on the postwar betrayal of the broader scope of the Vietnamese state's commemoration of war. Throughout the wartime period, the state celebrated individual acts of self-sacrifice by patriotic workers and peasants, heroic mothers, children and grandparents, and revolutionary cadres and soldiers. If their contributions fell short of the ultimate sacrifice of death in battle, they nonetheless occupied a central place in the official narrative of war as a collective struggle for national liberation and socialist revolution.

Film was a particularly important means through which the state imparted the commemorative meanings it gave to the sacrifices of these social groups. The first feature-length Vietnamese film, *On the Same River (Chung Mot Dong Song)*,[15] told the story of two young lovers, divided by the river that formed the boundary between northern and southern Vietnam in the Geneva Accords, who put aside the individual sorrows of their frustrated love to fight for the reunification of the country and ideals of socialism. It set the tone for filmmaking during the war and in its aftermath, including such well-known films as *The Fledgling (Chim Vanh Khuyen)*, in which a little girl is killed in her attempts to warn a revolutionary cadre of an impending enemy ambush; *Coal Season (Mua Than)*, set among coal miners in the North who overcome constant bombardment by American jets to produce the coal needed for the war effort; and *When Mother Is Absent (Me Vang Nha)*, which focused on a mother and her five children who responsibly take care of each other at home while their mother fights the enemy on the battlefield.[16] This commemorative rendering in film emerged most fully in the 1965 documentary *Victory at Dien Bien Phu (Chien Thang Dien Bien Phu)*,[17] released to coincide with the tenth anniversary of the French defeat at the climactic battle of the first Indochina war. Crosscutting between black-and-white footage of the battle itself and vignettes that celebrated individual acts of heroism by soldiers in battle and by peasants and workers on the home front, the film presented what it called the "spirit of Dien Bien Phu" as a didactic lesson of the necessity of collective self-sacrifice to successfully realize "the struggle against American imperialists for independence, for the land of the peasants, for socialism."

Many of the revisionist films of the 1980s undermined these larger commemorative pretensions of the Vietnamese state. Depicting a postwar world in which the patriotic and revolutionary figures celebrated in official memory occupied a marginal, often forgotten, place in society, they called into question the state's ability to honor the wartime sacrifices of its people and to sustain the foundational myths of the war experience through which it sought to legitimate its power and authority. The betrayal of wartime sacrifices emerges as a particularly important theme in three of these films. Tran Van Thuy's 1987 documentary, *How to Behave (Cau Chuyen Tu Te)*, opens with historical footage of

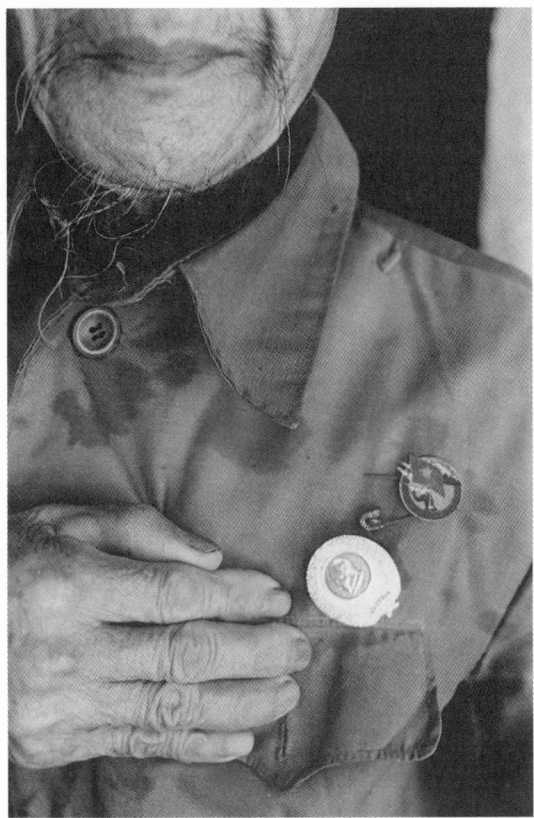

Figure 7.2.   Dien Bien
Phu veteran, Tam
Nong District, Phu
Tho. Photograph by
Natalia Puchalt.

brave revolutionary men and women on the attack that could have been
drawn from any number of wartime films. At the same time, the narrator
self-consciously admits the culpability of filmmakers in advancing the
state's memorializing project: "Our films were unworthy because we
didn't dare say what we thought and unimportant because no one
wanted the films we could make." He insists that *How to Behave* will
instead explore the everyday lives of ordinary people in contemporary
Hanoi. The film does so in a manner that belies the commemorative
promises of the official wartime narrative. Among the individuals pro-
filed in the film are several decorated veterans of the French and American Wars who barely eke out a subsistence living for their families as
cyclo drivers and bicycle repairmen and whose proud memories of their
contributions to the war effort are now largely ignored by the state (figs.
7.2 and 7.3).

Figure 7.3. American
War veteran and
Agent Orange victim,
Tam Nong District,
Phu Tho. Photograph
by Natalia Puchalt.

The veteran at the center of *Brothers and Relations* occupies a similarly peripheral place within his family and in postwar society. From the
outset of the film, when the veteran returns to his home in Hanoi, he
receives little understanding or appreciation from his family for his experiences in war. Ringing the bell upon his arrival, he is first greeted by
a young woman who does not know him but now occupies his former
rooms, which his family had rented out believing him to be dead. Confused, he rings again and this time awakens his brother's sleeping wife.
Annoyed that someone is at their gate early on a Sunday morning, she
asks her husband to receive the caller, but he is preoccupied with col-
lecting the eggs his hens had laid the night before and so refuses. Finally
the wife answers the bell. Astonished to see the veteran, she gives him a
forced smile that only slightly masks her underlying anxiety that his
return will upset the household's economic arrangement with their

boarders. After a brief and somewhat torpid reunion in which his brother's wife emphasizes that the ration book he received as a demobilized veteran makes him "worth a lot," the family returns to its everyday life in which the veteran is alternately ignored or chastised for his inability to find a job and reduce the economic burden his presence places upon them.

The cool reception that the veteran receives from his family is replicated in his encounters with society at large. Potential employers insist they cannot offer him a position because he does not have proper training in a trade; they remain unmoved when he explains he was drafted before he could enter vocational school. Unable to find a job, he passes much of his time with other unemployed veterans in seedy cafés frequented by prostitutes. But here, too, the veteran tells his few friends he "just doesn't fit in."

By focusing on the indifference the veteran encounters from his family and society, *Brothers and Relations* points to the state's larger failure to honor the wartime contributions of soldiers and its inability to honor its commemorative ideals in the postwar period. In one revealing exchange the veteran's brother says that his failure to find a job "betrays their father's trust," to which the veteran tells his seemingly uncomprehending brother: "Betray? You don't think joining the guerrillas for so many years, fighting, not running away, with a bullet in my body is honorable. I come back and look for a job so I won't be a parasite. But if you lack a diploma and have a mind that won't do anything right, you might as well be dead." In the end, the film suggests, the returning veteran can find a place for himself and his own memories of war only on the margins of society. A chance encounter with his old platoon leader, a kindly and trustworthy figure who has made a quiet life for himself in a small coastal fishing village, convinces the veteran to do the same. Surrounded by the platoon leader's warm and empathetic family, the veteran comes to enjoy an Arcadian existence that the film poses as a virtuous antithesis to the ills of forgetfulness of the rest of contemporary society.

The most probing and critical examination of the state's betrayal of the ideals it had so painstakingly cultivated through official commemorations of war emerges in a second film by Dang Nhat Minh, *Girl on the River (Go Gai tren Song),* released in 1987. The film opens with a young woman in a hospital who is telling her life story to a woman journalist. The first third of the film flashes back to the period of the American War, when the young woman had been a prostitute in Hue operating one of the small wooden boat/brothels on the Perfume River that serviced the officers and enlisted men of the Armed Forces of the Republic of Vietnam (ARVN). One night a wounded Communist cadre who seeks refuge on her boat from a pursuing ARVN patrol awakens her. She hides him from the prying eyes of the patrol officers, tends his wounds, and the following day takes him farther down the river, an action that allows him to escape his ARVN pursuers. The film makes clear both the substantial dangers involved in helping the cadre and the close, though nonsexual, bond that develops between him and the prostitute in the short time they spend together. Once the cadre has escaped, she dreams of his future as a heroic resistance fighter.

After the war's end, the young woman realizes the cadre has survived the war and become an important provincial government official. She makes efforts to see him at his office to renew their friendship and seek his assistance. Her papers, however, reveal her to be a former prostitute who had served time in a reeducation camp after the war, and she is refused admittance to him. But while the man's factotums refuse her request because of her "class background," they remain unaware of her earlier relationship with their boss. The former prostitute leaves, assuming that the cadre himself did not refuse her request. By chance shortly thereafter, the cadre's car is stopped because of road construction. On the construction crew laying piles of asphalt is the prostitute, who immediately recognizes the cadre and approaches his car. In a long, painful scene she circles the car without speaking while the cadre ignores her, gazing straight ahead, almost through her. Devastated by this treatment, she leaves work that day, dazed, and is hit by a truck as she walks down a country road. Recovering from the injuries in a hospital, she encounters the woman journalist to whom she has been telling her story.

Neither the young woman nor the journalist realizes the cadre is the husband of the journalist. Indeed, the journalist is puzzled when her husband responds unsympathetically to her interest in publishing the story (he of course realizes the story is about him and worries that if the connection were revealed it could harm his position). The journalist begins to encounter obstacles to publishing her story, again unaware that her husband is using his connections to make sure it is not printed. Told by her editor that the story will not be published, she threatens to resign her position. When she returns home and tells her husband what she has done, he explodes, not only revealing that the story was about him but also criticizing her for giving up her position and for endangering his career.

If the basic structure of the plot serves to reveal the betrayals and hypocrisies of official commemoration of wartime sacrifice, understanding Dang Nhat Minh's decision to use a prostitute as the heroine is essential to decoding the multiple meanings of the film and how Vietnamese audiences might have apprehended it. The sympathy and quiet heroism he accords to the prostitute and his implicit criticism of the cadre's postwar behavior overturn some of the state's most fundamental political assumptions. During the war, the prostitute often served as a symbol of the corruption and immorality the North Vietnamese state attributed to the South Vietnamese government. In the immediate postwar period, party rhetoric called for the eradication of prostitution in the South because it was inimical to what it termed the "human dignity" of women and the "moral integrity" of the new "socialist man." Prostitutes, like others associated with the southern regime, were to be made over into socialist men and women, a decision that helps explain why the film's heroine had been sent to a reeducation camp.[18]

Yet *Girl on the River* offers the prostitute as a symbol of loyalty and principle to reveal the absence of those qualities in the socialist regime. It emphasizes the contrast between the behavior of the prostitute and the cadre in a scene late in the film. After his angry attack on his wife, the cadre goes to the hospital hoping to see the girl (though whether to affect a reconciliation or silence her is not clear). She has already been released, but as the cadre looks around her empty room and at the white sheets of her bed, he suddenly imagines a stain of red blood on the sheets. A new bride traditionally presented blood-stained silk squares after the wedding night to her husband's kin as proof of her virginity; what the cadre has been visualizing, therefore, is nothing less than the prostitute's essential purity.

Dang Nhat Minh's use of the prostitute as a self-sacrificing patriot also has a deeper resonance in traditional Vietnamese literary culture. Most Vietnamese are familiar with the story of Tay Thi (Ch. Hsi shi), a young woman who in popular legend is credited with assuring the victory of the king of Yüeh over the king of Wu during the period of the Warring States (403–221 B.C.). After the king of Wu defeated the kingdom of Yüeh, believed to be the embryonic precursor of the Vietnamese state, the king of Yüeh presented Tay Thi to the Wu court. A woman of transcendent beauty—the T'ang poet Li Po called her "luminous, ravishing, a light on the sea of clouds"—Tay Thi was reportedly educated in the feminine arts at the Yüeh court for the purposes of corrupting the king of Wu. Distracted by Tay Thi's beauty and charms, the tale continues, the king of Wu became less vigilant, enabling the Yüeh many years later to avenge their defeat and destroy the kingdom of Wu.[19]

The close links between the story of Tay Thi and the behavior of the prostitute in *Girl on the River* suggest the film offers an even deeper challenge to the larger symbolic meanings the state accorded to prostitution. Its approving depiction of the prostitute's contribution to the war effort joins it to a sustained indigenous debate that began during the period of French colonial rule over the efficacy of collaboration in which the prostitute came to be seen as a metaphor for an acceptance of foreign rule. At the center of these debates were often-conflicting interpretations of Nguyen Du's nineteenth-century epic poem *The Tale of Kieu (Truyen Kieu),* in which the heroine's willingness to prostitute herself for her family was widely seen as an apologia for the author's decision to abandon the Le cause and serve the new Nguyen dynasty. In what are commonly known as the "writing brush wars" of the 1860s in the wake of the French conquest of the South, one leading collaborator with the French justified his decision by comparing his plight to that of Kieu. Similarly, Pham Quynh, a leading indigenous supporter of French rule in the 1920s, sought to canonize Kieu as a filial, self-sacrificing daughter who prostitutes herself to save her family in an effort to defend his own collaboration with the French. If collaboration for Pham Quynh was like prostitution, then he, like Kieu, was practicing it for the purest and noblest of motives, prostituting himself for the ultimate good of the nation.[20]

These defenses of Kieu and of collaboration met with sharp indigenous attacks. Opponents of collaboration in the writing brush wars did not so much direct their ire at Kieu as argue that collaborators attempted to cloak their disloyalty in the false guise of filial piety. But Pham Quynh's detractors, some of whom came to play leading roles in the North Vietnamese state after 1945, chose to attack him through a critique of Kieu. Their argument that Kieu was little more than an unchaste and lewd woman undeserving of veneration was squarely aimed at undermining Pham Quynh's defense of collaboration. These proponents of "art for humanity's sake" in the 1930s, who set many of the parameters for the state's socialist realist aesthetics in the coming decades, had little use for Kieu and prostitution. Far from a model of revolutionary voluntarism, she appeared as little more than a weak, passive victim of an iniquitous social system that the socialist revolution aimed to transform.[21] For instance, in To Huu's poem "The Song on the Perfume River" (1938), a work later celebrated by the North Vietnamese state, the reprobate prostitute who "drifts on streams of foul desire" is offered as a metaphor for the immorality of life under French colonialism. Only with the coming of socialist revolution, the poem suggests, will she "quit this wandering life of woe" and the "dirt and filth . . . vanish . . . to hail a new dawn."[22] The sympathetic portrayal of the prostitute as patriot in *Girl on the River,* which recalls Nguyen Du and Pham Quynh's use of the prostitute to defend collaboration, reverses the symbolic meanings the state gave to prostitution: it is the prostitute who is the wartime hero, only to be victimized by the ills of postwar socialist society.

Dang Nhat Minh's choice of two women to serve not only as the film's central characters but also as its narrative voice joins the film to a traditional literary idiom in which male authors adopted a female narrative voice that could serve counterhegemonic purposes without interference from the state. In part, his choice may have been a device to evade censorship by employing the practices of the northern radical and progressive authors of the 1920s and 1930s who used the coded language of gender to undertake political debate and avoid colonial censorship.[23] The timing of the film's release in 1987, in the very early days of the reform movement, suggests that Minh would have needed to be very cautious in presenting his critiques because the boundaries and implications of the reforms remained uncertain.

Girl on the River employs two gendered literary tropes—women as victims and women as powerless—that give it the freedom to articulate a more sweeping indictment of contemporary society. Drawing on the symbolic resonance of women as victims, an idea that is enshrined in Vietnamese literary classics like the eighteenth-century epic poem *Lament of the Soldier's Wife (Chinh Phu ngam),* as well as in the literature of the 1920s and 1930s that portrayed a feminized colonial population victimized by Confucian family structures and the colonial state, the film uses the prostitute and female journalist to suggest society at large has been victimized by the state's inability to uphold its commemorative ideals. Similarly, and more bleakly, the film appropriates the common literary and cultural equation that linked women with powerlessness to suggest that just as the women in the film are unable to control their own fates, contemporary Vietnamese society lacks the agency to rescue itself from the state's betrayal of the socialist ideals that underlay its official narrative of war.

The final plot twist in *Girl on the River* underscores this subtle critique of state practices, starkly revealing the emptiness of the state's commemorative promises. After the argument with her husband, the woman journalist, now concerned with how the story of the prostitute might adversely affect her own family's status, finds the young woman and tells her she had been mistaken all along. The man she saw in the car, the journalist claims, was not the cadre she had helped. He had died, she says, many years before. Believing the journalist's lie, the young woman recalls her dream after she had helped the cadre escape in which he walked onto a battlefield to become a hero. But in the ironically elegiac vision that closes the film, she wrongly imagines he is killed in a glorious, self-sacrificing soldier's death.

WHAT ARE THE REAL LEGACIES OF THE WAR?

The importance the revisionist films of the 1980s attached to the betrayals of the official meanings of wartime sacrifice reflected a more fundamental unease with the nature of postwar society in northern Vietnam. If revisionist filmmakers took full advantage of the opportunities the Renovation agenda offered to enlarge the parameters of public discourse on the legacies of war, they were far from champions of the market reforms adopted by the state in the mid-1980s to arrest the stagnation of the Vietnamese economy.[24] In almost all their films, the forgetfulness of many of their protagonists serves to emphasize the spiritual malaise they ascribe to contemporary society, in which the wartime virtues of revolutionary self-sacrifice are increasingly disregarded by corrupt and self-seeking cadres. The quest for individual advancement and rising economic inequalities, the revisionist films suggest, belie official promises that the sacrifices of war would bring collective egalitarianism and social justice in the postwar era.

Le Duc Tien's 1986 film, *A Quiet Little Town (Thi Tran Yen Tinh)*, advances this critique through gentle but trenchant satire. On the way to the wedding of a relative, a high-ranking government minister from Hanoi and his driver are seriously injured in a traffic accident near a small provincial town. A local party official, whose nephew's wedding the minister was coming to attend, orders the better dressed of the two injured men to be sent to his town's clinic while the other man is taken to a neighboring town for treatment. After the local notables realize that their patient may die without surgery, the central question of the narrative becomes how the handling of the minister's case can best promote the fortunes of various members of the small town's party and state bureaucracy. The local party official, aware of the possible rewards that could come from saving a minister's life, urges that he be operated on immediately. The wife of the young doctor who would perform the surgery urges her reluctant husband to take up the challenge in the hopes that the grateful minister would organize the doctor's transfer to Hanoi and provide her a way out of the provincial town she detests. The head of the town clinic, believing the minister's condition is too serious for treatment in his clinic and that the minister's death could have serious repercussions for his own position, insists that he be returned to Hanoi for surgery.

In the meantime, back in Hanoi the minister's wife, whose manner and physical presence closely resemble those of Imelda Marcos, browbeats her sons to use their connections in the military to get a military jet to airlift her husband out. Eventually the young doctor takes charge and performs the surgery while the local party cadre organizes a welcoming party, made up of family and friends who had assembled for the aborted wedding of his nephew, to greet the minister's wife and family who are flying by military helicopter to the small town. They arrive just as the patient is wheeled out of surgery. As the doctor proudly pronounces the surgery a success, the minister's wife looks at the patient on the stretcher and realizes it is not her husband but his driver. Suddenly an announcement from the neighboring town reports that the minister's surgery in its clinic was successful and that he is resting comfortably. His wife and family rush off, dashing the hopes of local officials and bureaucrats that the minister's gratitude would advance their careers.

The preoccupation with status and power among agents of the state that infuses the damning portrait of society under the market economic reforms in *A Quiet Little Town* also emerges in the documentary *How to Behave*. The film, whose depiction of the lives of veterans in postwar society was discussed earlier, is centered around a group of filmmakers who honor the request of a dying colleague to discover if kindness (*tu te*), a term the film tellingly defines as "acting in the public rather than individual interest," could still be found in Vietnamese society. The filmmakers ultimately do find kindness, not among party cadres or state bureaucrats—one of whom claims "No one has time for such outmoded notions these days"—but in a leper colony run by Catholic nuns, a particularly charged choice given the intense and sustained hostility of the socialist state in Vietnam toward the Catholic Church. If the devotion of the nuns to the lepers, as the film claims, rests on "faith," *How to Behave* suggests the callousness of society at large represents a loss of faith in the state's socialist ideals. Pointedly noting that "the people" (*nhan dan*) are "sacred words" in the state's vocabulary as the objects of "sacrifice, devotion and generosity," the film sets the difficult lives of ordinary people against the indifference of powerful party officials whose own lives are marked by material ease to suggest "the gap between words and deeds has become too wide." The mixed tone of sorrow and anger through which the film articulates its sense of the postwar betrayal of wartime ideals emerges most sharply in the closing frames. A quotation appears on screen—"Only animals can turn from the suffering of men and busy themselves preening their furs and feathers"— to which the film's narrator adds, "This quote is not by my friend but by the venerated Karl Marx."

If wartime experiences are a somewhat muted presence in the narratives of *A Quiet Little Town* and *How to Behave*,[25] a gendered construction of war memories serves as a crucial symbolic vehicle for the critique of contemporary society advanced by many of the revisionist films. They pit a series of grasping younger women against the probity of veterans whose virtuous behavior underlines the dominant ethos of corruption and selfishness the films ascribe to contemporary society. This metaphorical dichotomy builds in part upon the traditional Vietnamese division of gender roles that contrasts women as "generals of the interior" (*noi tuong*), who dominate the domestic sphere and oversee the family's budget, with men who properly inhabit the public realm, where they conduct the more contemplative official business of family life and governance. By rendering the contours of contemporary society as a feminine landscape forgetful of the self-sacrifices of war, the symbolic vocabularies of these films suggest that the power of the market economy has dangerously extended the private domain of women into the masculine public sphere and dislodged the traditional forces of moral order and authority in society.

The oppositional pairing of the behavior of younger women and soldiers to advance this gendered representation of the abandonment of wartime ideals occurs in the majority of revisionist films. In *When the Tenth Month Comes,* the actions of a female cadre whose preoccupation with material advancement prompts her to chastise the heroine Duyen for her "inability to get ahead" stand in sharp contrast to those of a soldier who had fought with Duyen's husband and eventually tells her son that his father is dead. When the son asks the soldier if he is telling the truth, his reply that "a soldier never lies" emphasizes the moral gulf between wartime revolutionary virtue and the ills of contemporary society. A decorated war veteran in *How to Behave* serves as an example of what the film calls "honest people who live a kind life" despite material deprivation, while a young woman becomes the chief symbol for its contention that kindness is largely absent in most contemporary social relations. Other films use one or the other of these paradigmatic figures. The status-seeking wife of the doctor in *A Quiet Little Town* who pushes her reluctant husband to operate does so in the hopes that it will bring his transfer to Hanoi and open up new opportunities for status and material comfort. The veteran father of the young girl in love with a soldier in *A Fairy Tale for Seventeen-Year-Olds* is a figure of particular depth whose blessing of his daughter's somewhat fanciful relationship suggests the ways in which masculine authority, cultivated by the experiences of war, provides a strong moral force in society.

In two films the engendered revisionist critique is rendered in a particularly sharp and disturbing manner. The contrast between the behavior of the veteran in *Brothers and Relations* and the wife of his brother in honoring the memory of her brother who was killed in war was noted at the outset of this chapter. Juxtaposing the selfless virtue of the veteran who collects and buries the remains of the fallen soldier with the obsession of the wife who works with unabashed eagerness to bribe and cajole an expansive network of corrupt officials to facilitate a potentially lucrative business trip to Singapore for her husband, the film suggests that the wife's single-minded pursuit of material advantage blinds her to her obligations to her dead brother. The wife's place in the film as a larger symbol of the perils of the marketplace emerges with particular force in a scene in which she meets her husband on the day of their wedding anniversary. She emerges from a shop carrying a boom box to greet her waiting husband, who has brought a small bouquet of flowers to mark the occasion. "You bought another cassette player?" he asks. "You can't have too many," she jauntily replies. As the two ride off on their motorcycle, the wife clutches the boom box to her heart while carelessly holding the bouquet in her other hand. The flowers, a potent expression of the humane rather than material nature of social relationships, appear almost expendable; it is the boom box that gets the loving embrace.

In Nguyen Khac Loi's 1989 film, *The General Retires (Tuong Ve Huu)*, a decorated general and the wife of his son serve as the central characters. The general, a figure of quiet authority and simple tastes who is clearly devoted to serving the ideals of the state, comes to live with his son's family after he retires from military service. But he soon feels out of place as he experiences the market-generated rhythms of life in the household. One day he discovers that his son's wife, a doctor at a maternity clinic, brings home aborted fetuses from the clinic to feed a pack of Alsatian dogs she is raising to sell as guard dogs to supplement the family's income. Appalled by her behavior and devastated to realize that the spiritual emptiness he finds in the household pervades contemporary society, the general leaves the house to rejoin his elderly military comrades, among whom he dies.[26]

The symbolism of gender cuts even deeper in *The General Retires* and *Brothers and Relations,* which use the emasculation of husbands by their wives to reveal the corrupting seductiveness of the marketplace and its corrosive penetration into all realms of human relations. The son of the general is depicted as an impotent figure, powerless to resist the moral transgressions of the market that his wife has introduced into the household. When the general tells his son what his wife has been doing, implicitly calling upon him to reassert his authority and end the practice, the son replies somewhat stiffly, as if to hide his embarrassment, "I had known about this but dismissed it as something of no importance."

The brother of the veteran in *Brothers and Relations* is a similarly weak figure who is literally seduced into the conventions of the marketplace by his wife. In one key scene that illustrates the wife's domination (and that of the market), husband and wife are seen lounging on a bed after returning home with their new boom box. The wife removes her husband's glasses, unbuttons her shirt, and turns on a cassette of Western popular music. As she leans back seductively and pulls her husband toward her, he looks both at her and at the boom box next to her with an expression full of greed and licentiousness. The close of the film condemningly suggests that his emasculation and his embrace of the market economy are fully consummated. He sits mutely in the back of a car at the airport, his face filled with avaricious anticipation for his imminent business trip to Singapore, while his wife tells his brother that she does not have time to deal with the remains of her dead brother that he has recovered and brought to her.

Not all filmmakers shared the opprobrium with which these films greeted the coming of the market economy. For Luu Trong Ninh, the market economy offered a salutary alternative to what he perceived as the obvious failures of socialism. His 1993 film, *Please Forgive Me (Xin Loi),* depicts the trials of a soldier turned movie producer trying to make a film glorifying the North's war against the United States by using Vietnamese actors and actresses born after the Communist victory in 1975. The film focuses on the conflicting generational sensibilities of the producer and his cast. The producer, an austere figure proud of his role in "liberating" the country from foreign aggressors, criticizes his youthful cast for their ingratitude for his generation's self-sacrifice to state and society during the war. In response, the young cast members, with a notable absence of filial piety, impertinently ask what, beyond poverty, the older generation has really bequeathed to the country. Luu Trong Ninh's sympathies clearly lie with the younger generation. Almost twenty years younger than the directors of most of the revisionist films, he came of age not during the American War but in its aftermath. His film gives voice to an impatient and consumer-oriented generation for whom official memories of wartime heroism hold no meaning, and the freedom to pursue individual interests permitted by the market economy is a welcome departure from what they see as the constraining collectivist ethos of socialist economics.[27]

But if *Please Forgive Me* suggests the presence of generational differences among revisionist filmmakers over the meaning of war and its aftermath, the film is an exception to the largely conservative critique of contemporary society in most revisionist films. In depicting what they saw as the real legacies of war, these films did not so much subvert official memories of war as embrace a war of nostalgia. They offer remembrances of revolutionary morality, purity, and egalitarianism, all essential components of the state's wartime narrative, as a jeremiad against the materialism and spiritual declension of postwar society.

The frequently conservative cast of the revisionist critique of memory, commemoration, and legacies of war should not obscure the radical challenge these films posed to the public construction of historical memory in northern Vietnamese society. Official reaction to these films provides one indication of the boldness of their larger vision and the dangers it posed to state efforts to monopolize the meanings of war.[28] A 1989 survey undertaken by the *People's Army Daily* (*Quan Doi Nhan Dan*) asked technical cadres, political cadres, and senior colonels and generals for their reaction to the film *The General Retires*. Most technical cadres, whose lower-level positions had little connection to official ideology, liked the film. But some 60 percent of political cadres, colonels, and generals surveyed, whose positions linked their ideological outlook much more closely to that of the state, voiced strong disapproval.[29] The revisionist films also encountered opposition in the Ministry of Culture, whose official censors requested a number of cuts, arguing, for instance, that the metaphysical setting through which the heroine of *When the Tenth Month Comes* meets her dead husband promoted improper beliefs in superstitious practices. In most cases, however, the artistic freedom granted under the reform agenda allowed filmmakers to ultimately resist these pressures.[30]

Nor should the meanings these films gave to memories of war be viewed as an isolated phenomenon disconnected from broader popular discourse on the war in contemporary northern Vietnamese society. Along with filmmakers, a group of writers also drew inspiration from the relaxation of official supervision in the arts to write a series of best-selling novels and short stories that pursue and deepen many of the larger themes of the revisionist films. Their shared sensibilities emerge in the claims of the veteran narrator of Bao Ninh's *The Sorrow of War* (*Noi Buon Chien Tranh*), one of the most popular of these works, after recounting his disillusionment over his wartime service: "The future lied to us, there long ago in the past. There is no new life, no new era nor hope for a beautiful future."[31]

These articulations of countermemories of war in film and literature also link the discourse surrounding war commemoration in Vietnam with broader global patterns of the contested processes of remembering war throughout the twentieth century. Just as the Vietnamese state's insistence that the fallen soldier served as the preeminent legitimating symbol for its wars against the French and the Americans mirrored the official memorializing aims and practices of interwar European states, the form and content of Vietnamese countermemories of war bear striking, if unconscious, parallels with the works of interwar European artists, filmmakers, poets, and novelists. Although separated by space, time, and culture, works such as Otto Dix's *Der Krieg,* Wilfred Owen's "Anthem for a Doomed Youth," Erich Maria Remarque's *All Quiet on the Western Front,* or Abel Gance's *J'accuse* and the challenges they posed to the official meaning of World War I find resonant company in revisionist Vietnamese film.[32]

What joins these works most fully is a common insistence that the ideological base of state constructions of war conceals more than it reveals. Like their European counterparts, the Vietnamese revisionist films of the 1980s—whether reasserting the power of traditional familial claims on the memories of fallen soldiers, recasting official memory to subvert state commemorative practices, or appropriating the ideals of the official memorializing project to voice displeasure with the legacies of war—opened up the process of remembering war, acknowledging and articulating the multiplicity of meanings that the wars against the French and Americans, which claimed the lives of more than three million of their people, hold for northern Vietnamese society.

NOTES

1. See Michel Foucault, "Counter-Memory: The Philosophy of Difference," in his *Language, Counter-Memory, Practice: Selected Essays and Interviews*, ed. Donald F. Bouchard (Ithaca, N.Y.: Cornell University Press, 1977), 113–96.

2. Greg Lockhart, "Preface" and "Introduction," in Nguyen Huy Thiep, *The General Retires and Other Stories* (Kuala Lumpur: Oxford in Asia, 1991), v–vi, 5–12.

3. For a discussion of the growth and development of the Vietnamese film industry before and after the reforms of the 1980s, see Banh Bao and Huu Ngoc, *L'Itinéraire du film de fiction vietnamien: Expériences vietnamiennes* (Hanoi: Editions en langues étrangères, 1984); John Charlot, "Vietnamese Cinema: First Views," *Journal of Southeast Asian Studies* 22 (March 1991): 33–62; Ngo Manh Lan, "Looking Inwards: Vietnamese Cinema in the Eighties," *Cinemaya* 2 (winter 1988–89): 6–14; and Nguyen Duy Can, ed., *Lich Su Dien Anh Cach Mang Viet Nam* [*History of Revolutionary Cinema in Vietnam*] (Hanoi: Cuc Dien Anh, 1983).

4. Centralized accounting of box office receipts and attendance for Vietnamese films, if undertaken at all, is not publicly available, making it difficult to precisely quantify the sizes of audiences. All the films discussed in this chapter, however, were in general release among the estimated eight hundred movie theaters in Vietnam, and my informants in Hanoi indicate that on the whole they were enthusiastically received.

5. Readers who are interested in viewing the revisionist films discussed in this chapter will, unfortunately, find it somewhat difficult. In preparing my analysis, I relied on videotaped copies of the films obtained from the Vietnam Cinema Department and, in a few cases, pirated copies available from street vendors in Hanoi. A limited number of these films, with English subtitles, are available at the UCLA Television and Film Archive in Los Angeles, but they must be viewed at the archive itself. I am currently working on a project with the University of Hawaii's Center for Southeast Asian Studies that seeks to make some of these films more accessible to an international audience.

6. George Mosse, *Fallen Soldiers: Reshaping the Memory of the World Wars* (New York: Oxford University Press, 1990), 7; see also chap. 7.

7. My discussion of official state commemorative practices in Vietnam is informed by Shaun Malarney, this volume.

8. My examination of the competing claims for remembering the war dead made in these films draws its theoretical inspiration from the work of Maurice Halbwachs. See his "Social Frameworks of Memory," in *On Collective Memory*, ed. and trans. Lewis A. Coser (Chicago: University of Chicago Press, 1992), 37–189, and *The Collective Memory*, trans. Francis J. Ditter Jr. (New York: Harper Colophon, 1980). For a recent discussion of the relationship between state and local forms of remembrance that expands upon Halbwachs's work and informed my thinking, see Alon Confino, "Collective Memory and Cultural History: Problems of Method," *American Historical Review* 102 (December 1997): 1386–403.

9. For a useful discussion of the threat outsiders were believed to pose to a

village, see Masaya Shiraishi, "State, Village and Vagabonds: Vietnamese Rural Society and the Phan Ba Vanh Rebellion," in *History and Peasant Consciousness in Southeast Asia,* ed. Andrew Turton and Shigeharu Tanabe (Osaka: National Museum of Ethnography, 1984), 345–400.

10. Neil Jamieson, "The Traditional Family in Vietnam," *Vietnam Forum,* no. 8 (1986): 123.

11. For a discussion of the state's reform of the death anniversary ceremony and the resurgence of traditional ritual practices in the 1980s, see Shaun K. Malarney, "Ritual and Revolution in Viet Nam" (Ph.D. diss., University of Michigan, 1993), 364–66, 419–20.

12. On the role of the guardian spirit in village belief and ritual practice, see Neil Jamieson, "The Traditional Village in Vietnam," *Vietnam Forum,* no. 7 (1986): 95–100. On the state appropriation of these cults, see Patricia Pelley, "The History of Resistance and the Resistance to History in Post-colonial Constructions of the Past," in *Essays into Vietnamese Pasts,* ed. K. W. Taylor and John K. Whitmore (Ithaca, N.Y.: Cornell University Southeast Asia Program, 1995), 232–45.

13. On the traditional symbolism of the kite, see Tran Quoc Vuong, "The Legend of Ong Dong from the Text to the Field," in *Essays into Vietnamese Pasts,* 37–38.

14. For an important discussion of the competing claims to the remains of the war dead in interwar France between the state, the Catholic Church, and local communities that displays a number of similarities to the Vietnamese case, see Daniel J. Sherman, "Bodies and Names: The Emergence of Commemoration in Interwar France," *American Historical Review* 103 (April 1998): 443–66.

15. *On the Same River* [*Chung Mot Dong Song*], directed by Hong Nghi and Hieu Dan, 1959.

16. *The Fledgling* [*Chim Vanh Khuyen*], directed by Nguyen Van Thong and Tran Vu, 1962; *Coal Season* [*Mua than*], directed by Huy Thanh, 1970; and *When Mother Is Absent* [*Me Vang Nha*], directed by Nguyen Khanh Du, 1979. Between 1959 and 1975, some thirty-six films were released in northern Vietnam that give similar portrayals of individual revolutionary self-sacrifice during the war. Another forty were released in the postwar period between 1979 and 1985. These figures and plot summaries draw upon selected articles in *Dien Anh,* the official film journal in northern Vietnam.

17. *Victory at Dien Bien Phu* [*Chien Thang Dien Bien Phu*], directed by Tran Viet, 1965.

18. The reality in the South was often quite different, with prostitutes coming to serve the new socialist man, including cadres and government officials, in what one Vietnamese somewhat disingenuously called "the line of socialist duty." In this sense, the criticisms offered in *Girl on the River* mirror aspects of these well-known hypocritical practices. On the state's official rhetoric linking prostitution and the southern regime and the actual practices of the postwar period, see Hoang Ngoc Thanh Dung, "To Serve the Cause of Women's Liberation," and Nguyen Ngoc Ngan, "In the Line of Socialist Duty," both in *To Be Made Over: Tales of Socialist Reeducation in Vietnam,* ed. and trans. by Huynh

Sanh Thong (New Haven, Conn.: Yale Center for International and Area Studies, 1988), 43–94.

19. On the story of Tay Thi, see Edward H. Schafer, *The Vermillion Bird: T'ang Images of the South* (Berkeley and Los Angeles: University of California Press, 1967), 82–83; David Johnson, "Epic and History in Early China: The Matter of Wu Tzu-shü," *Journal of Asian Studies* 40 (February 1981): 268; David Johnson, "The Wu Tzu-shü *Pien-wen* and Its Source: Part I," *Harvard Journal of Asiatic Studies* 40 (June 1980): 93–156; and David Johnson, "The Wu Tzu-shü *Pien-wen* and Its Source: Part II," *Harvard Journal of Asiatic Studies* 40 (December 1980): 497.

20. On the symbolism of prostitution and Kieu in the "writing brush wars," see Jeremy H. C. S. Davidson, "'Good Omen' versus 'Worth': The Poetic Dialogue between Ton Tho Tuong and Phan Van Tri," in *Context, Meaning and Power in Southeast Asia,* ed. Mark Hobart and Robert H. Taylor (Ithaca, N.Y.: Cornell University Southeast Asia Program, 1986), 53–77. On Pham Quynh's defense of Kieu, see Hue-Tam Ho Tai, *Radicalism and the Origins of the Vietnamese Revolution* (Cambridge, Mass.: Harvard University Press, 1992), 109–13; and Huynh Sanh Thong, "Main Trends of Vietnamese Literature between the Two World Wars," *Vietnam Forum,* no. 3 (1984): 103–7.

21. On the debates in the late 1930s that presaged the Vietnamese state's embrace of social realism, see David G. Marr, *Vietnamese Tradition on Trial, 1920–1945* (Berkeley and Los Angeles: University of California Press, 1981), 361–66.

22. To Huu, "The Song on the Perfume River," in *An Anthology of Vietnamese Poems: From the Eleventh through the Twentieth Centuries,* ed. Huynh Sanh Thong (New Haven, Conn.: Yale University Press, 1996), 156–57.

23. Tai, *Radicalism and the Origins of the Vietnamese Revolution,* chap. 3.

24. For useful overviews of the context in which the Vietnamese state undertook the process of market economic reforms, see Börje Ljunggren and Peter Timmer, eds., *The Challenge of Reform in Indochina* (Cambridge, Mass.: Harvard University Press, 1993); and William S. Turley and Mark Selden, eds., *Reinventing Vietnamese Socialism:* Doi Moi *in Comparative Perspective* (Boulder, Colo.: Westview Press, 1993).

25. In *A Quiet Little Town,* memories of war emerge indirectly as a tool through which the head of the clinic tries to advance his preference for returning the minister to Hanoi for treatment. To get an indifferent postmistress to send an urgent message to Hanoi, he says nonchalantly, "Your voice sounds funny. Were you exposed to Agent Orange?" Nervously she replies, "I was in the Youth Combat Troops," then quickly moves to send the telegram despite her earlier hesitations. Satisfied that his message is being sent, the doctor begins to leave. The woman cries out, "Wait! What about my exposure to Agent Orange?" "You're cured," he laughs. "I'm a good doctor!"

26. The film is an adaptation of a short story of the same name by Nguyen Huy Thiep, widely acknowledged as one of the leading writers in contemporary Vietnam. Critics have pointed to a certain ambiguity in the story's rendering of the wife's behavior, suggesting that her actions appear "more hard-headed than hard-hearted" given the prevailing economic difficulties in the period in which

the story is set. See Lockhart, "Introduction," 19. The film's portrayal of the wife, which sharply contrasts the menacing ruthlessness of her behavior with the moral purity of the general, is devoid of any such empathy.

27. A similar theme underlies the screenwriter Le Hung's 1991 play, *Fable for the Year 2000* [*Huyen Thoai Nam 2000*]. In one crucial scene, an old man and a young man are involved in a standoff on a bridge. The old man insists he should go first because his generation produced everything of value in society: houses, roads, the contested bridge, even the young man. The young man, angry and impatient that old men "occupy all the most important positions except in homes for the aging," proclaims that he cannot wait until the old man "has walked his last step" and criticizes the "pathetic" legacy the older generation has left. See Murray Hiebert, "Playing for Keeps," *Far Eastern Economic Review*, May 7, 1992, 37–38.

28. For a revealing comparative discussion of resistant, subversive, and oppositional memory in the context of other socialist regimes, see the contributors to *Memory, History, and Opposition under State Socialism*, ed. Rubie S. Watson (Santa Fe, N.M.: School of American Research Press, 1994).

29. *People's Army Daily* [*Quan Doi Nhan Dan*], February 18, 1989, as cited in Lockhart, "Introduction," 3–4.

30. On the efforts of official censors and their evasion by filmmakers, see Charlot, "Vietnamese Cinema," 39–40. An exception was Luu Trong Ninh's *Please Forgive Me,* which was banned after a brief release in Hanoi. The Ministry of Culture demanded several cuts before it would permit the film to be shown again. One requested cut was a speech in which Communist troops were criticized for committing the same acts of brutality during the war that the state had attributed to American soldiers. Ninh, who accumulated a huge private debt to make the film, acceded to their demands. See Murray Hiebert, "Vietnam's Censors Tell Producer to Cut Film," *Far Eastern Economic Review*, July 22, 1993, 90.

31. Bao Ninh, *Noi Buon Chien Tranh* [*The Sorrow of War*] (Westminster, Calif.: Hong Linh, 1992; reprint of edition published in Hanoi in 1991), 67. Along with the short stories of Nguyen Huy Thiep set in postwar Vietnam, well-known novels on the war that parallel the revisionist films of the 1980s include Le Luu, *Thoi Xa Vang* [*The Old Days*] (Hanoi: Tac Pham Moi, 1987) and Duong Thu Huong, *Tieu Thuyet Vo De* [*Novel without a Name*] (Hanoi, 1989; reprint, Stanton, Calif.: Van Nghe, 1991). In another example of the close ties between revisionist film and literature, Duong Thu Huong is the screenwriter of *Brother and Relations.*

32. For a penetrating discussion of European countermemories of war, see Jay Winter, *Sites of Memory, Sites of Mourning: The Great War in European Cultural History* (New York: Cambridge University Press, 1995). Also potentially suggestive for the Vietnamese case is the beautiful and probing comparative analysis of sorrow and memory in the Chinese and Jewish traditions in Vera Schwarcz, *Bridge across Broken Time: Chinese and Jewish Cultural Memory* (New Haven, Conn.: Yale University Press, 1998).

Commemoration and Community

Hue-Tam Ho Tai

Maurice Halbwachs observed that memory is not the product of individuals acting in isolation but is socially constructed.[1] As John Gillis and others have proposed, commemoration and the politics of national identity are closely linked;[2] so are memory and community. If a community creates and sustains memory, the reverse is also true: memory creates and sustains the community. The creation of a common past is a means of defining what and who belong, and what and who deserve to be consigned to oblivion. Battles over memory are thus battles over how to draw the contours of community, who is to be included, and who is to be excluded from the community thus defined. This theme runs through, or is implied in, the chapters here by Zinoman, Giebel, Malarney, and Bradley.

As a southerner with my own ambivalent feelings about the recent past, I must therefore point out a significant lack in the present volume: the lack of a perspective from those who, during the war officially known as the War Against the Americans, fought alongside those Americans, or at least did not consider them enemies. The dead of the Armed Forces of the Republic of Vietnam (ARVN) do not figure in the state's commemorative project so eloquently described by Malarney and captured in film in *When the Tenth Month Comes*. ARVN veterans and their families are not entitled to any of the privileges accorded to northern veterans or survivors of revolutionary martyrs. This is not an unusual postscript to conflict. As Milan Kundera wrote of another set of victors, "They wanted to erase hundreds of thousands of lives from human memory and leave nothing but a single unblemished age of unblemished idyll."[3] To be truly comprehensive, a task beyond the capabilities of a single volume, the study of commemoration would need to include the dead of the South. To do otherwise risks turning them into the scholarly equivalents of the wandering ghosts of those who, dying unmourned, constantly haunt the living in an attempt to force their way into the consciousness of the community, to be acknowledged as worthy of being remembered if only because they once walked the earth.

It would also need to include the living, especially those who now live beyond the national boundaries. Diaspora and transnationalism have exploded the boundaries of identity and community. Besides local divergences from the national commemorative script alluded to by Malarney, Giebel, and Bradley, Kennedy and Williams and I point out as well the role of foreign visitors in shaping the re-presentation of the past. Even more interesting, however, is the role of Vietnamese exiles. Those who left their homeland after the fall of Saigon (renamed Ho Chi Minh City) have created different communities of memory. April 30, 1975, the day when the Communist forces entered Saigon, is officially called Reunification Day and is one of two state celebrations. The other, Independence Day, celebrates the occasion on which Ho Chi Minh declared independence on September 2, 1945, in Hanoi's Ba Dinh Square. But while Vietnamese at home and abroad can take pride in independence, most expatriates ignore that date altogether. Their commemorative energies are concentrated on April 30, which they call National Day of Shame (Ngay Quoc Han). They mark it with their own set of commemorative practices that signify rupture rather than unity, sorrow rather than joy. This duality of commemoration is, of course, not a unique phenomenon. Chinese on either side of the Taiwan Straits celebrate independence on different days.[4]

Filled with the anguish of the recent exile from a country where a totalitarian state was still in firm control, Kundera wrote: "The people who have emigrated (there are one hundred and twenty of them) and the people who have been silenced and removed from their jobs (there are half a million of them) are fading like a procession moving off into the mist. They are invisible and forgotten."[5] But his fear has not been realized, either among his compatriots or among the Vietnamese. The exiled Vietnamese poet Du Tu Le wrote:

> Since time began, when people leave
> each leaving represents a truth.

There can be no tomorrow if
they cower and submit.[6]

Exiles provide, mostly from afar, a truly contrapuntal voice to the official discourse, a voice that cannot be ignored entirely because modern communications make it so easily accessible to domestic audiences.

"The past is a foreign country; they do things differently there,"[7] wrote L. P. Hartley. For exiles, however, the past is a familiar place and a familiar time; it is the present that is strange. Where they reside does not quite feel like home, but their homeland is now out of bounds. What happens when their own narratives of the past and those circulating in the homeland collide, or when their memories are set side by side with present realities is worth further analysis. As occasional returnees, they come back neither as detached tourists for whom the past has been turned into a marketable commodity nor as American veterans trying to come to terms with their own personal histories by finding out what Vietnam has become since the end of war, nor yet as worshipful pilgrims at sites of memory constructed by the state. The proliferation of ancestral halls and other structures of commemoration refurbished or newly built with the help of overseas remittances attests to their active role in the reconstruction of the past as well as the economy. They are visitors from another place and time. If they come back to Vietnam as the visible symbols of past national trauma, they are also emissaries of a future still waiting to be born, the future that is supposed to replace the Communist utopia of yore. They open windows through which young Vietnamese, like the heroine of *Paradise of the Blind,* can glimpse different worlds and imagine different futures. They are the ones who pass through the airports and sit in the university auditoriums which form the objects of her longings.

And so, while the essays in this volume have focused on the construction of memory within Vietnam, there remains a need to redefine the meaning of community and expand the geography of memory.

NOTES

1. Maurice Halbwachs, *Les Cadres sociaux de la mémoire* (Paris: Mouton, 1976).

2. John Gillis, ed., *Commemorations: The Politics of National Identity* (Princeton, N.J.: Princeton, University Press, 1994).

3. Milan Kundera, *The Book of Laughter and Forgetting* (New York: Knopf, 1981), 24

4. I am grateful to Jeffrey Wasserstrom for reminding me of this parallel with the Vietnamese situation.

5. Kundera, *The Book of Laughter and Forgetting,* 23

6. Du Tu Le, "The Dawn of a New Humankind," in *An Anthology of Vietnamese Poems from the Eleventh through the Twentieth Centuries,* ed. and trans. Huynh Sanh Thong (New Haven, Conn.: Yale University Press, 1996).

7. L. P. Hartley, *The Go-Between* (London: Hamish Hamilton, 1978), 9.

Glossary

an dân (*anmin*)
An Giang
An Hoá
Anh và Em
áo dài
ăn may cửa Phật
Âu Lạc
ba đảm đang
bà mẹ Việt Nam anh hùng
Bao Giờ Cho Đến Tháng Mười
Bảo Đại
Bảo Ninh
băng hà
bất khuất
Bến Thành
bị chết
Bò Bóp
Búi Xuân Phái
Cam Ranh
Cao Bá Nhạ
Cao Bá Quát
Cao Bằng
Cao Đài
Câu Chuyện Tử Tế
Cô Gái Trên Sông
Chàm (Tower)
chia buồn

chiến thắng Điện Biên Phủ
chiến tranh
chiến tranh chống Mỹ cứu
    nước
chiến tranh thần thánh
Chinh Phụ Ngâm Khúc
chính nghĩa
Chơn Thành
Chu Lai
Chúa Tàu Kim Quy
Chung Một Giòng Sông
con ma
Côn Đảo
Côn Lôn
Côn Sơn
Cồn Tiên
công đức
cống hiến
Củ Chi (Tunnel)
cúng
Cửa Biển
Cửu Long
cựu chiến binh Việt Nam
Cựu Kim Sơn
Dạ Ngân
Dốc Miếu
Dương Bích Liên

Dương Thu Hương
Dương Văn Phúc
Đà (spring)
Đà Lạt
Đà Nẵng
đài liệt sĩ
Đại Việt
Đại Việt Sử Ký Toàn Thư
đánh đông dẹp bắc
Đặng Kim Quy
Đặng Nhật Minh
Đặng Thai Mai
Đặng Trần Côn
Đập Đá Côn Đảo
đền
đình
Điện Biên Phủ
Đời trong Ngục
Độc Lập
Đổi Mới (policy)
Đông Du
Đông Kinh Nghĩa Thục
đức
Đức Thánh Trần
gia đình chính sách
gia đình liệt sĩ
giặc đến nhà đàn bà cũng
   đánh
giấy báo tử
giỗ
giết dần giết mòn
gọi hồn
Hải Hưng
hàng mã
Hoả Lò (prison)
Hoàng Anh
Hoàng Dung
Hoàng Văn Thụ
hi sinh
Hòn Vọng Phu
Hồ Biểu Chánh
Hồ Hữu Tường
Hồ Quý Ly
hồ thỉ tang bồng
hồi ký
hồi ký nhà tù

hồi ký cách mạng
Huế (City)
Hùng (kings)
Huỳnh Thúc Kháng
Hữu Nghị
Khải Định
Khe Sanh
khởi nghĩa
Khu Lưu Niệm
Lạc Tân Vương (Le Xinwang)
Lam Sơn
Lao Bảo
Lâm Bình Tường
Lê
Lê Đức Tiến
Lê Huân
Lê Lợi
Lê Lựu
Lê Thị Kim Bạch
Lê Văn Do
Lê Văn Hiến
lễ truy điệu
lễ tưởng niệm
liệt sĩ
Lĩnh Nam Chích Quái
Long Xuyên
Lưu Phương Thành
Lưu Trọng Ninh
Lý Bôn
Lý Tế Xuyên
Lý Thái Bạch (Li Po)
Lý Thường Kiệt
mất
mẹ anh hùng
Mẹ Vắng Nhà
Mỹ An
Mỹ Hoà Hưng
Mỹ Sơn
Mỹ Thuật ở Làng
nạn nhân chiến tranh
ngày quốc hận
ngày thương binh liệt sĩ
ngày xá tội vong nhân
Nghệ Tĩnh
ngoại
nghĩa trang liệt sĩ

nghĩa vụ thiêng liêng
Ngọn Cỏ Gió Đùa
Ngô Đức Kế
Ngô Quyền
Nguyễn Ái Quốc
Nguyễn An Ninh
Nguyễn Du
Nguyễn Duy Trinh
Nguyễn Đức Thuần
Nguyễn Huy Thiệp
Nguyễn Hữu Cầu
Nguyễn Lưu
Nguyễn Khánh Dư
Nguyễn Khắc Lợi
Nguyễn Khắc Viện
Nguyễn Quang Thân
Nguyễn Sáng
Nguyễn Tạo
Nguyễn Thị Di
Nguyễn Thiều
Nguyễn Trãi
Nguyễn Văn Anh
Nguyễn Văn Linh
Nguyễn Văn Thông
Nguyễn Văn Viễn
Nha Trang
nhân dân
nhân nghĩa (renyi)
Nhượng Tống
nội
nội tướng
Nỗi Buồn Chiến Tranh
Núi Thánh
Ông Hổ
Phạm Trọng Yêm (Fan
    Zhongyan)
Phan Bội Châu
Phan Châu Trinh
Phan Văn Hùm
phó Ban Chính Sách Xã
phong trào Đông Du
phụ nữ
qua đời
Quảng Ngãi
Quảng Trị
Quế Sơn

Qui Nhơn
Tạ Thu Thâu
Tam Giác Sắt
Tân Biên
Tây Thi
thành hoàng
thay đổi nhà tù đế quốc thành
    trường học cách mạng
thi đàn
Thi Tù Tùng Thoại
Thị Trấn Yên Tĩnh
Thiên Mụ (pagoda)
Thời Xa Vắng
thống nhất
Tiếng Dân
tinh thần
Tô Ngọc Thanh
Tô Ngọc Vân
tổ quốc
tổ quốc ghi công
Tôn Đức Nhung
Tôn Đức Thắng
Tôn Quang Phiệt
Tôn Thọ Tường
Tôn Văn Đề
Trần Bạch Đằng
Trần Huy Liệu
Trần Hưng Đạo
Trần Quốc Vượng
Trần Văn Giàu
Trần Văn Trà
Triệu (Lady)
Triệu Quang Phục
Trưng (sisters)
Trưng Nhị
Trưng Trắc
Trường Chinh
trường học thiên nhiên
tứ đức
từ trần
tử sĩ
tử tế
Tướng Về Hưu
Tự Đức
uống nước nhớ nguồn
Văn Nghệ

Văn Thiên Tường (Wen   Võ Nguyên Giáp
    Tienxiang)   Võ Văn Trúc
Việt Nam Quốc Dân Đảng   Vũ Tú Nam
Việt Nam Thanh Niên Cách   xin lỗi
    Mạng Đồng Chí Hội

Bibliography

Agulhon, Maurice. *Marianne au combat: L'imagerie et la symbolique républicaines de 1789 à 1880* (Paris: Flammarion, 1979).

An Giang (July 27, August 5, 12, 1988) (document no. 149, Ton Duc Thang Museum, Ho Chi Minh City).

An Giang Culture/Information Department, 1988 (document no. 84, Ton Duc Thang Museum, Ho Chi Minh City).

An Giang provincial branch of VCP, circular no. 06/TT-TU, Long Xuyen, March 13, 1987 (document no. 39, Ton Duc Thang Museum, Ho Chi Minh City).

Anderson, Benedict. *Imagined Communities* (London: Verso, 1991).

Andrews, Julia. *Painters and Politics in the People's Republic of China, 1949–1979* (Berkeley and Los Angeles: University of California Press, 1994).

A. T. "Hai Cuoc Thao Luan ve Viet Bac va Vuot Con Dao" ["Two Debates about Viet Bac and Escape from Con Dao"], *Bao Van Nghe*, March 20, 1955.

Bailey, Murray. *Travel and Tourism Opportunities in Vietnam: A Blueprint for Development* (Hong Kong: Business International Asia-Pacific, 1990).

Banh Bao and Huu Ngoc. *L'Itinéraire du film de fiction vietnamien: Expériences vietnamiennes* (Hanoi: Editions en langues étrangères, 1984).

Bao Ninh. *Noi Buon Chien Tranh* [*The Sorrow of War*] (Hanoi, 1991; reprint, Westminster, Calif.: Hong Linh, 1992). English version by Frank Palmos based on the translation from the Vietnamese by Vo Bang Thanh and Phan Thanh Hao with Katerina Pierce (London, Secker and Warburg, 1991; New York: Pantheon, 1995).

Barmé, Geremie R. *Shades of Mao: The Posthumous Cult of the Great Leader* (Armonk, N.Y.: M. E. Sharpe, 1996).

Berman, Marshall. *All That Is Solid Melts into Air* (New York: Penguin, 1982).

Bhabha, Homi, ed. *Nation and Narration* (London: Routledge, 1990).

Blatti, Jo, ed. *Past Meets Present: Essays about Historic Interpretation and Public Audiences* (Washington, D.C.: Smithsonian Institution Press, 1987).

Bloch, Maurice, and Jonathan Parry, eds. *Death and the Regeneration of Life* (Cambridge: Cambridge University Press, 1982).

Blumanhourst, Gloria E. "Coherence: A Narrative Criticism of Two Accounts of Herstory" (master's thesis, Colorado State University, 1986).

Boudarel, Georges. *Cent fleurs écloses dans la nuit du Vietnam: Communisme et dissidence, 1945–1956* (Paris: Jacques Bertoin, 1991).

———. "Intellectual Dissidence in the 1950s: The 'Nhan Van Giai Pham' Affair." *Vietnam Forum*, no. 13 (1990): 154–74.

Bourguet, Marie Noelle, Lucette Valensi, and Nathan Wachtel, eds. *Between History and Memory* (Chur: Harwood Academic Publishers, 1990).

Bowley, Robert. "Vietnam Visited and Revisited" (http://www.goodnet.com/~rbowley/vietnamstory.html, 1995).

Bozon, Michel, and Anne Marie Thiesse. "The Collapse of Memory: The Case of the Farm Workers (French Vexin, Pays de France)." In *Between History and Memory*, edited by Marie Noelle Bourguet, Lucette Valensi, and Nathan Wachtel (Chur: Harwood Academic Publishers, 1990).

Brombert, Victor. *The Romantic Prison: The French Tradition* (Princeton, N.J.: Princeton University Press, 1978).

Bryant, Donald C. "Rhetoric: Its Function and Its Scope." *Quarterly Journal of Speech* 39 (December 1953): 401–24.

Bui Cong Trung. "O Con Dao" ["In Con Dao"]. In *Len Duong Thang Loi* [*On the Road to Victory*] (Hanoi: NXB Hanoi, 1985).

Butler, Samuel. *Erewhon Revisited* (New York: Modern Library, 1955).

Carnochan, W. B. "The Literature of Confinement." In *The Oxford History of the Prison: The Practice of Punishment in Western Society*, edited by Norval Morris and David Rothman (New York: Oxford University Press, 1995).

Carroll, Lewis. *Through the Looking Glass and What Alice Found There* (New York: Norton, 1995).

Charlot, John. "Vietnamese Cinema: First Views." *Journal of Southeast Asian Studies* 22 (March 1991): 33–62.

Clark, T. J. *The Painting of Modern Life* (Princeton, N.J.: Princeton University Press, 1984).

Clinton, Catherine. *The Other Civil War: American Women in the Nineteenth Century* (New York: Hill and Wang, 1984).

———. *Tara Revisited: Women, War and the Plantation Legend* (New York: Abbeville Press, 1995).

Clinton, Catherine, and Nina Silber, eds. *Divided Houses: Gender and the Civil War* (New York: Oxford University Press, 1992).

Cohen, Erik. "Toward a Sociology of International Tourism." *Social Research* 39 (1972): 164–82.

Confino, Alon. "Collective Memory and Cultural History: Problems of Method." *American Historical Review* 102 (December 1997): 1386–483.

Cong Huyen Ton Nu Nha Trang. "The Role of French Romanticism in the New Poetry Movement in Vietnam." In *Borrowings and Adaptations in Vietnam-*

ese Culture, edited by Truong Buu Lam, Southeast Asian Paper No. 25 (Honolulu: Center for Asia and Pacific Studies, 1985).

Cu Huy Can. *Culture et politique culturelle en République socialiste du Viet Nam [Culture and Political Culture in the Socialist Republic of Vietnam]* (Paris: UNESCO, 1985).

Da Ngan. "Nha Khong Co Dan Ong" ["The House with No Men"] (1990). In *Literature News: Nine Stories from the Vietnam Writers' Union Newspaper,* Bao Van Nghe, selected and translated with introduction and illustrations by Rosemary Nguyen (New Haven, Conn.: Council on Southeast Asia Studies, 1997).

Dang Anh Dao. "Victo Huygo va con Nguoi Viet Nam Hien Dai" ["Victor Hugo and Vietnamese Today"]. In *Hugo O Viet Nam [Hugo in Vietnam],* edited by Luu Lien (Hanoi: NXB Vien Van Hoc, 1985).

Dang Chan Lieu and Le Kha Ke. *Tu Dien Viet-Anh: Vietnamese English Dictionary* (Hanoi: NXB Khoa Hoc Xa Hoi, 1971).

Dang Kim Quy. "Ngoi Nha Luu Niem Thoi Nien Thieu Chu Tich Ton Duc Thang" ["President TDT's Childhood Home"]. *Tap Chi Lich Su Dang [Journal of Party History],* May 1991, 36.

Dang Thai Mai. *Van Tho Cach Mang Viet Nam Dau The Ky XX (1900–1925) [Vietnamese Revolutionary Prose and Poetry in the Early Twentieth Century]* (Hanoi: NXB Van Hoc, 1964).

Dang Viet Chau. "Nguc Son La 1935–1936" ["Son La Prison 1935–1936"]. In *Suoi Reo Nam Ay [The Bubbling Spring That Year]* (Hai Phong: NXB Thong Tin-Van Hoa, 1993).

Davidson, Jeremy H. C. S. " 'Good Omen' versus 'Worth': The Poetic Dialogue between Ton Tho Tuong and Phan Van Tri." In *Context, Meaning and Power in Southeast Asia,* edited by Mark Hobart and Robert H. Taylor (Ithaca, N.Y.: Cornell University Southeast Asia Program, 1986).

Davidson, Phillip B. *Vietnam at War: The History, 1946–1975* (New York: Oxford University Press, 1988).

Démariaux, J. C. *Les Secrets des îles Poulo Condore: Le grand bagne indochinois* (Paris: J. Peyronnet & Cie, 1956).

Dickinson, Greg. "Memories for Sale: Nostalgia and the Construction of Identity in Old Pasadena," *Quarterly Journal of Speech* 83 (1977): 1–27.

Duncan, Martha Grace. *Romantic Outlaws, Beloved Prisons: The Unconscious Meanings of Crime and Punishment* (New York: New York University Press, 1996).

Duong Thu Huong. *Nhung Thien Duong Mu [Paradise of the Blind]* (Hanoi: NXB Phu Nu, 1988), translated by Phan Huy Duong and Nina McPherson (New York: Morrow, 1991).

———. *Tieu Thuyet Vo De [Novel without a Name]* (Hanoi, 1989; reprint, Stanton, Calif.: Van Nghe, 1991), translated by Phan Huy Duong and Nina McPherson (New York: Morrow, 1995).

Durand, Maurice, and Nguyen Tran Huan. *Introduction à la littérature vietnamienne* (Paris: G. P. Maisonneuve et Larose, 1969).

Erlanger, Steven. "Saigon in Transition and in a Hurry." *New York Times Magazine Sophisticated Traveler,* May 17, 1992, 18–19, 50, 80–81.

"Faith in Hanoi." *Wall Street Journal,* January 20, 1995.

Fall, Bernard. *The Viet Minh Regime,* Data Paper No. 14 (Ithaca, N.Y.: Cornell University Southeast Asia Program, 1954).

Faulkner, William. *Requiem for a Nun* (New York: Random House, 1968).

Faust, Drew. *Mothers of Invention: Women of the Slaveholding South in the American Civil War* (Chapel Hill: University of North Carolina Press, 1996).

Fisher, Walter. "Narration as a Human Communication Paradigm: The Case of Public Moral Argument." *Communication Monographs* 51 (March 1984): 1–22.

Florida, Nancy K. *Writing the Past, Inscribing the Future: History as Prophecy in Colonial Java* (Durham, N.C.: Duke University Press, 1995).

Foss, Sonja K. *Rhetorical Criticism: Exploration and Practice* (Prospect Heights, Ill.: Waveland Press, 1989).

Foucault, Michel. "Counter-memory: The Philosophy of Difference." In *Language, Counter-memory, Practice: Selected Essays and Interviews,* edited by Donald F. Bouchard (Ithaca, N.Y.: Cornell University Press, 1977).

Furet, François. *Penser la révolution française* (Paris: Gallimard, 1978).

Giebel, Christoph. *Striking Images: Ba Son 1925 — A Case Study of the History and Historiography of Vietnamese Labor* (Ithaca, N.Y.: Cornell University Southeast Asia Program, forthcoming).

———. "Telling Life: An Approach to the Official Biography of Ton Duc Thang." In *Essays into Vietnamese Pasts,* edited by K. W. Taylor and John K. Whitmore (Ithaca, N.Y.: Cornell University Southeast Asia Program, 1995).

———. "Ton Duc Thang and the Imagined Ancestries of Vietnamese Communism" (Ph.D. diss., Cornell University, 1996).

Gillis, John, ed. *Commemorations: The Politics of National Identity* (Princeton, N.J.: Princeton University Press, 1994).

Graburn, Nelson H. H. "Tourism: The Sacred Journey." In *Hosts and Guests,* edited by Valene L. Smith (Philadelphia: University of Pennsylvania Press, 1989).

Greenberger, Robert S. "Buy Those Zippos, Catch Some Waves, Visit a War Museum." *Wall Street Journal,* January 25, 1993.

Ha Phu Huong. "O Nha Tu Lao Bao" ["In Lao Bao Prison"]. *Tap Chi Cua Viet* [*Viet Door Journal*] 3 (1990): 25–29.

Halbwachs, Maurice. *Les Cadres sociaux de la mémoire* (Paris: Mouton, 1976).

———. *The Collective Memory,* translated by Francis J. Ditter Jr. (New York: Harper Colophon, 1980).

———. *On Collective Memory,* edited and translated by Lewis A. Coser (Chicago: University of Chicago Press, 1992).

Hantover, Jeffrey. "Bui Xuan Phai." In *Bui Xuan Phai,* edited by Nguyen Quan (Ho Chi Minh City: HCMC Arts Association [Hoi My Thuat T. P. Ho Chi Minh], 1992).

———. *Uncorked Soul: Contemporary Art from Vietnam* (Hong Kong: Plum Blossoms, 1991).

Hardacre, Helen. *Shinto and the State, 1868–1988* (Princeton, N.J.: Princeton University Press, 1989).

Hémery, Daniel. *Révolutionaires vietnamiens et pouvoir colonial en Indochine* (Paris: Maspéro, 1975).

Hiebert, Murray, "Playing for Keeps." *Far Eastern Economic Review,* May 7, 1992, 37–38.

———. "Vietnam's Censors Tell Producer to Cut Film." *Far Eastern Economic Review,* July 22, 1993, 90.

———. "Wish You Were Here." *Far Eastern Economic Review,* January 18, 1990, 44–45.

Ho Chi Minh. *Le Procès de la colonisation française* (Paris: Librairie du Travail, 1925).

Hoang Anh. "Nha Tu De Quoc Tro Thanh Truong Hoc cua Chien Si Cach Mang" ["Imperialist Prisons Become Schools for Revolutionary Fighters"]. *Tap Chi Cong San [Communist Review]* 1, no. 40 (1990): 3–9.

Hoang Dung, ed. *Tho Van Cach Mang 1930–1945 [Revolutionary Poems and Prose, 1930–1945]* (Hanoi: NXB Van Hoc, 1980).

Hoang Giang. "La Révolte des intellectuels au Vietnam en 1956." *Vietnam Forum,* no. 13 (1990): 144–53.

Hoang Ngoc Thanh Dung. "To Serve the Cause of Women's Liberation." In *To Be Made Over: Tales of Socialist Reeducation in Vietnam,* edited and translated by Huynh Sanh Thong (New Haven, Conn.: Yale Center for International and Area Studies, 1988).

Hobsbawm, Eric. "Mass-Producing Traditions: Europe, 1870–1914." In *The Invention of Tradition,* edited by Eric Hobsbawm and Terence Ranger (Cambridge: Cambridge University Press, 1983).

Hooper-Greenhill, Eilean. *Museums and the Shaping of Knowledge* (London: Routledge, 1992).

Hunt, Lynn. *The Family Romance of the French Revolution* (Berkeley and Los Angeles: University of California Press, 1994).

Huynh Kim Khanh. *Vietnamese Communism, 1925–1945* (Ithaca, N.Y.: Cornell University Press, 1982).

Huynh Sanh Thong, ed. and trans. *An Anthology of Vietnamese Poems from the Eleventh through the Twentieth Centuries* (New Haven Conn.: Yale University Press, 1996).

———. *The Heritage of Vietnamese Poetry* (New Haven, Conn.: Yale University Press, 1979).

———. "Main Trends of Vietnamese Literature between the Two World Wars." *Vietnam Forum,* no. 3 (1984): 99–125.

Huynh Thuc Khang. *Thi Tu Tung Thoai [Prison Verse]* (Hue: NXB Tieng Dan, 1939).

———. *Tu Truyen. [Autobiography]* (Hue: Anh Minh, 1963).

Ignatius, David. "Vietnamese Begin to Question If War Was Worth Sacrifices." *Washington Post,* November 2, 1991.

Jamieson, Neil. "The Traditional Family in Vietnam." *Vietnam Forum,* no. 8 (1986): 91–150.

———. "The Traditional Village in Vietnam." *Vietnam Forum,* no. 7 (1986): 89–126.

————. *Understanding Vietnam* (Berkeley and Los Angeles: University of California Press, 1993).

Johnson, David. "Epic and History in Early China: The Matter of Wu Tzu-shü." *Journal of Asian Studies* 40 (February 1981): 255–71.

————. "The Wu Tzu-shü *Pien-wen* and Its Source." Parts 1 and 2. *Harvard Journal of Asiatic Studies* 40 (June 1980): 93–156; 40 (December 1980): 465–505.

Kapferer, Bruce. *Legends of People, Myths of State: Violence, Intolerance, and Political Culture in Sri Lanka and Australia* (Washington, D.C.: Smithsonian Institution Press, 1988).

Karp, Ivan, Christine Mullen Kreamer, and Steven D. Lavine, eds., *Museums and Communities: The Politics of Public Culture* (Washington, D.C.: Smithsonian Institution Press, 1992).

Koonz, Claudia. *Mothers in the Fatherland: Women, the Family and Nazi Politics* (New York: St. Martin's Press, 1987).

Kundera, Milan. *The Book of Laughter and Forgetting* (New York: Knopf, 1981).

Kurihara, Hirohide. "Changes in the Literary Policy of the Vietnamese Workers' Party, 1956–1958." In *Indochina in the 1940s and 1950s* edited by Takashi Shiraishi and Motoo Furuta (Ithaca, N.Y.: Cornell University Southeast Asia Program, 1992).

Lam Binh Tuong. "Bao Ve Ngoi Nha Luu Niem Chu tich Ton Duc Thang o My Hoa Hung, Tinh Chat Phong Canh va Canh Quan" ["Protecting President Ton Duc Thang's Home in My Hoa Hung, the Landscape Character and Beauty"], in Ban tuyen giao Tinh uy An Giang [An Giang Provincial Propaganda Commission].

————. "Trung Tu Di Tich voi Viec Phuc Hoi Noi That Ngoi Nha cua Chu tich Ton Duc Thang o My Hoa Hung (An Giang)" ["Reconstructing Historic Sites with Interior Renovations of President Ton Duc Thang's House in My Hoa Hung (An Giang)"], in Ban tuyen giao Tinh uy An Giang [An Giang Provincial Propaganda Commission].

Lanfant, Marie-Françoise. "International Tourism, Internationalization and the Challenge to Identity." In *International Tourism: Identity and Change,* edited by Marie-Françoise Lanfant, John B. Allcock, and Edward M. Bruner (Thousand Oaks, Calif.: Sage, 1995).

Lanfant, Marie-Françoise, John B. Allcock, and Edward M. Bruner, eds. *International Tourism: Identity and Change* (Thousand Oaks, Calif.: Sage, 1995).

Le Luu. *The Old Days [Thoi Xa Vang]* (Hanoi: Tac Pham Moi, 1987).

Lee, Begonia. "Houses of the Holy." *Far Eastern Economic Review,* June 6, 1996: 52

Lenz, Ralph. "On Resurrecting Tourism in Vietnam." *Focus* 43, no. 3 (fall 1993): 1–6.

Liu, James T. C. "An Early Sung Reformer: Fan Chung-Yen." in *Chinese Thought and Institutions,* edited by John K. Fairbank, 3d ed. (Chicago: University of Chicago Press, 1964).

Ljunggren, Börje, and Peter Timmer, eds. *The Challenge of Reform in Indochina* (Cambridge, Mass.: Harvard University Press, 1993).

Lockhart, Greg. "Preface" and "Introduction." In Nguyen Huy Thiep, *The General Retires and Other Stories* (Kuala Lumpur: Oxford in Asia, 1992).

Lowenthal, David. *The Past Is a Foreign Country* (Cambridge: Cambridge University Press, 1985).

Lumley Robert, ed. *The Museum Time-Machine: Putting Cultures on Display* (London: Routledge, 1988).

Luong, Hy Van. "Agrarian Unrest from an Anthropological Perspective: The Case of Vietnam." *Comparative Politics* 17, no. 2, (January 1985): 153–74.

———. "Economic Reform and the Intensification of Rituals in Two Northern Vietnamese Villages, 1980–1990," In *The Challenge of Reform in Indochina,* edited by Börje Ljunggren and Peter Timmer (Cambridge, Mass.: Harvard University Press, 1993).

Luu Lien. *Hugo o Viet Nam* [*Hugo in Vietnam*] (Hanoi: NXB Vien Van Hoc, 1985).

MacCannell, Dean. "Staged Authenticity: Arrangements of Social Space in Tourist Settings." *American Journal of Sociology* 79 (1973): 589–603.

———. *The Tourist: A New Theory of the Leisure Class* (New York: Schocken Books, 1989).

Malarney, Shaun. "The Emergent Cult of Ho Chi Minh? A Report on Religious Innovation in Contemporary Northern Viet Nam." *Asian Cultural Studies* 22 (1996): 121–31.

———. "The Limits of 'State Functionalism' and the Reconstruction of Funerary Ritual in Contemporary Northern Vietnam," *American Ethnologist* 23 (August 1996): 540–60.

———. "Ritual and Revolution in Viet Nam" (Ph.D. diss., University of Michigan, 1993).

Margolick, David. "To Hanoi by Train, a Journey of 1,000 Miles." *New York Times Magazine, Sophisticated Traveler,* (November 9, 1997), 17–19, 32, 34, 36–37.

Marr, David. *Vietnam 1945: The Quest for Power* (Berkeley and Los Angeles: University of California Press, 1995).

———. *Vietnamese Anticolonialism: 1885–1925* (Berkeley and Los Angeles: University of California Press, 1971).

———. *Vietnamese Tradition on Trial, 1920–1945* (Berkeley and Los Angeles: University of California Press, 1981).

Marr, David G., and A. C. Milner, eds. *Southeast Asia in the 9th to 14th Centuries* (Singapore: Institute of Southeast Asian Studies, 1986).

Martin, Paul. "Land of the Descending Dragon." *National Geographic Traveler,* May/June 1996, 160–75.

Maza, Sara. "The Diamond Necklace Affair Revisited (1785–1786): The Case of the Disappearing Queen." In *Eroticism and the Body Politic,* edited by Lynn Hunt (Baltimore: Johns Hopkins University Press, 1991).

McEvilley, Thomas. "Doctor, Lawyer, Indian Chief." In *Art and Otherness: Crisis in Cultural Identity* (New York: Documentext, 1992).

Milio, Philip. "My Return to Vietnam" (http://grunt.space.swri.edu/pmilio.html, 1996).

Morris, Norval, and David Rothman, eds. *The Oxford History of the Prison:*

The Practice of Punishment in Western Society (New York: Oxford University Press, 1995).

Mosse, George L. *Fallen Soldiers: Reshaping the Memory of the World Wars* (Oxford: Oxford University Press, 1990).

Mowlana, Hamid. *Global Information and World Communication* (New York: Longman, 1986).

Ngo Manh Lan. "Looking Inwards: Vietnamese Cinema in the Eighties," *Cinemaya* 2 (winter 1988–89): 6–14.

Ngo Ngoc Boi. "The Blanket of Scraps" ["Nhung Manh Vun"]. In *Literature News: Nine Stories from the Vietnam Writers' Union Newspaper,* Bao Van Nghe, selected and translated with introduction and illustrations by Rosemary Nguyen (New Haven, Conn.: Council on Southeast Asia Studies, 1997).

Ngo Van Quynh. "Am Vang Cuoc Vuot Nguc" ["Echo of an Escape"]. In *Suoi Reo Nam Ay* [*The Bubbling Spring That Year*] (Hai Phong: NXB Thong Tin-Van Hoa, 1993).

Nguyen Dang Manh and Tran Huu Ta, eds. *Tuyen Tap Vu Trong Phung* [*Collected Works of Vu Trong Phung*], vol. 1 (Hanoi: NXB Van Hoc, 1993).

Nguyen Don Phuc. "Dan Ba Dong Phuong" ["Oriental Women"]. *Nam Phong* 101 (December 1925): 435–37.

Nguyen Duc Thuan. "Truong Hoc Xa Lim" ["Cell School"]. In *Truong Hoc sau Song Sat* [*School behind the Iron Bars*] (Hanoi: NXB Thanh Nien, 1969).

Nguyen Duy Can, ed. *Lich Su Dien Anh Cach Mang Viet Nam* [*History of the Revolutionary Cinema in Vietnam*] (Hanoi: Cuc Dien Anh, 1983).

Nguyen Duy Trinh. "Lam Bao va Sang Tac Tieu Thuyet trong Nha Lao Vinh" ["Writing Newspapers and Novels in Vinh Prison"]. In *Truong Hoc sau Song Sat* [*School behind the Iron Bars*] (Hanoi: NXB Thanh Nien, 1969).

Nguyen Hue Chi, ed. *Suy Nghi Moi Ve Nhat Ky Trong Tu* [*New Reflections on the Prison Diary*] (Hanoi: NXB Khoa Hoc Xa Hoi, 1990).

Nguyen Huy Thiep. "The General Retires." In *The General Retires and Other Stories,* translated with an introduction by Greg Lockhart (Kuala Lumpur: Oxford in Asia, 1991).

Nguyen Khac Vien. *Tradition and Revolution in Vietnam,* edited by David Marr and Jayne Werner (Berkeley, Calif.: Indochina Resource Center, n.d. [1974?]).

Nguyen Khac Vien and Huu Ngoc, ed. and trans. *Vietnamese Literature: Historical Background and Texts* (Hanoi: Red River, 1980).

Nguyen Luu. "Nha Tu Son La, Truong Hoc Cach Mang" ["Son La Prison, School for Revolutionaries"]. *Nghien Cuu Lich Su* [*Journal of Historical Studies*] 103 (1975): 57–71.

Nguyen Nam. "Luoc Dich Quoc Ngu Cuoi The Ky XIX" ["Translations into the Romanized Script in the Nineteenth Century"] *Tap Chi Han Nom* [*Han Nom Journal*] 1, no. 34 (1998): 20–31.

Nguyen Ngoc Bich. *A Thousand Years of Vietnamese Poetry* (New York: Knopf, 1975).

Nguyen Ngoc Ngan. "In the Line of Socialist Duty." In *To Be Made Over: Tales of Socialist Reeducation in Vietnam,* edited and translated by Huynh Sanh

Thong, (New Haven, Conn.: Yale Center for International and Area Studies, 1988).

Nguyen Quan. *Vietnamese Plastic Art* (Hanoi: NXB My Thuat, 1987).

———, ed. *Bui Xuan Phai in the Collection of Tran Hau Tuan* (Hanoi: Red River, 1991).

Nguyen Quan and Phan Cam Thuong. *My Thuat o Lang* [*Art in the Village*] (Hanoi: NXB My Thuat, 1991).

Nguyen Quang Phong. *Cac Hoa Si Truong Cao Dang My Thuat Dong Duong* [*Painters of the Indochina Art School*] (Hanoi: NXB My Thuat 1991).

Nguyen Q. Thang and Nguyen Ba The. *Tu Dien Nhan Vat Lich Su Viet Nam* [*Dictionary of Vietnamese Historical Figures*] (Hanoi: NXB Khoa Hoc Xa Hoi, 1991).

Nguyen Quang Than, "The Waltz of the Chamber Pot" ["Vu Dieu cai Bo"] (1991). In *Literature News: Nine Stories from the Vietnam Writers' Union Newspaper,* Bao Van Nghe, selected and translated with introduction and illustrations by Rosemary Nguyen (New Haven, Conn.: Council on Southeast Asia Studies, 1997).

Nguyen Tao, *Chung Toi Vuot Nguc* [*We Escape from Prison*] (Hanoi: NXB Van Hoa, 1977).

———. *Trong Nguc Toi Hoa Lo* [*In the Dark Prison, Hoa Lo*] (Hanoi: NXB Van Hoc, 1959).

———. *Vuot Nguc Dak Mil* [*Escape from Dak Mil*] (Hanoi: NXB Thanh Nien, 1976).

Nguyen The Anh. "A Case of Confucian Survival in Twentieth-Century Vietnam: Huynh Thuc Khang and His Newspaper *Tieng Dan.*" *Vietnam Forum* no. 8 (1986): 173–203.

Nguyen Thieu. "Truong Hoc trong Tu" ["Prison School"]. In *Truong Hoc sau Song Sat* [*School behind the Iron Bars*] (Hanoi: NXB Thanh Nien, 1969).

Nguyen Tien Huu. *Dörfliche Kulte im traditionellen Vietnam* [*Village Cults in Traditional Vietnam*] (Munich: Verlag UNI-Druck, 1970).

Nguyen Van Tu. "Toi Lam Cau Doi Tet o Nha Tu Son La" ["I Make Rhyming Couplets on New Year Occasion in Son La Prison"], In *Suoi Reo Nam Ay* [*The Bubbling Spring That Year*] (Hai Phong: NXB Thong Tin-Van Hoa, 1993).

Nhuong Tong. *Doi trong Nguc* [*Life in Prison*] (Hanoi: Van Hoa Moi, 1935).

Ninh Binh, Cultural Service [Ty Van Hoa Ninh Binh]. *Cong Tac Xay Dung Nep Song Moi, con Nguoi Moi va Gia Dinh Tien Tien Chong My, Cuu Nuoc* [*The Task of Building the New Ways, the New Person and the Progressive Family in the War of National Salvation Against the Americans*] (Ninh Binh: n.p., 1968).

Nora, Pierre, ed. *Lieux de mémoire.* Vol. 1 (Paris: Gallimard, 1984).

Norkunas, Martha K. *The Politics of Public Memory: Tourism, History, and Ethnicity in Monterey, California* (Albany: State University of New York Press, 1993).

O'Harrow, Stephen. "Men of Hu, Men of Han, Men of the Hundred Man: The Biography of Si Nhiep and the Conceptualization of Early Vietnamese Society." *Bulletin de l'Ecole Française d'Extrême-Orient* 75 (1986): 249–66.

Oliver, Victor. *Cao Dai Spiritism* (Leiden: E. J. Brill, 1976).

Ouzouf, Mona. "Le Panthéon: l'Ecole Normale des morts." In *Lieux de mémoire*, vol. 1, edited by Pierre Nora (Paris: Gallimard, 1984).

Pacific-Asia Travel News. *Vietnam: A Travel Agent's Guide* (Phoenix, Ariz.: Americas Publishing, 1994).

Pearce, Susan, ed. *Objects of Knowledge* (London: Athlone, 1990).

Pelley, Patricia. "The History of Resistance and the Resistance to History in Post-colonial Constructions of the Past." in *Essays into Vietnamese Pasts,* edited by K. W. Taylor and John K. Whitmore (Ithaca, N.Y.: Cornell University Southeast Asia Program, 1995).

———. "Writing Revolution: The New History in Post-colonial Vietnam" (Ph.D. diss., Cornell University, 1993).

Pellico, Silvio. *My Prisons* (London: Oxford University Press, 1963).

Pham Hung. *In the Death Cell* (Hanoi: Foreign Languages Publishing House, 1960).

Pham Nhu Thom, ed. *Hoi Ky Tran Huy Lieu* [*Memoirs of Tran Huy Lieu*] (Hanoi: NXB Khoa Hoc Xa Hoi, 1991).

Pham Quynh. "Dia Vi Nguoi Dan Ba trong Xa Hoi Nuoc Ta" ["The Position of Women in Our Society"]. *Nam Phong* [*Southern Wind*] 82 (April 1924): 269–84.

Phan Huy Le et al. *Lich Su Viet Nam,* [*History of Vietnam*], vol. 1 (Hanoi: NXB Dai Hoc va Giao Duc Chuyen Nghiep, 1991).

Phan Van Cac. "Tu Ban Dich Nam 1960 den Ban Dich Bo Sung va Chinh Ly Nam 1983," ["From 1960 Translation to the Supplemented and Corrected Translation of 1983"]. In *Suy Nghi Moi Ve Nhat Ky trong Tu* [*New Reflections on the Prison Diary*], edited by Nguyen Hue Chi (Hanoi: NXB Khoa Hoc Xa Hoi, 1990).

Phan Van Hum. *Ngoi Tu Kham Lon* [*A Stay in the Central Prison*] (1929: reprint, Saigon: NXB Dan Toc, 1957).

Phung Quan. *Vuot Con Dao* (1955; reprint, Hue: NXB Thanh Hoa, 1987).

Pike, Douglas. *History of Vietnamese Communism, 1925–1976* (Stanford, Calif.: Hoover Institution Press, 1978).

———. *PAVN: People's Army of Vietnam* (New York: Da Capo Press, 1986).

Porter, Gareth. "Proletariat and Peasantry in Early Vietnamese Communism." *Asian Thought and Society* 1, no. 3 (December 1976): 333–46.

"The Profit Hunters." *The Economist*, June 11, 1994, 31.

Renan, Ernest. "What Is a Nation?" (lecture presented at the Collège de France, 1882), translated by Martin Thom, in Homi Bhabha, *Nation and Narration* (London: Routledge, 1990).

Rubin, William. *Primitivism in XXth Century Art: Affinity of the Tribal and the Modern* (New York: Museum of Modern Art, 1984)

Schafer, Edward H. *The Vermillion Bird: T'ang Images of the South* (Berkeley: and Los Angeles: University of California Press, 1967).

Schaffer, John, and Cao Thi Nhu Quynh. "Ho Bieu Chanh and the Early Development of the Vietnamese Novel." *Vietnam Forum*, no. 12, (1988): 100–111.

Schreiner, Klaus H. *Politischer Heldenkult in Indonesien: Tradition und Mod-*

erne Praxis [*Political Hero Cult in Indonesia: Tradition and Modern Practice*] (Berlin: Reimer, 1995).

Schwarcz, Vera. *Bridge across Broken Time: Chinese and Jewish Cultural Memory* (New Haven, Conn.: Yale University Press, 1998).

Scott, James C., *Domination and the Arts of Resistance: Hidden Transcripts* (New Haven, Conn.: Yale University Press, 1990).

Sheehan, Neil. *After the War Was Over* (New York: Random House, 1991).

Shenon, Philip, "Hanoi to Show Tourists Hideout That Eluded US." *New York Times,* December 11, 1992.

Sherman, Daniel J. "Bodies and Names: The Emergence of Commemoration in Interwar France." *American Historical Review* 103 (April 1998): 443–66.

Shiraishi, Masaya. "State, Village and Vagabonds: Vietnamese Rural Society and the Phan Ba Vanh Rebellion." In *History and Peasant Consciousness in Southeast Asia,* edited by Andrew Turton and Shigeharu Tanabe (Osaka: National Museum of Ethnography, 1984).

Silber, Nina. *The Romance of Reunion: Northerners and the South, 1865–1900* (Chapel Hill: University of North Carolina Press, 1993).

Smith, Valene, ed. *Hosts and Guests* (Philadelphia: University of Pennsylvania Press, 1989).

Solomon, Andrew. "Their Irony, Humor (and Art) Can Save China." *New York Times Magazine,* December 19, 1993.

Son La, Ty Van Hoa Thong Tin, *Tho Ca Cach Mang Nha Tu Son La 1930– 1945* [*Revolutionary Poems and Songs from Son La Prison*] (Son La: NXB Son La, 1980).

Spengemann, William C., and L. R. Lundquist. "Autobiography and the American Myth." *American Quarterly* 17 (fall 1965): 501–19.

Sturken, Marita. *Tangled Memories: The Vietnam War, the AIDS Epidemic, and the Politics of Remembering* (Berkeley and Los Angeles: University of California Press, 1997).

Suoi Reo Nam Ay [*The Bubbling Spring That Year*] (Hai Phong: NXB Thong Tin-Van Hoa, 1993).

Tai, Hue-Tam Ho. "Monumental Ambiguity: The State Commemoration of Ho Chi Minh." In *Essays into Vietnamese Pasts,* edited by K. W. Taylor and John K. Whitmore (Ithaca, N.Y.: Cornell University Southeast Asia Program, 1995).

———. *Radicalism and the Origins of the Vietnamese Revolution* (Cambridge, Mass.: Harvard University Press, 1992).

Taylor, Keith W. *The Birth of Vietnam* (Berkeley and Los Angeles: University of California Press, 1983).

———. "Looking behind the Vietnamese Annals: Ly Phat Ma (1028–54) and Ly Nhat Ton (1054–72) in the *Viet Su Luoc* and the *Toan Thu.*" *Vietnam Forum* no. 7 (winter—spring 1986): 47–68.

———. "Notes on the Viet Dien U Linh Tap." *Vietnam Forum,* no. 8 (summer— fall 1986): 26–59.

Taylor, Nora. "The Artist and the State: The Politics of Painting and National Identity in Hanoi, Vietnam 1925–1995" (Ph.D diss., Cornell University, 1997).

————. "Masterpieces by the Cup: Top Art Collection Hangs in Streetside Cafe." *Vietnam Investment Review,* no. 129 (March 21–27, 1994): 27.

Thayer, Carlyle. "Dilemmas of Development in Vietnam." *Current History,* December 1978, 221–25.

To Huu. "The Song on the Perfume River." In *An Anthology of Vietnamese Poems: From the Eleventh through the Twentieth Centuries,* edited and translated by Huynh Sanh Thong (New Haven, Conn.: Yale University Press, 1996).

To Thanh Tam, ed. *Mot con Nguoi Binh Thuong—Vi Dai. Ky Yeu Hoi Thao Khoa Hoc ve Chu Tich Ton Duc Thang Nhan Dip Ky Niem 100 Nam Ngay Sinh 20-8-1888—20-8-1988 [A Great Ordinary Person. Proceedings of the Symposium on President Ton Duc Thang Commemorating the Centennial of His Birth]* (An Giang: Provincial Propaganda Commission, 1989).

Toan Anh. *Nep Cu: Tin Nguong Viet Nam [Old Ways: Vietnamese Beliefs],* vol. 1 (Saigon: Hoa Dang, 1969).

Ton Quang Phiet. *Mot Ngay Ngan Thu [The Eternal Day]* (Hue: Phuc Long, 1935).

Tran Cung. "Tu Con Dao Tro Ve (Hoi Ky)" ["Return from Poulo Condore (Memoirs)"] *Nghien Cuu Lich Su [Journal of Historical Studies]* 134 (1970): 18–26.

Tran Dang Ninh. *Hai Lan Vuot Nguc [Two Prison Escapes]* (Hanoi: NXB Van Hoc, 1970).

————. "Vuot Nguc Son La" ["Escape from Son La Prison"]. In *Suoi Reo Nam Ay [The Bubbling Spring That Year]* (Hai Phong: NXB Thong Tin-Van Hoa, 1993).

Tran Dinh Tho. "De Co nhung Tac Pham Nghe Thuat Tao Hinh Dam Da Tinh Chat Dan Toc" ["In Order for Works of Art to Have a Warm National Essence"]. In Tran Van Can, *Ve Tinh Dan Toc cua Nghe Thuat Tao Hinh [Concerning National Sentiment in Visual Arts]* (Hanoi: NXB Van Hoa, 1973).

Tran Hinh. "Victo Huygo va cac Nha Van Viet Nam" ["Victor Hugo and Vietnamese Writers"]. In *Hugo o Viet Nam [Hugo in Vietnam],* edited by Luu Lien (Hanoi: NXB Vien Van Hoc, 1985).

Tran Huu Ta. "Doc Hoi Ky Cach Mang: Nghi Ve Ve Dep Cua Nguoi Chien Si Cong San Viet Nam" ["Reading Revolutionary Memoirs: Thoughts on the Beauty of Vietnamese Communist Warriors"]. *Tap Chi Van Hoc [Journal of Literature]* 2, no. 164 (1977): 17–28.

Tran Huy Lieu. "Doc Tap Tho Nhat Ky trong Tu cua Ho Chu Tich" ["Reading Chairman Ho's Prison Diary"]. *Nghien Cuu Van Hoc [Journal of Literary Studies]* 6 (1960): 12–24.

————. "Duoi Ham Son La" ("In the Son La Hole"]. In *Tran Huy Lieu: Hoi Ky [Tran Huy Lieu: Memoirs]* (Hanoi: NXB Khoa Hoc Xa Hoi, 1991).

————. "Nghia Lo Khoi Nghia—Nghia Lo Vuot Nguc" ["Nghia Lo Uprising— Escape from Nghia Lo"]. In *Tran Huy Lieu: Hoi Ky [Tran Huy Lieu: Memoirs]* (Hanoi: NXB Khoa Hoc Xa Hoi, 1991).

————. *Nguyen Trai,* 2d ed. (Hanoi: NXB Khoa Hoc Xa Hoi, 1969).

————. "Phan Dau de Tro Nen Mot Dang Vien Cong San" ["Striving to Become a Communist Party Member"]. In *Tran Huy Lieu: Hoi Ky* [*Tran Huy Lieu: Memoirs*] (Hanoi: NXB Khoa Hoc Xa Hoi, 1991).

———. "Tinh trong Nguc Toi" ["Love in the Dark Prison"]. In *Tran Huy Lieu: Hoi Ky* [*Tran Huy Lieu: Memoirs*] (Hanoi: NXB Khoa Hoc Xa Hoi, 1991).

———. "Tren Hon Cau" ["On Hon Cau"]. In *Tran Huy Lieu: Hoi Ky* [*Tran Huy Lieu: Memoirs*] (Hanoi: NXB Khoa Hoc Xa Hoi, 1991).

———. "Tu Hoc trong Tu" ["Self-Study in Prison"]. In *Truong Hoc sau Song Sat* [*School behind the Iron Bars*] (Hanoi: NXB Thanh Nien, 1969).

———. "Xuan No trong Tu" ["Spring Blooms in Prison"]. In *Tran Huy Lieu: Hoi Ky* [*Tran Huy Lieu: Memoirs*] (Hanoi: NXB Khoa Hoc Xa Hoi, 1991).

Tran Quoc Vuong. "The Legend of Ong Dong from the Text to the Field." In *Essays into Vietnamese Pasts,* edited by K. W. Taylor and John K. Whitmore (Ithaca, N.Y.: Cornell University Southeast Asia Program, 1995).

———. "Traditions, Acculturation, Renovation: The Evolutional Pattern of Vietnamese Culture." In *Southeast Asia in the 9th to 14th Centuries,* edited by David G. Marr and A. C. Milner (Singapore: Institute of Southeast Asian Studies, 1986).

Tran Tu Binh. "Thoat Nguc Hoa Lo" ["Escape from Hoa Lo Prison"]. In *Ha Noi Khoi Nghia* [*Hanoi Uprising*] (Hanoi: NXB Hanoi, 1966).

Tran Van Can. *Ve Tinh Dan Toc cua Nghe Thuat Tao Hinh* [*Concerning National Sentiment in Visual Arts*] (Hanoi: NXB Van Hoa, 1973).

Tran Van Giap et al. *Luoc Truyen Cac Tac Gia Viet Nam* [*Sketch of Vietnamese Authors*] (Hanoi: NXB Khoa Hoc Xa Hoi, 1971).

Tran Van Giau. "The First Propagandist for the Ideas of 1789 in Vietnam." *Vietnamese Studies* 21 (1991): 5–17.

———. *Su Phat Trien cua Tu Tuong o Viet Nam tu The Ky XIX den Cach Mang Thang Tam* [*Ideological Development in Vietnam from the Nineteenth Century to the August Revolution*], vol. 2 (Hanoi: NXB Khoa Hoc Xa Hoi, 1975).

Tre. *Vietnam: Investment and Tourism in Prospect* (Hanoi: Nguyen Minh Hoang Printing House, 1991).

Truong Chinh. "Marxism and Vietnamese Culture." In *Selected Writings* (Hanoi: Foreign Language Publishing House, 1977).

Tumarkin, Nina, *Lenin Lives: The Lenin Cult in Soviet Russia* (Cambridge, Mass.: Harvard University Press, 1983).

———. *The Living and the Dead: The Rise and Fall of the Cult of World War II in Russia* (New York: Basic Books, 1994).

Turley, William S., and Mark Selden, eds. *Reinventing Vietnamese Socialism: Doi Moi in Comparative Perspective,* (Boulder, Colo.: Westview Press, 1993).

Turner, Karen Gottschang, with Phan Thanh Hao. *Even the Women Must Fight: Memories of War from North Vietnam* (New York: Wiley, 1998).

Turner, Victor. *Dramas, Fields, and Metaphors: Symbolic Action in Human Society* (Ithaca, N.Y.: Cornell University Press, 1974).

Ungar, Esta S. "Vietnamese Leadership and Order: Dai Viet under the Le Dynasty (1428–1459)" (Ph.D. diss., Cornell University, 1983).

Urry, John. *Consuming Places* (New York: Routledge, 1995).

Van Tien Dung. "Niem Tin La Suc Manh" ["Belief Is Strength"]. In *Suoi Reo Nam Ay* [*The Bubbling Spring That Year*] (Hai Phong: NXB Thong Tin-Van Hoa, 1993).

Vietnam, Government of. *Nhung Van Ban ve Viec Cuoi, Viec Tang, Ngay Gio, Ngay Hoi* [*Documents on Weddings, Funerals, Death Anniversary and Public Festivals*] (Hanoi: NXB Van Hoa, 1979).

Vietnam, Institute of Philosophy. *Dang Ta Ban ve Dao Duc* [*Our Party Discusses Ethics*] (Hanoi: Uy Ban Khoa Hoc Xa Hoi Viet Nam, 1973).

Vietnamtourism. *Tourism* (http://www.vietnamtourism.com/tourist/index.htm, 1998).

Viollis, Andrée. *Indochine S.O.S* (1935; reprint, Paris: Les Editeurs Français Réunis, 1949).

Vo Van Truc, ed. *Tieng Hat trong Tu* [*Prison Songs*], vol. 1 (Hanoi: NXB Thanh Nien, 1972).

Vu Duy Nhai. "Nho Lai nhung Ngay Thoat Nguc Son La" ["Recalling the Days of Escape from Son La Prison"]. In *Suoi Reo Nam Ay* [*The Bubbling Spring That Year*] (Hai Phong: NXB Thong Tin-Van Hoa, 1993).

Vu Huyen. "Notes on the 1990 National Arts Exhibition." *Vietnamese Studies* 3 (1990): 100–102.

Vu Tu Nam. "Mot So Y Kien Tham Gia Ket Thuc Cuoc Tranh Luan: Phe Binh cuon *Vuot Con Dao*" ["Some Opinions Regarding the Debate: A Critique of *Escape from Con Dao*"]. *Bao Van Nghe* [*Literature and Arts Newspaper*], July 28, 1955.

Walsh, Kevin. *The Representation of the Past: Museums and Heritage in the Post-modern World* (London: Routledge, 1992).

"War Sites to Bring in Tourist Bucks." *Vietnews* 3, no. 6 (1995): 35–36.

Watson, Rubie, ed. *Memory, History, and Opposition under State Socialism* (Sante Fe, N.M.: School of American Research Press, 1994).

Werner, Jayne Susan. *Peasant Politics and Religious Sectarianism: Peasant and Priest in the Cao Dai in Vietnam* (New Haven, Conn.: Yale University Southeast Asia Studies, 1981).

Whitfield, Danny J. *Historical and Cultural Dictionary of Vietnam* (Metuchen, N.J.: Scarecrow Press, 1976).

Whitmore, John K. "Communism and History in Vietnam," In *Vietnamese Communism in Comparative Perspective*, edited by William S. Turley (Boulder, Colo.: Westview Press, 1980).

———. "From Classical Scholarship to Confucian Belief in Vietnam." *Vietnam Forum*, no. 9 (1987): 49–65.

Winter, Jay. *Sites of Memory, Sites of Mourning: The Great War in European Cultural History* (New York: Cambridge University Press, 1995).

Wolf, Arthur P. "Gods, Ghosts, and Ancestors." In *Religion and Ritual in Chinese Society*, edited by Arthur P. Wolf (Stanford, Calif.: Stanford University Press, 1974).

———, ed., *Religion and Ritual in Chinese Society* (Stanford, Calif.: Stanford University Press, 1974).

Wolf, Margery. *Women and the Family in Rural Taiwan* (Stanford, Calif: Stanford University Press, 1972).

Wolters, Oliver W. "Assertions of Cultural Well-Being in Fourteenth-Century Vietnam." In *Two Essays on Dai-Viet in the Fourteenth Century* (New Haven, Conn.: Yale Southeast Asia Studies, 1988).

———. *History, Culture, and Region in Southeast Asian Perspectives* (Singapore: ISEAS, 1982).

———. "On Telling a Story of Vietnam in the Thirteenth and Fourteenth Centuries." *Journal of Southeast Asian Studies* 26 (March 1995): 63–74.

———. "Possibilities for a Reading of the 1293–1357 period in the Vietnamese Annals." *Vietnam Forum*, no. 11 (1988): 92–149.

———. *Two Essays on Dai-Viet in the Fourteenth Century* (New Haven, Conn.: Yale Southeast Asia Studies, 1988).

Woodside, Alexander. *Community and Revolution in Modern Vietnam* (Boston: Houghton Mifflin: 1976).

———. "Conceptions of Change and of Human Responsibility for Change in Late Traditional Vietnam." *Vietnam Forum*, no. 6 (1985): 73–111.

———. *Vietnam and the Chinese Model: A Comparative Study of Vietnamese and Chinese Government in the First Half of the Nineteenth Century* (Cambridge, Mass.: Harvard University Press, 1971).

Xuan Cang and Ly Dang Cao. "Tim Mo Liet Si bang Phuong Phap Moi?" ["Discovering the Graves of War Dead by a New Method?"]. *The Gioi Moi* [*New World*], October 1996, 8–11.

Xuan Dieu. "Yeu Tho Bac" ["Loving Uncle's Poetry"]. In *Tap Nghien Cuu Binh Luan Chon Loc ve Tho Van Ho Chu Tich* [*Selected Commentaries and Studies on Chairman Ho's Poetry*] (Hanoi: Giao Duc, 1978).

Xuan Thuy. "Suoi Reo Nam Ay" ["The Bubbling Spring That Year"]. In *Suoi Reo Nam Ay* [*The Bubbling Spring That Year*] (Hai Phong: NXB Thong Tin-Van Hoa, 1993).

Yamamoto Tatsuro. "Myths Explaining the Vicissitudes of Political Power in Ancient Vietnam." *Acta Asiatica: Bulletin of the Institute of Eastern Culture* 18 (1970): 70–90.

Zinoman, Peter. *The Colonial Bastille: A History of Imprisonment in Vietnam, 1862–1940* (Berkeley and Los Angeles: University of California Press, 2001).

———. "Declassifying Nguyen Huy Thiep." *positions* 2, no. 2 (fall 1994): 294–317.

Contributors

JOHN BODNAR teaches history at Indiana University. He is the author of *Remaking America: Public Memory, Commemoration, and Patriotism in the Twentieth Century* (1992).

MARK PHILIP BRADLEY teaches history at the University of Wisconsin–Milwaukee. He is the author of *Imagining America and Vietnam: The Making of Postcolonial Vietnam, 1919–1950* (2000).

CHRISTOPH GIEBEL teaches history at the University of Washington.

LAUREL B. KENNEDY teaches in the Department of Communications at Denison University.

SHAUN KINGSLEY MALARNEY teaches anthropology in the Division of International Studies at the International Christian University in Tokyo.

HUE-TAM HO TAI is Kenneth T. Young Professor of Sino-Vietnamese History at Harvard University. She is the author of *Millenarianism and Peasant Politics in Vietnam* (1983) and *Radicalism and the Origins of the Vietnamese Revolution* (1992).

NORA A. TAYLOR teaches art history in the Interdisciplinary Humanities Program at Arizona State University.

MARY ROSE WILLIAMS teaches at Lane Community College in Ohio.

PETER ZINOMAN teaches history at the University of California at Berkeley. He is the author of *The Colonial Bastille: A History of Imprisonment in Vietnam, 1862–1940* (2001)

Index

abstract paintings, 115, 120, 128–29
age, gender inflected by, 168
Agent Orange: reference to in *A Quiet Little Town,* 225n25; victim of, 210 (fig.)
agriculture: collectivization of in North Vietnam in late 1950s and early 1960s, 53; redistribution of land to the peasantry in 1991–92, 54
Agulhon, Maurice, 14
airports, 9, 15, 199, 229
All Souls' Day, Vietnamese (*see also* Feast of Wandering Souls), 75n40
altar(s)
in Giap Tu communal house, 70–71
in homes: ancestral altars, 60, 62, 64, 82; funeral altars, 60, 62, 63–64, 65, 75n30, 178 (fig.); as part of Commemorative Area for Ton Duc Thang, 82, 84, 87–88; role in soldier's death anniversary ceremony, 69–70
American War. *See* War of National Salvation Against the Americans
amnesia, collective/social, 7–8, 14, 15, 190, 193n33
anarchists, as political prisoners in colonial prisons, 34–35, 44n65
ancestral cult, Vietnamese, 47, 60, 75n30, 82, 170; ancestral altars in homes, 60, 62, 64, 82; role in Com-

memorative Area for Ton Duc Thang, 82, 85–86
Anderson, Benedict, 16n12
An Giang Province. *See* Commemorative Area for Ton Duc Thang; My Hoa Hung village
animals, caged, images of in classical prison poetry, 26–27
appropriate behavior (*hanh*), as one of the Four Virtues, 193n15
architecture, 10, 13; French, 13, 148, 152
Armed Forces of the Republic of Vietnam (ARVN), 190–91; brothels serving portrayed in *Girl on the River,* 212; military cemetery razed in 1975, 191; privileges for northern veterans and survivors not extended to, 67, 227–28
Army Museum (Hanoi), exaggerated death figures for American soldiers, 75n35
art(s): politicization of aesthetics, 12–13; state subsidies for, effect on 1980s film industry, 198; visual (*see* visual art(s))
"art for art's sake," 115
"art for humanity's sake," 214
art galleries, 109, 121
Arts Association, Vietnamese (*Hoi Nghe Si Tao Hinh;* National Arts Association; Vietnamese

Text: 10/13 Sabon
Display: Sabon
Compositor: Binghamton Valley Composition
Printing and binding: Sheridan Books, Inc.